AF322835

IN HONOR OF AMERICA

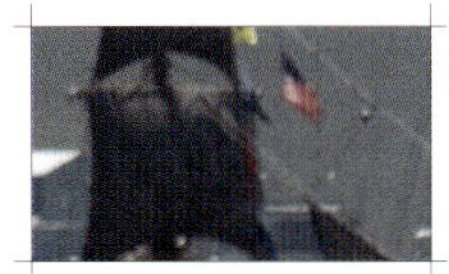

To Marvin
with thanks

Agostino von Hassel

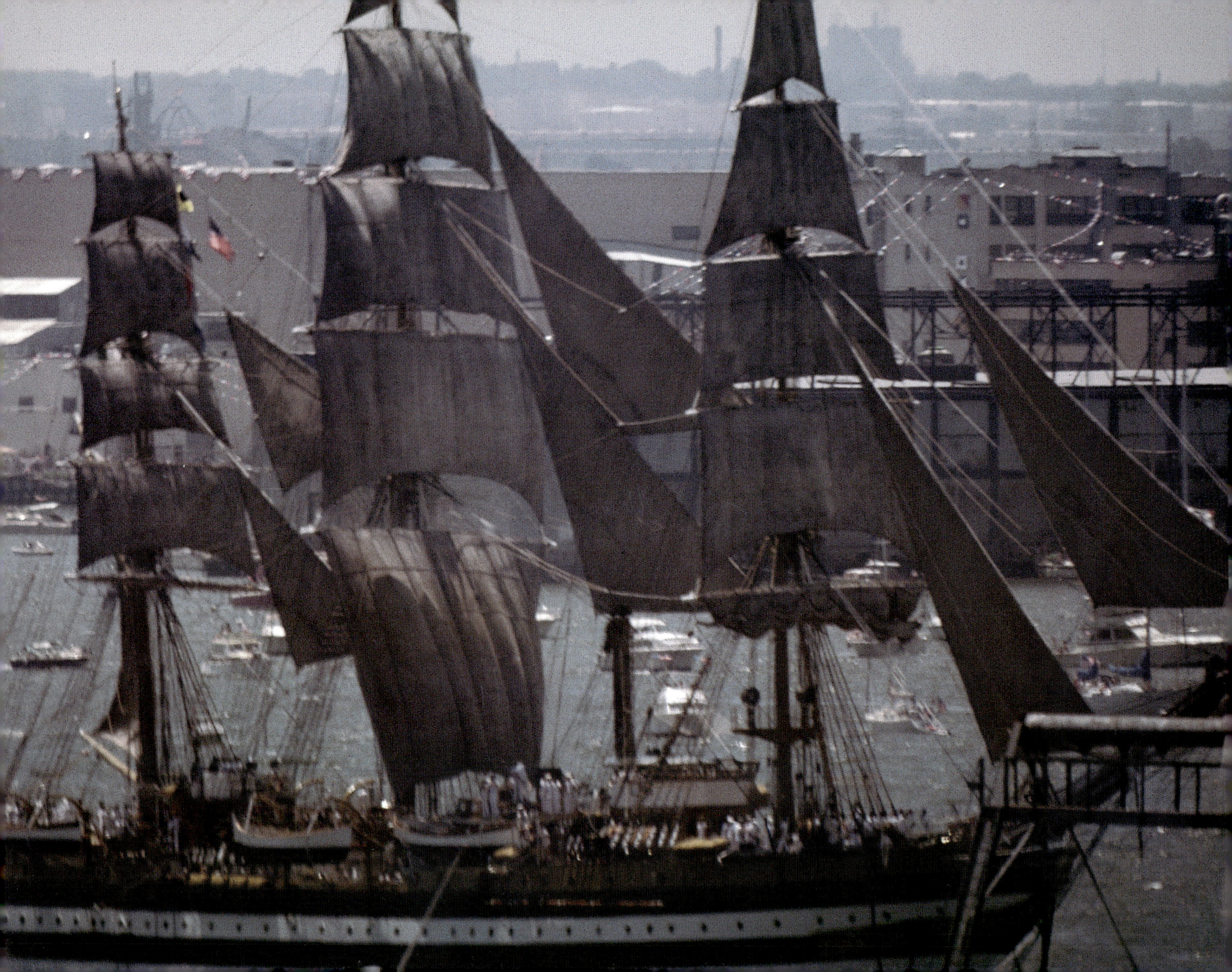

IN HONOR OF AMERICA

BY AGOSTINO VON HASSELL

HOWELL PRESS, INC.
CHARLOTTESVILLE, VIRGINIA

© 2003 by Agostino von Hassell

All rights reserved. This book, or any portions thereof, may not be reproduced or transmitted in any form or by any means, electronic or mechanical, including photocopying, recording, or by any information storage and retrieval system, without permission in writing from the publisher, except for brief quotations in critical reviews or articles.

Sources: The complete works of William Shakespeare / ed. by William George Clark and William Aldis Wright ; with complete notes of the Temple Shakespeare by Israel Gollancz ; introduction by Arthur Brisbane. Edition: (International ed.). Publisher: New York: Heart's International Library Co., 1914.

The Holy Bible: containing the Old and New Testaments / translated out of the original tongues; and with the former translations diligently compared and revised; the text conformable to that of the edition of 1611, commonly known as the authorized or King James' version; marginal references. 20th century ed. Publisher: Philadelphia: A.J. Holman, 1903.

Library of Congress Control Number: 2003107385
ISBN 1-57427-145-8

12 11 10 09 08 07 06 05 04 03
10 9 8 7 6 5 4 3 2 1

Published by Howell Press, Inc.
1713-2D Allied Lane
Charlottesville, VA 22903
(434) 977-4006
www.howellpress.com
Printed in Hong Kong by Rainbow Graphic & Printing Co., Ltd.

Cover and book design by Sherilyn Kulesh
Editing by Lisa M. Pellegrino

A solid 50 percent of the proceeds go to the Marine Corps Law Enforcement Foundation to assist the children of fallen Marines and law enforcement officers.

CONTENTS

PREFACE

CARE packages were my first contact with the United States of America. It was the early 1950s and my grandmother had carefully stashed the CARE packages throughout her home in Bavaria. She was preparing our family "for the next war," then thought imminent. Having been raised with stories of war, this gesture by private individuals towards a defeated people had a very strong impact on me.

My grandmother, Ilse von Hassell, daughter of Grand Admiral von Tirpitz, would always tell me how America helped us after the war. My whole family had been punished for the July 20, 1944, plot to assassinate Hitler. My grandfather, Ulrich von Hassell, was directly involved in the attempt on Hitler's life and was executed on September 8, 1944. Most of the rest of my family were arrested, at least briefly, and interrogated. Two of my toddler cousins had been taken away by the SS and had not been seen or heard from in two years.

Family and friends struggled to locate the missing children, but their efforts were severely hampered by a petrol shortage. American occupation forces gave my family the "gasoline" they desperately needed to continue the search and my two cousins were found in 1946, living under false names.

America—The Generous. That was my first impression. Later on, listening to the adults, I learned how all knew with great certainty that America would defend Germany against the then all so certain Soviet threat. America—The Protector.

In November of 1963 America was very much on my mind. I was just ten years old and living in Brussels, Belgium, where my father served on the German Embassy staff. On the night of the 22nd I was sleeping snugly in my bed when my mother woke me up to tell me that Kennedy had been killed. Recalling the tense talk among adults during the Cuban Missile Crisis, I felt like our main protector—symbolized by John F. Kennedy—was gone.

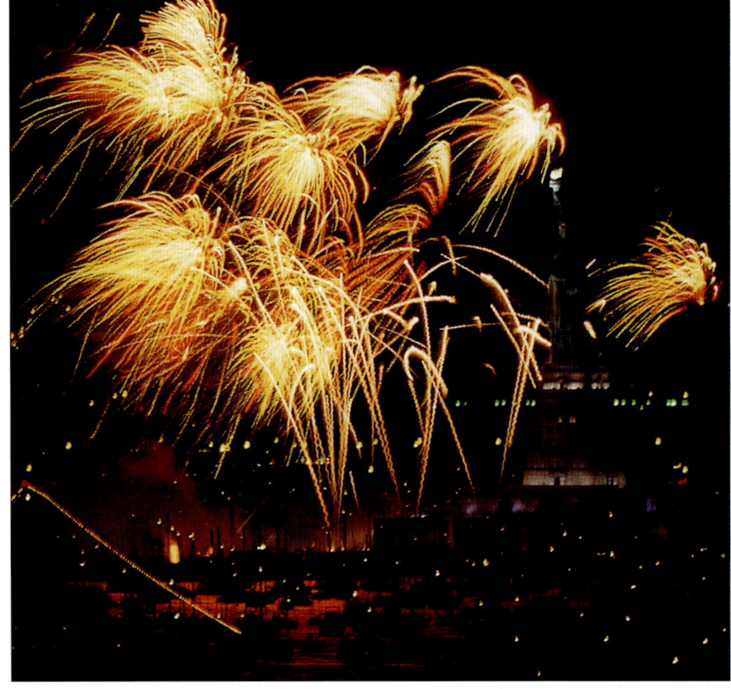

The photographs on these pages tell of my often wrenching transition from an aristocratic background, deeply rooted in the glories and the devotion to duty of Prussia and Hanover, into an American.

The generous embrace of America made it easy for me to leave behind that spent force of old Europe, that failure in morality, creativity and human spirit.

I have traveled extensively throughout the United States, exploring small towns and large cities. These pages reflect that exploration. My journeys left a deep impression on me: how unique was such a country where all embrace the flag and where bumper stickers with "God Bless America" are common. You would never see such pride in Germany, Italy or France. Never. America—The Proud.

America also showed me a creativity that comes from freedom. I have seen young artists in New York's Greenwich Village absorbing lessons from old Europe and shaping their own art. I have admired farmers in Columbia County, New York, fighting off the death of rural life, being inventive on how to squeeze every last penny from their milk production.

I have enjoyed elegant and simple restaurants around the nation taking this country's bountiful harvest and fashioning new dishes.

In my years here I have witnessed America—The Forgiving. I have hardly ever encountered resentment for my German background even though I have met many veterans who fought in North Africa, Italy, France and Germany. Jewish holocaust survivors in New York have always treated me with kindness and grace.

I have encountered the curiosity and permanent open-hearted welcome that marks the United States. Americans are the most forgiving people on earth. Fighting one day and delivering humanitarian aid the next: I saw it with my own eyes in the Middle East. In the annals of human history America is so different from its predecessors. Look at Rome, look at evil Napoleon, look at Japan; none of them, after they conquered, followed through with humanitarian aid. America's Marshall Plan restored a destroyed Europe; the outpouring of help from the U.S. Treasury and private individuals helped rebuild Haiti, Afghanistan and now Iraq.

Not all is well with America. It is far from perfect and may never be so. Yet all these problems, the poverty, the dissent—all that pales when you remember the tolerance, the goodness, the generosity and the forgiveness of this country.

These qualities and the incredible freedom make this nation unique in human history. The embrace of dissent is critical: America will not survive without healthy debates. May it be that America, the "last best hope," can survive as a power because it embraces freedom? I do hope so.

My path across America took me into the arms of the United States Marine Corps. This is the most American of American institutions, yet peculiar for outsiders. The Corps has taken the place in this world of the very finest regiments ever fielded, such as Prussia's Garde-du-Corps, home to many of my ancestors.

Marines are proud, caring, forgiving, tolerant yet ferocious in a fight. A Marine is a unique person who kills one day and cradles a baby the next. It is a proud Corps refuting any challenge, or as Marine Commandant Alexander Vandergrift said in 1948: "There is no tradition of the bended knee..." This was in reaction to President Harry S Truman's effort to do away with the Corps, citing the Marines as a landing party "that had gotten out of hand."

Our Corps embraced me and made me part of that complex family. I held a seriously wounded Marine in my arms in the gore of the Beirut Civil War in 1983. It was an experience that will never leave me. Our loss as a nation of more than 240 Marines in the suicide bombing at the Beirut Airport on October 23, 1983, is forever seared into my mind, yet the very thought of this will always reinforce my sense of obligation to serve and support, to help and assist.

A solid 50 percent of the profits of this book will be donated to the Marine Corps Law Enforcement Foundation. This group provides for the children of fallen Marines and law enforcement officers and many others such as all the children of our valiant British Allies killed in the recent Iraq War. It is a unique foundation, above politics and above greed: every penny raised goes to the purpose. There is no overhead. This is unique among American charities and in the spirit of this grand Corps of Marines to "take care of their own."

For those who care, my photographs are simple. I hardly ever use artificial lights or strobes. I have never used the ample tool chest of tricks America's creativity has provided to manipulate photos. They were taken with simple, old, mostly manual, Nikon and Leica cameras.

INTRODUCTION

By Vice Admiral Dick Dunleavy, USN (Ret.)

Here in your hands is a candid description of America in the words and pictures of an: incredibly talented individual, a naturalized American who deeply loves, respects and serves our country in what it stands for, freedom.

Oh, if only all Americans felt the way Agostino does regarding our Nation, our home! From the very beginning, his Preface, you are immediately captured by his ardor for his adopted land, our land, our country. His prose, his pictures indelibly etch in our minds and hopefully in our hearts the most sacred of all our gifts: individual freedom.

As you turn the pages, your imagination will soar as you stand in awe of our very beautiul landscape, meet our people, enjoy our celebrations, visit our homes, see our animals, savor our tranquility and rejoice in our freedom. The remarkable journey of an individual as he discovers his unfettered individual freedom will flow before your eyes, flash through your mind, and remain in your heart.

Encapsulated in "Landscape" is a vivid illustration of our natural beauty! The broad sandy beaches, tall majestic forests, deep forbidding swamps, snug harbors and more prove the benevolence of a Supreme Being when He or She created this great land. Our land with all its natural wonder—its rugged coasts, high deserts, towering mountains,

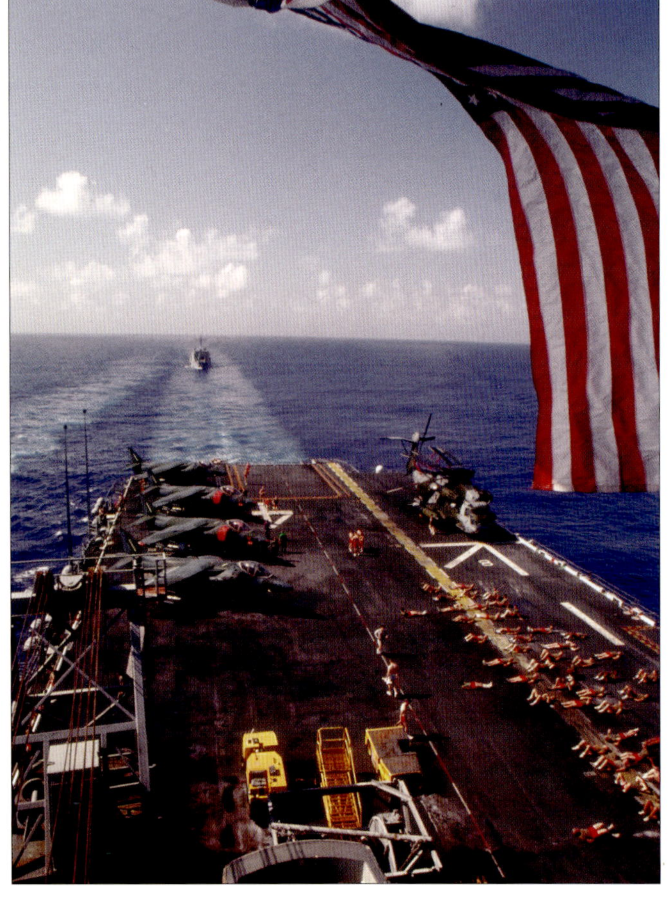

sweeping plains, small towns, cosmopolitan cities—all illustrate the magnificence of America.

"Faces" captures the true beauty of America, her people. Our ancestors came from around the globe for various sundry reasons, but primarily for individual freedom. Still today we have people coming to our shores to partake in our grand adventure. Pictures of New York City inhabitants dramatically present our diversity, while children at play and repose give us hope and belief in the bright future of America.

Our zest for life, the sobering moments reflecting on ages past, the celebration of life itself fill one's psyche as you peruse the "Celebration" section. We as a people celebrate our freedom during small town parades, summer fests, "at the hunt," during big city madness, political rallies for whatever reason. Again, it is our right because we are Americans.

The vista of America is her dynamically different locales. Quiet fishing villages, almost dormant during the winter months, contrast sharply with the vitality of the large city, just as the bustling city neighborhood violates the silence of the western plain. Our country is truly blessed with some of the most spectacular places on this planet.

Our love for animals is graphically displayed in "Animals", both in pictures and prose. From the solid farm animals, to high-spirited hunters, to

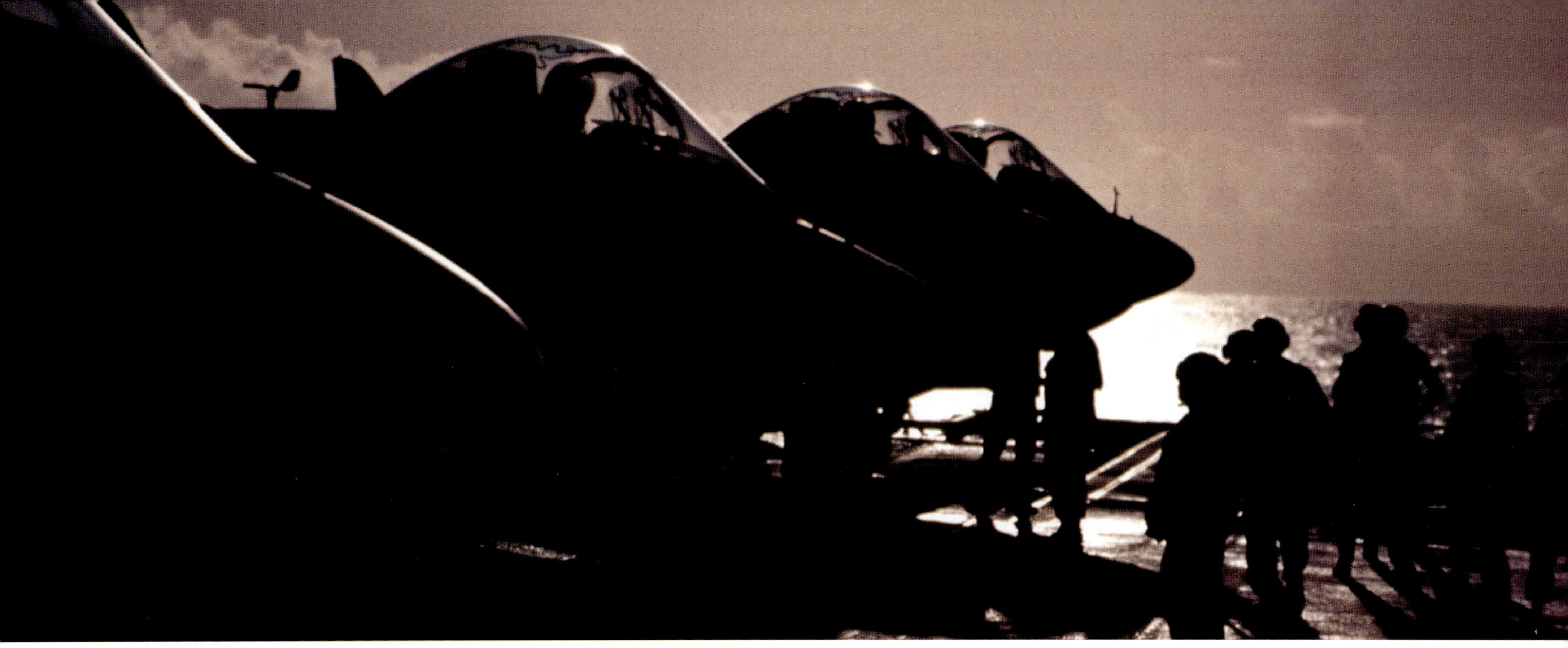

domestic pets, we Americans enjoy the company, hard work and, yes, entertainment of our animals.

The sereneness, the silence, the calm of America is one of its strengths. As illustrated post 9/11, we as a people stood tall, weeping together in our sorrow, then uniting behind our Commander in Chief and resolving to right this wrong. We posses an inner strength often misjudged by others: this is American Tranquility.

America's Freedom was won by and maintained by the sacrifice of our patriots of the past, present and future. Today we enjoy this precious jewel of Individual Freedom because of others who sacrificed much, sometimes all, in order to preserve this inalienable Right. As in days before, our military today carries the load, makes the sacrifice to ensure America's Freedom. May God continue to bless America!

Opposite: Marines on board the USS *Nassau* deploy by helicopter from the flight deck or by boats.

Above: AV-8B Harriers lined up on the flight deck of the USS *Nassau*. Marines are the most American of all our fighting forces, entering battles at a moment's notice throughout our nation's history.

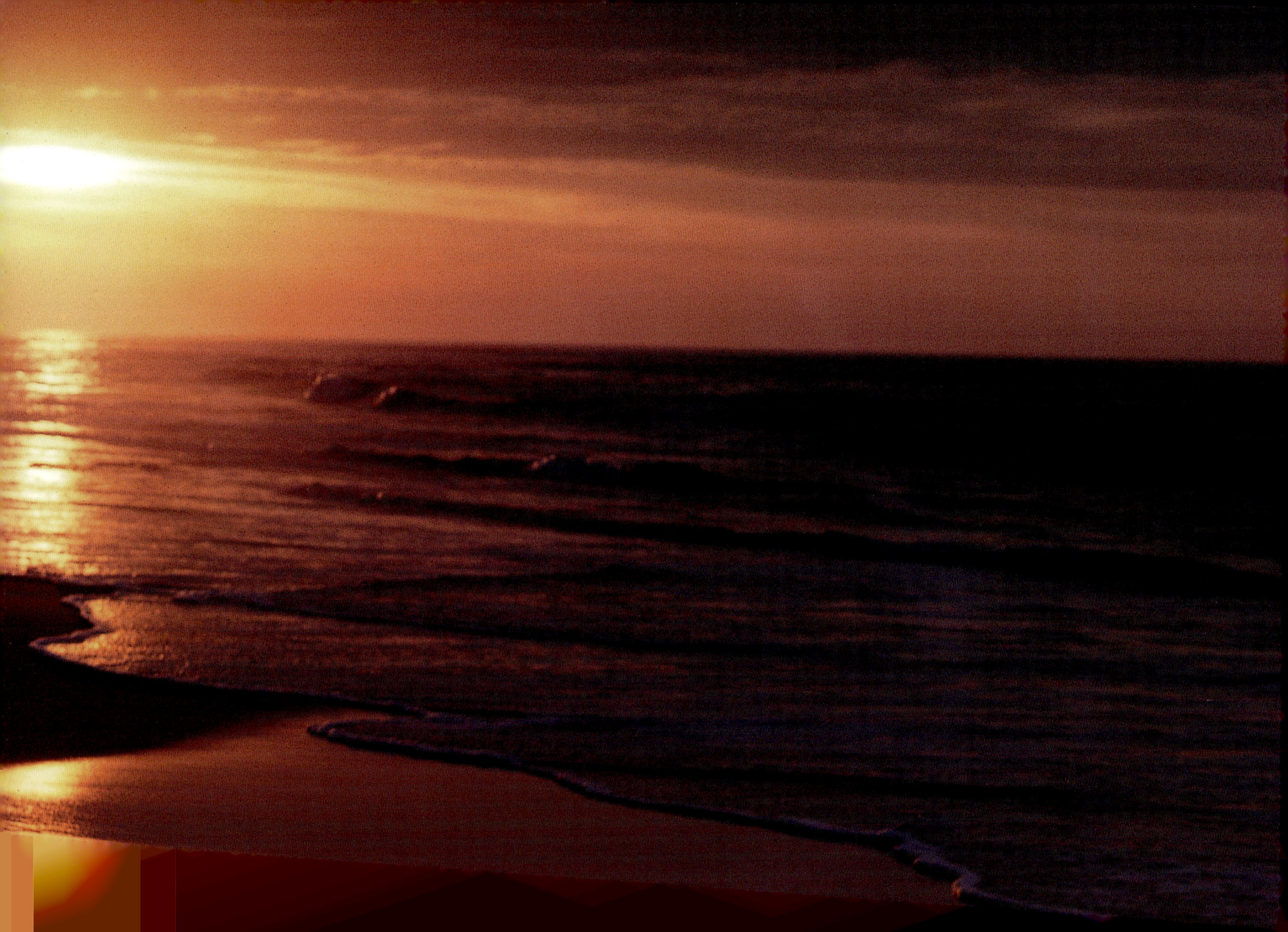

LANDSCAPE

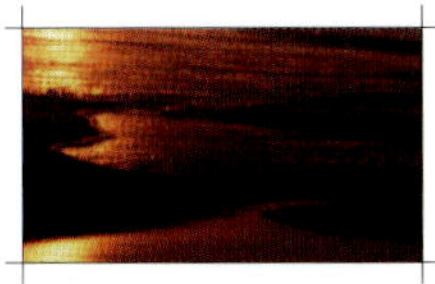

HOSTING MOUNTAINS, PLAINS, OCEANS AND FORESTS, AMERICA'S VISTAS ARE AS DIVERSE AS ITS PEOPLE.

Opposite: The beach at Southampton, New York, whence you can gaze across the Atlantic toward a Europe left behind.

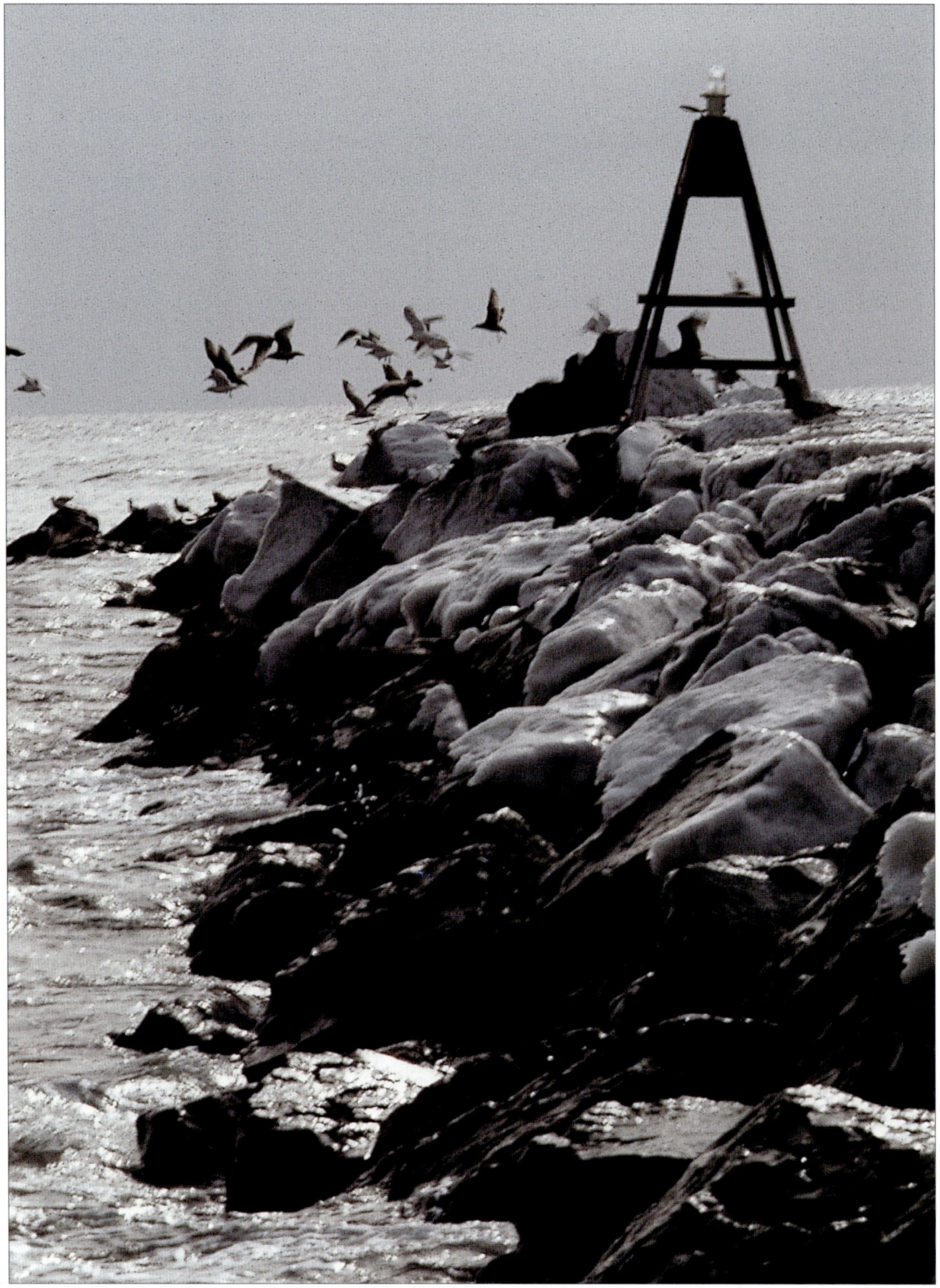

Left: The soothing sound of ocean waves crashing against the rocks clears the mind and refreshes the soul.

Opposite: Sand dunes in Southampton, New York, still unspoiled by careless development and commercial gore.

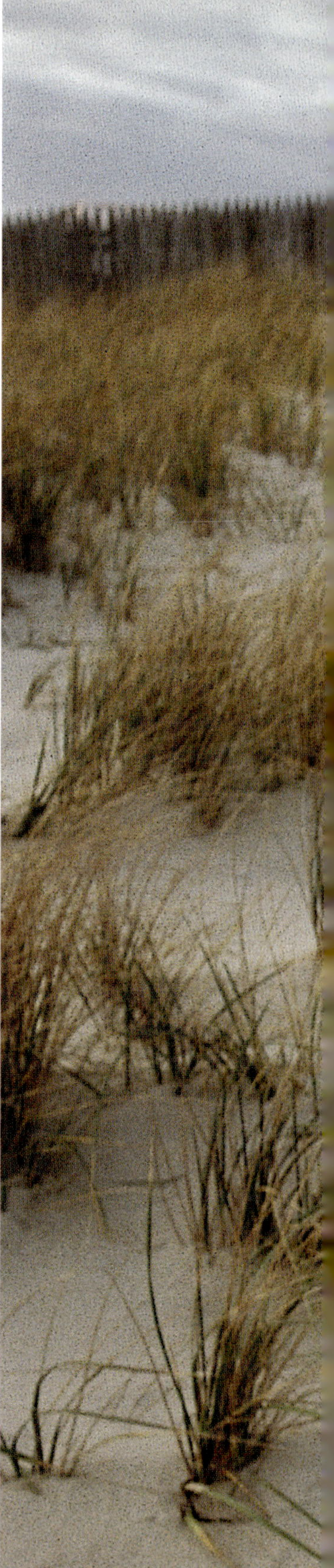

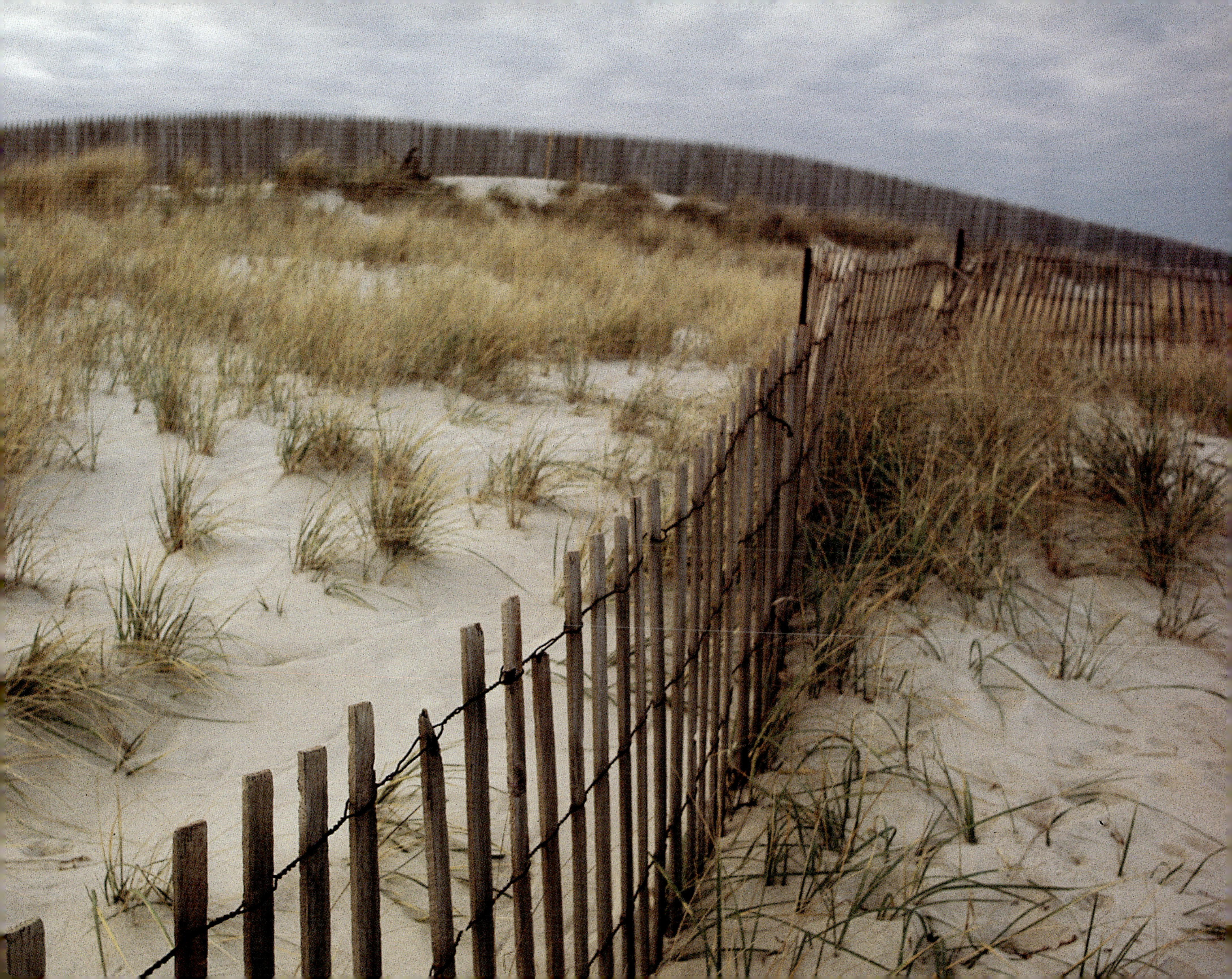

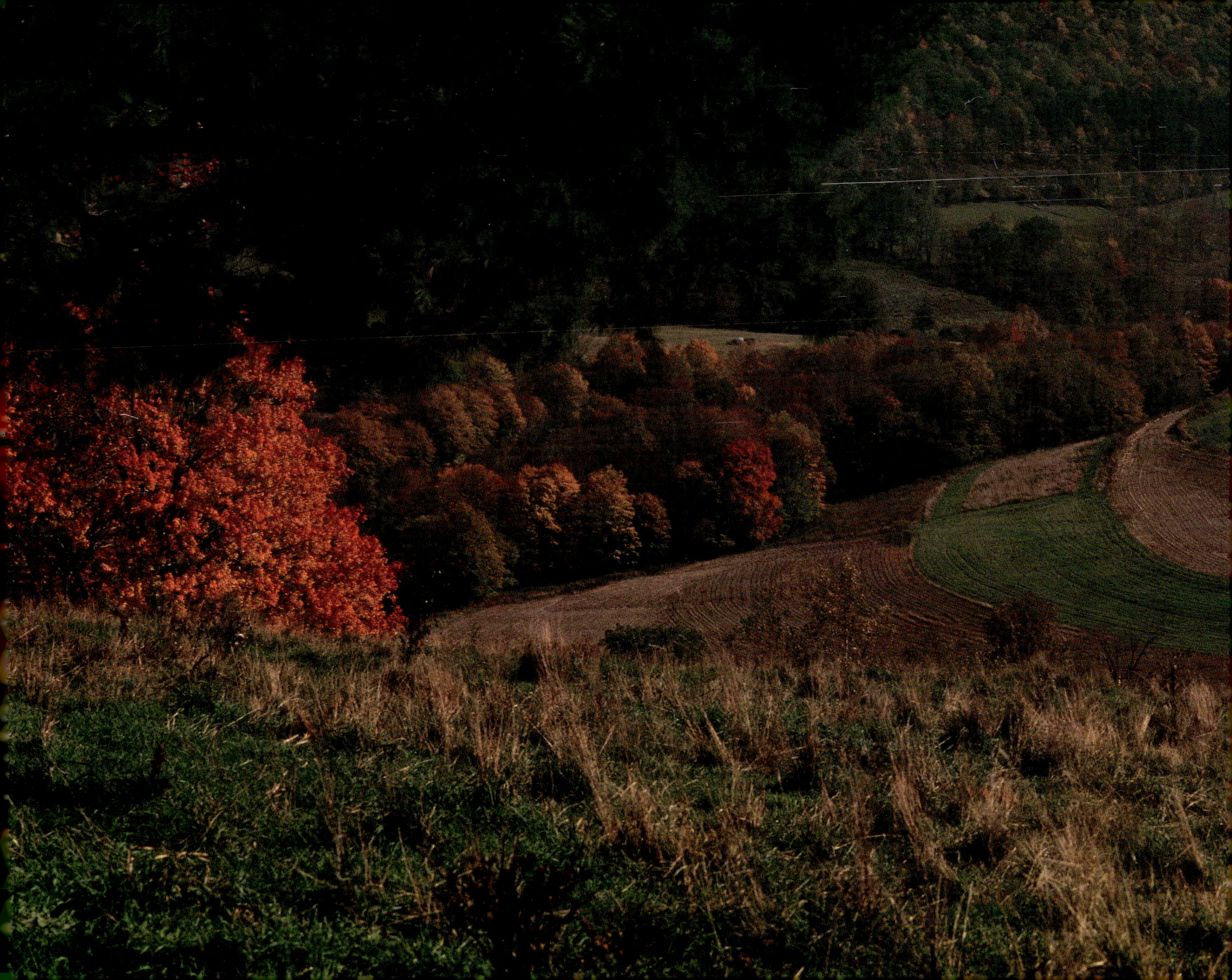

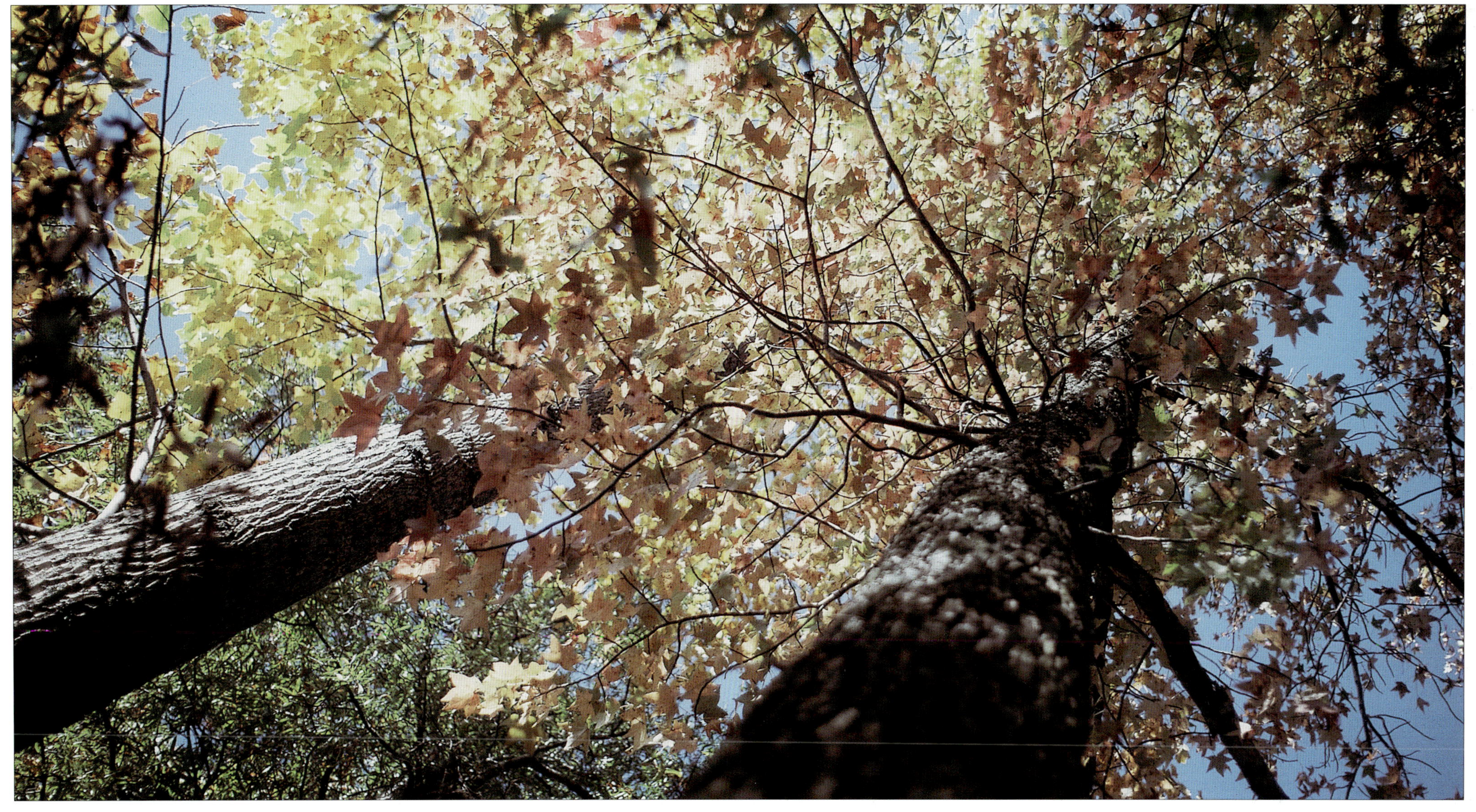

Opposite: American Indians first hunted on these lands in upstate New York. Dutch settlers with iron determination later cleared these lands for farming. As dairy farming began dying out in the 1980s and 1990s, forests started to take over again. Wild turkeys and deer have now returned.

Above: America is blessed with majestic forests, many of which predate the American Revolution. Preserving the living record of the growth of our nation has become a major goal for many.

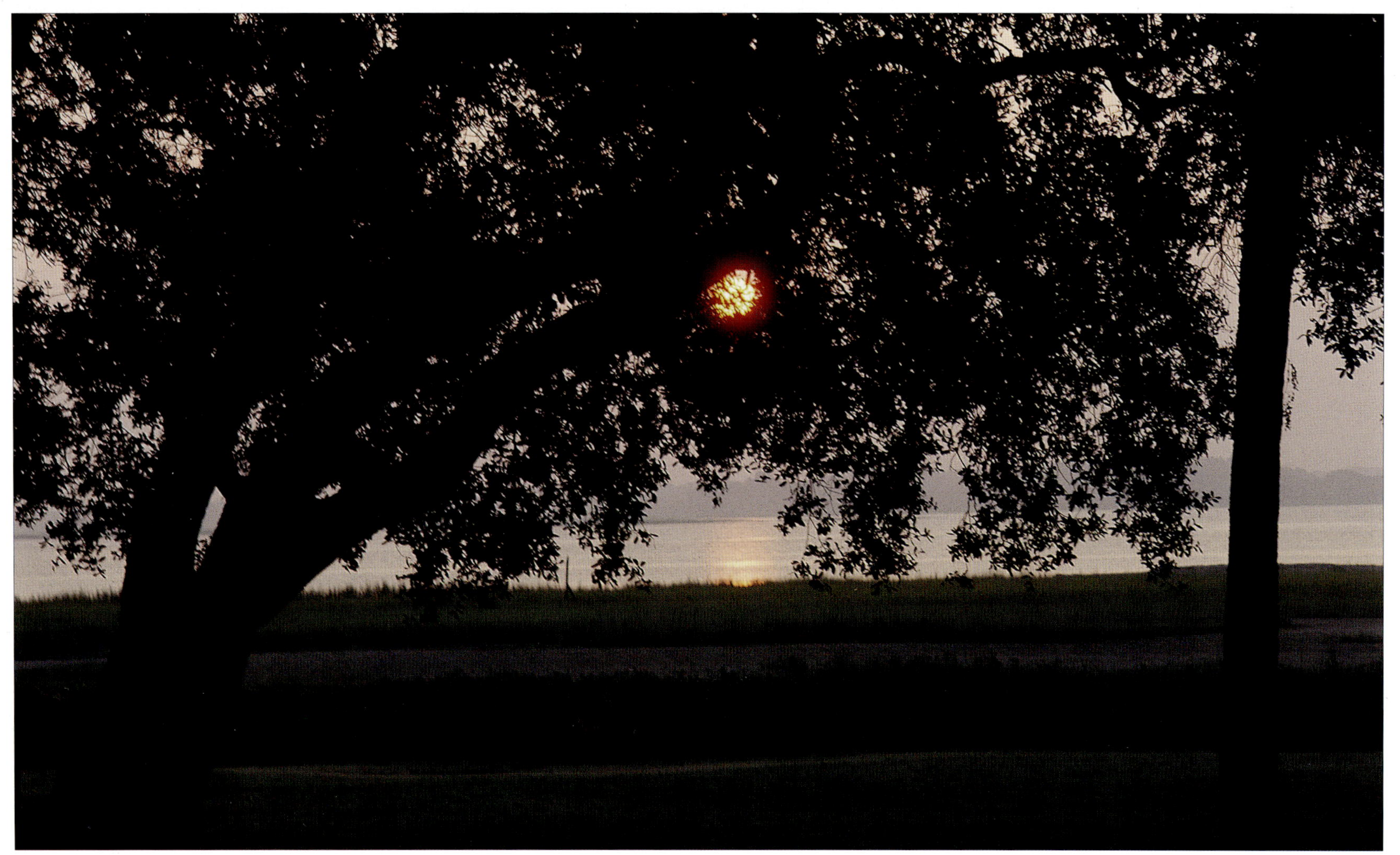

Above & Opposite: Edisto Island, South Carolina, is one of those magical places on America's East Coast that will restore your faith in human nature and courage. Relatively unspoiled by developers, these marshlands look very much today as they would have looked for early settlers in the 1600s. The region is rich in history. There were cotton and rice plantations based on slavery, whose effects haunt our land to this day. Blockade running during the War Between the States and liquor smuggling during the dark days of Prohibition failed to change the basic landscape, and the sea is still rich with crab and sweet rock shrimp.

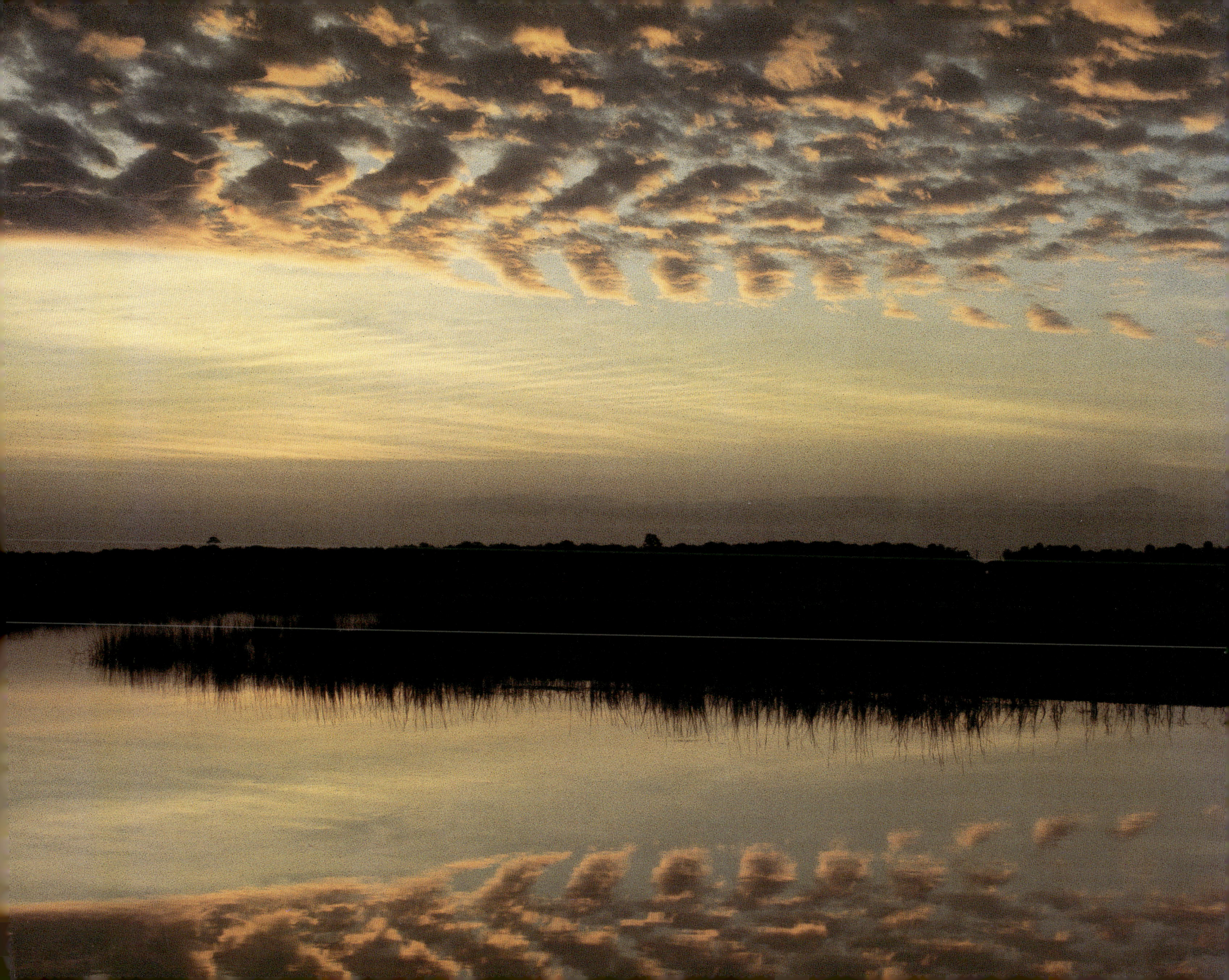

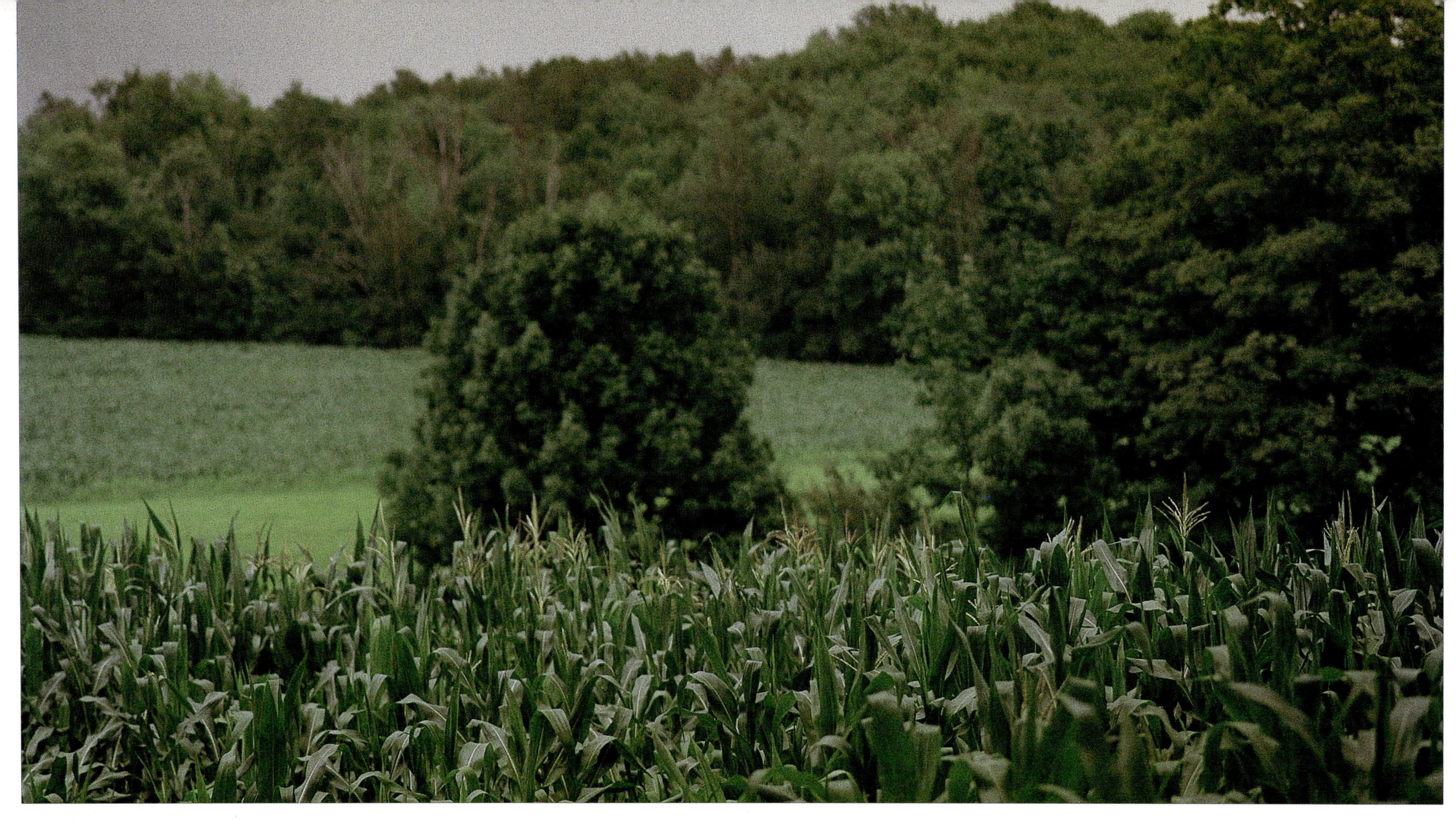

Above: Corn, the gift of American Indians cruelly forced off native lands, has created wealth for America and is a primary source of nutrition. These luscious cornfields were photographed in late August in Columbia County, New York.

Opposite: The abandoned, broken-down barn is a classic symbol of the decline of the family farm, once the mainstay of work and wealth. Structures such as this old hay barn in Hillsdale, New York, are now little more than curiosities.

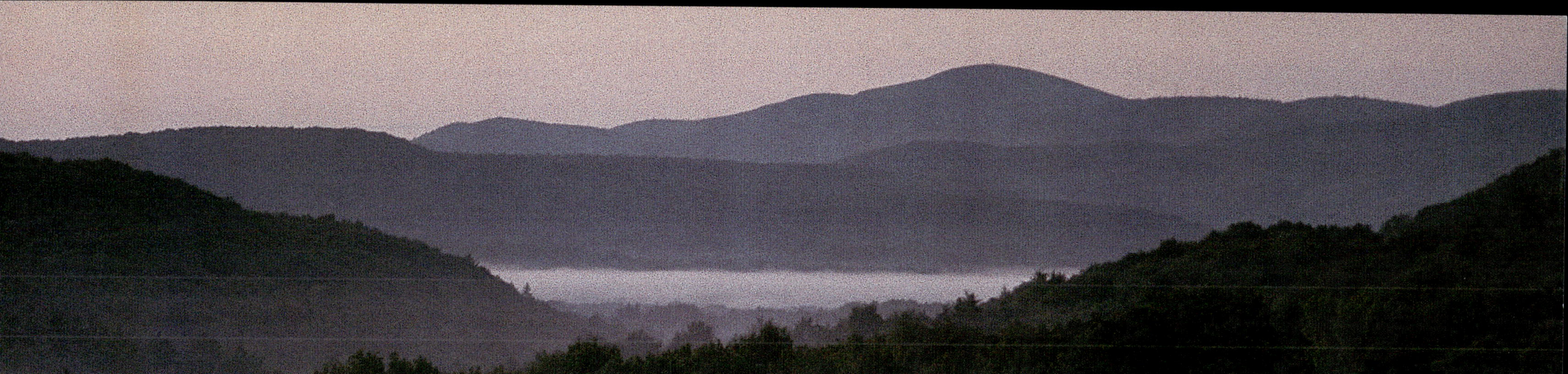

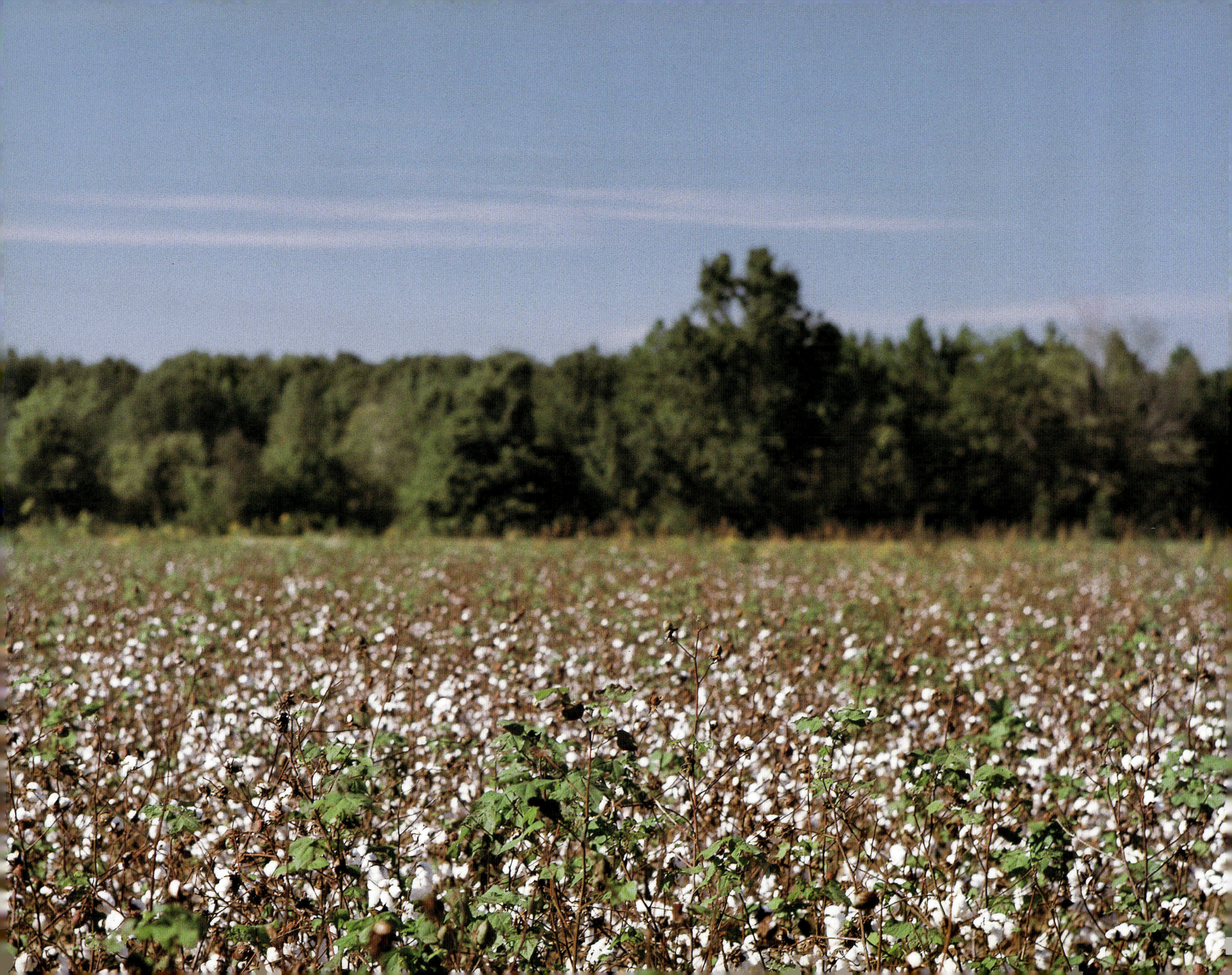

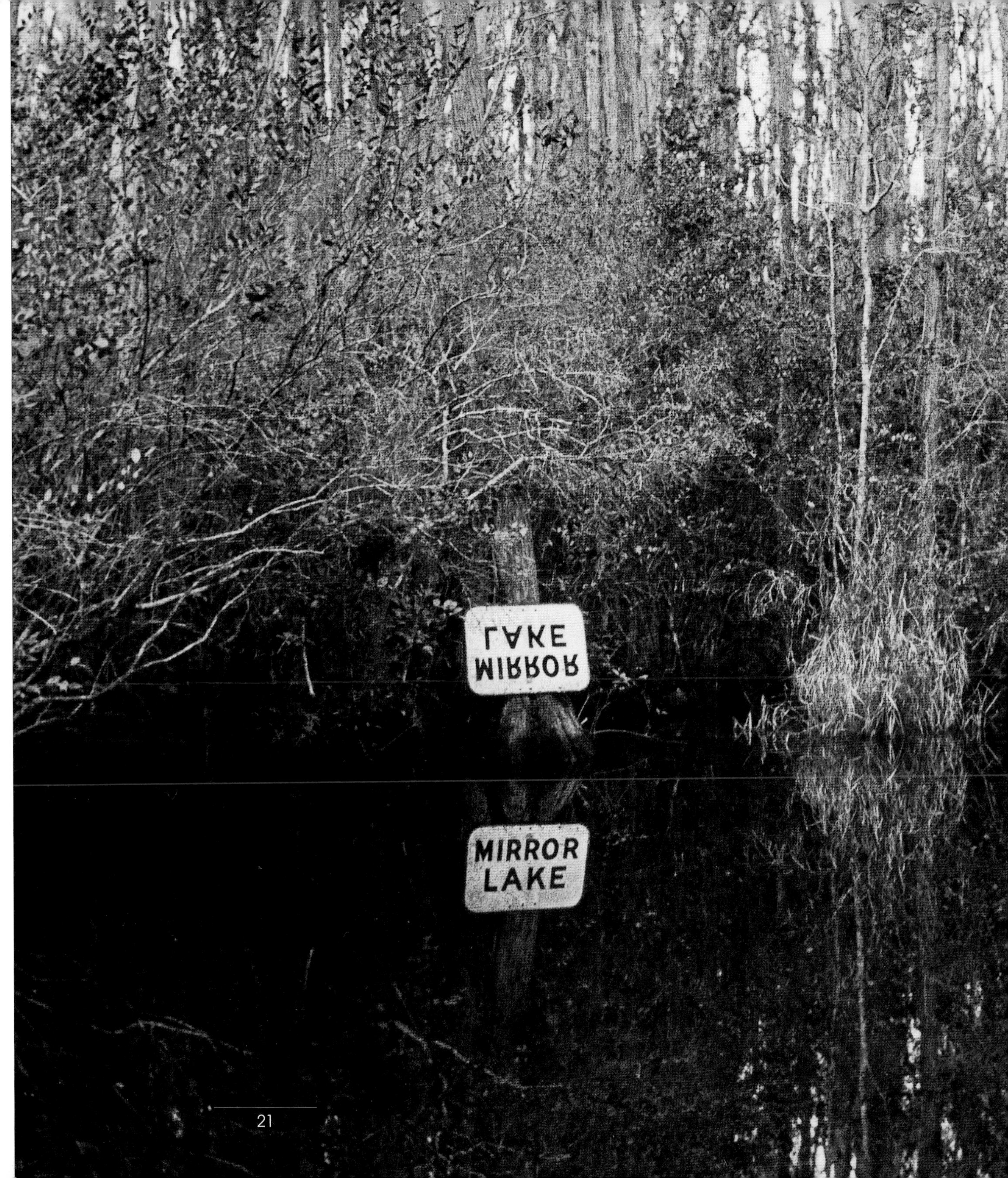

Opposite: Cotton brought both wealth and misery to the South. Grand plantations paid for by rich cotton crops continue to dominate the land south of the Mason Dixon line, but racism and poverty, aftereffects of slavery, still trouble this country.

Right: The South is rich with dramatic swamps, wetlands and ponds. A visit to the Florida Everglades or the famous Okefenokee Swamp in Georgia will remind you forever of the force of nature and the beauty of land left pristine. That swamp, in Georgia's southeast, measures about 700 square miles and is the location of this famous "mirror lake." These swamps are rich in culture – the Seminole Indians named this one Okefenokee or "The Land of the Trembling Earth."

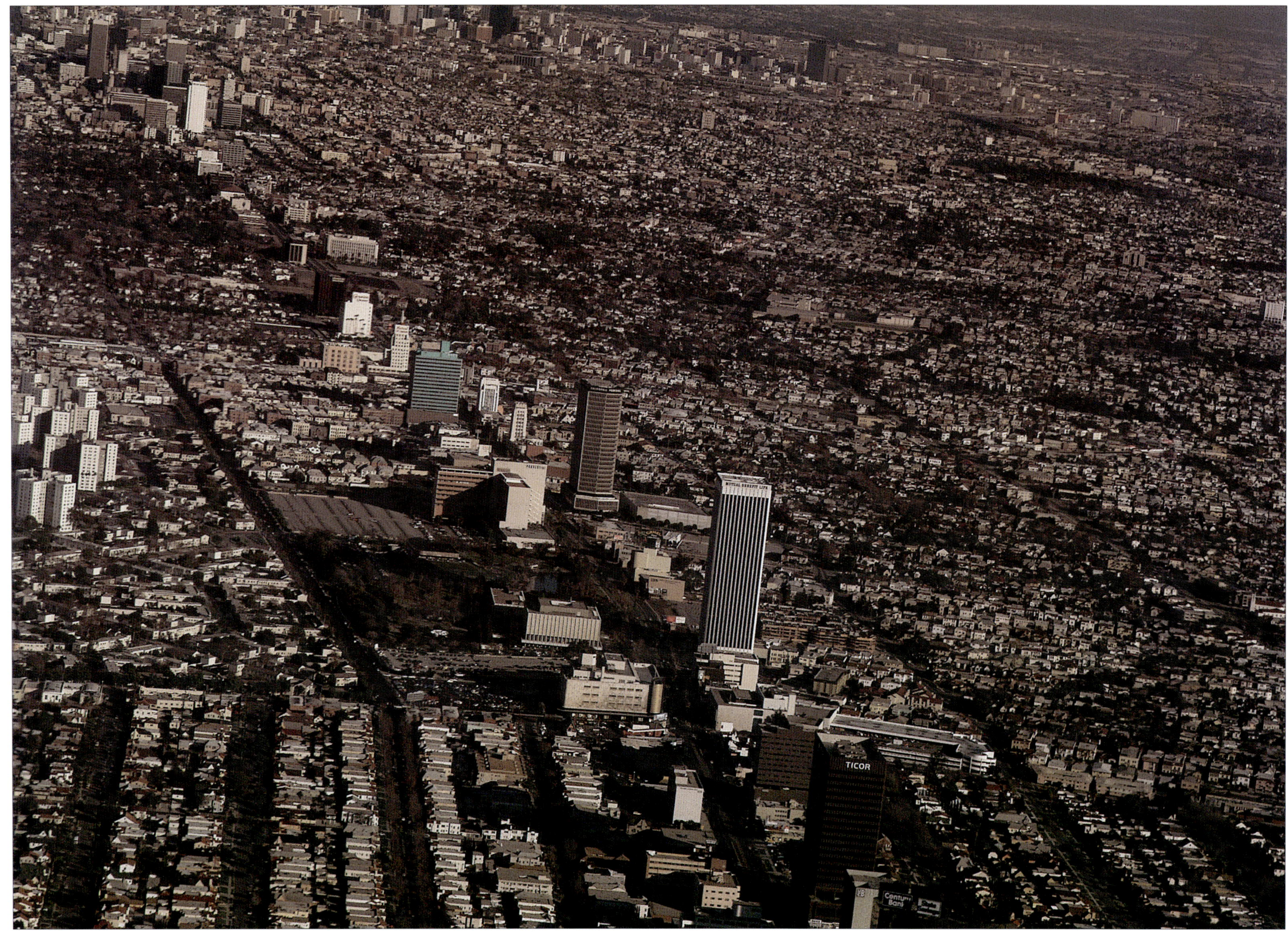

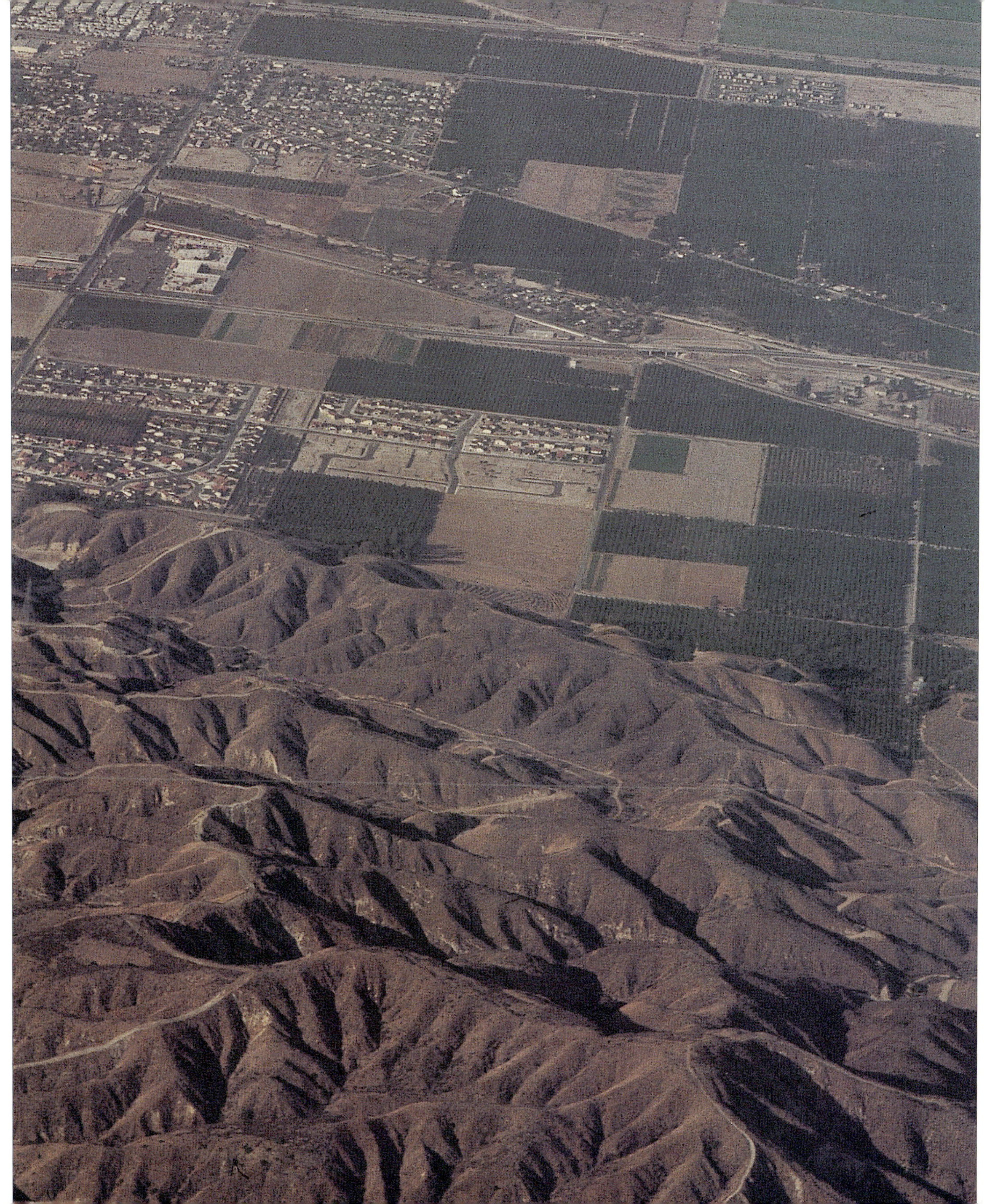

Right & Opposite: Urban areas in the United States reflect the common American desire to move around and be free. Only a few older U.S. cities such as Boston, New York and Philadelphia have the tight, compact feel of a European city. Most western cities, where much of the population growth came from pioneers, include plenty of wide-open spaces. No city provides a better example of urban sprawl than Los Angeles, pictured opposite. Automobiles have made this type of space possible. Americans love their cars and the freedom to just hop in and drive anywhere.

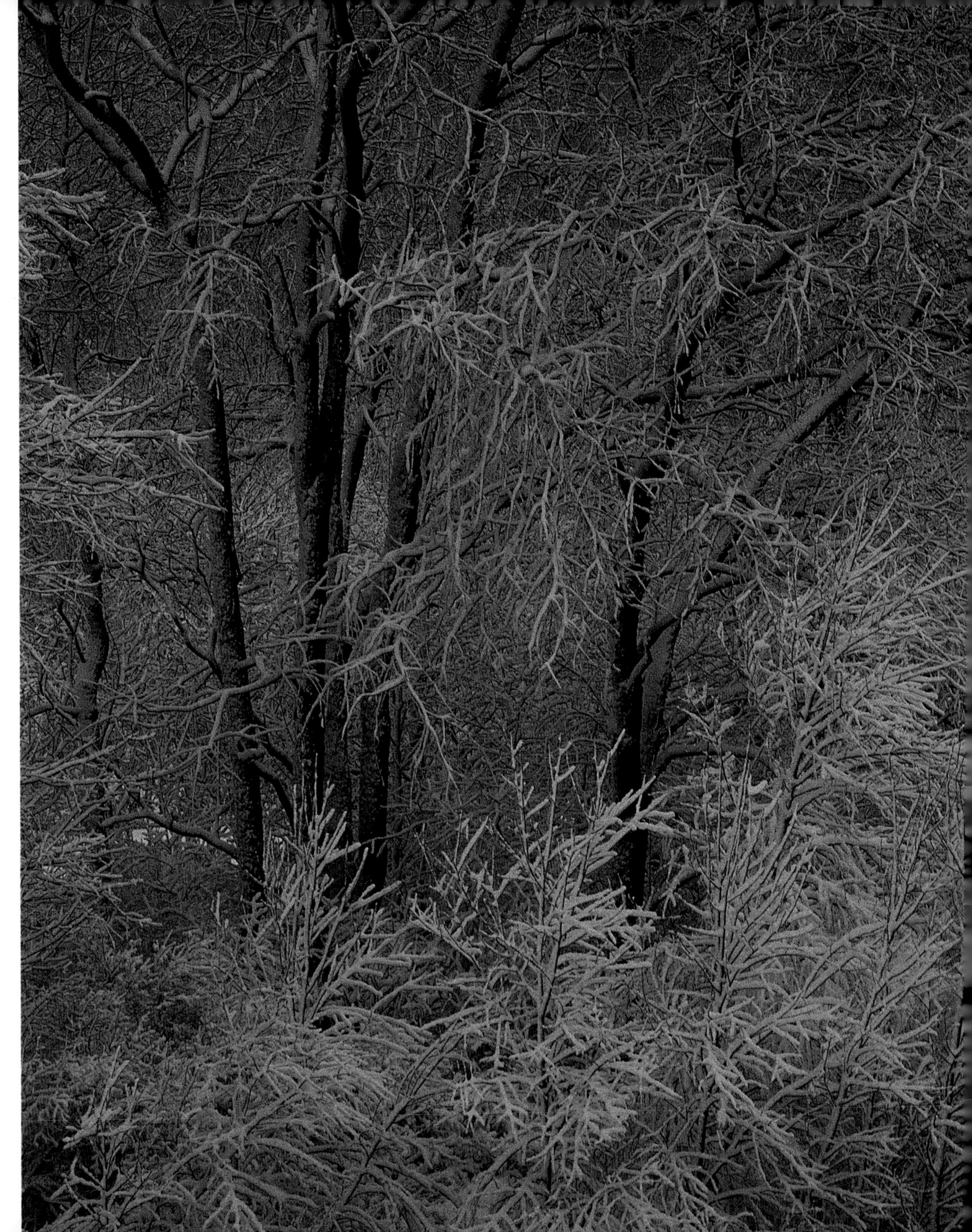

Right & Opposite:
Sunrise after a snowstorm is a glis-
tening, twinkling, magical time that
passes all too quickly. By sunset the
trees are bare again, but a certain
beauty and sense of wonder remain.

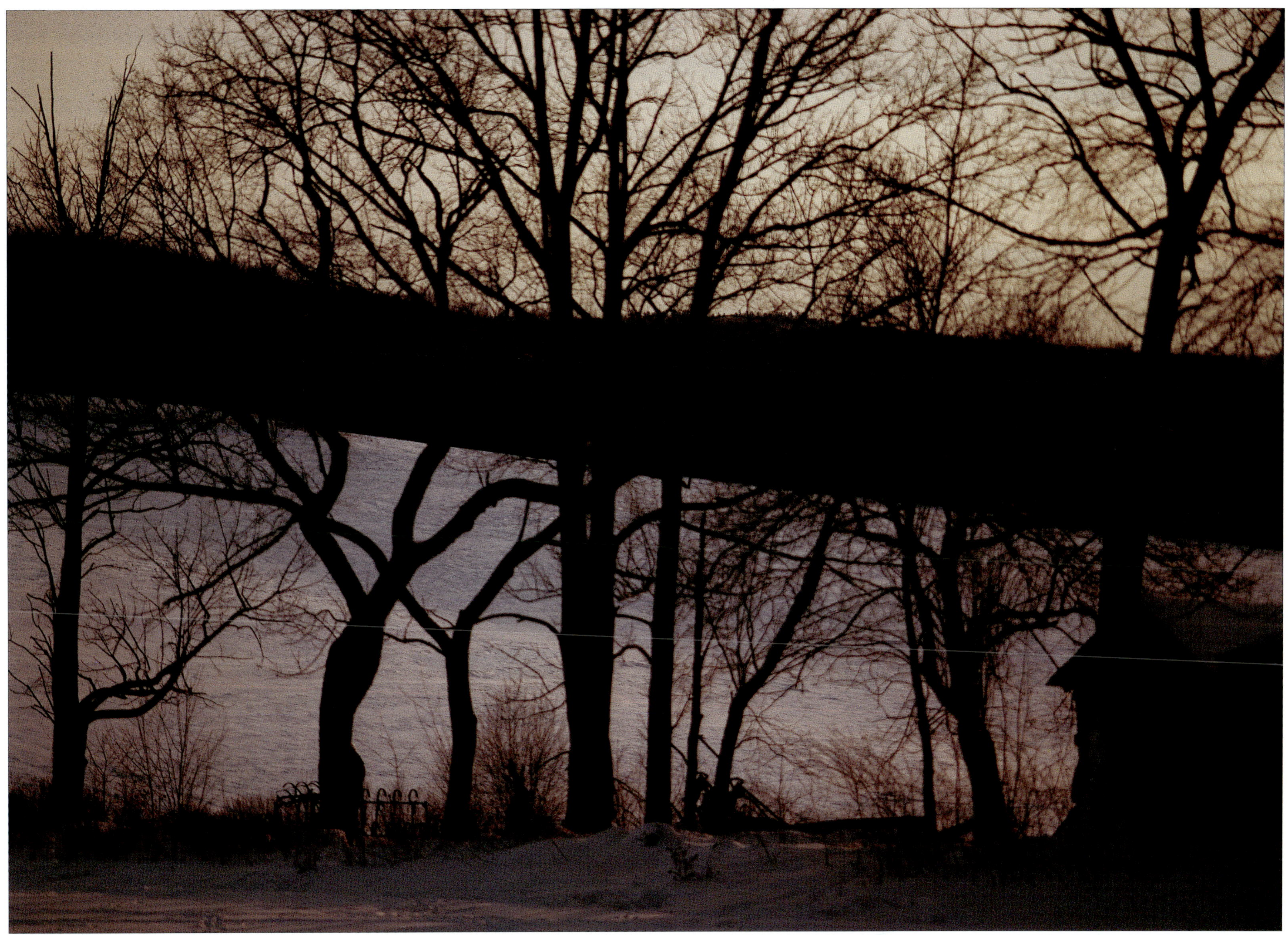

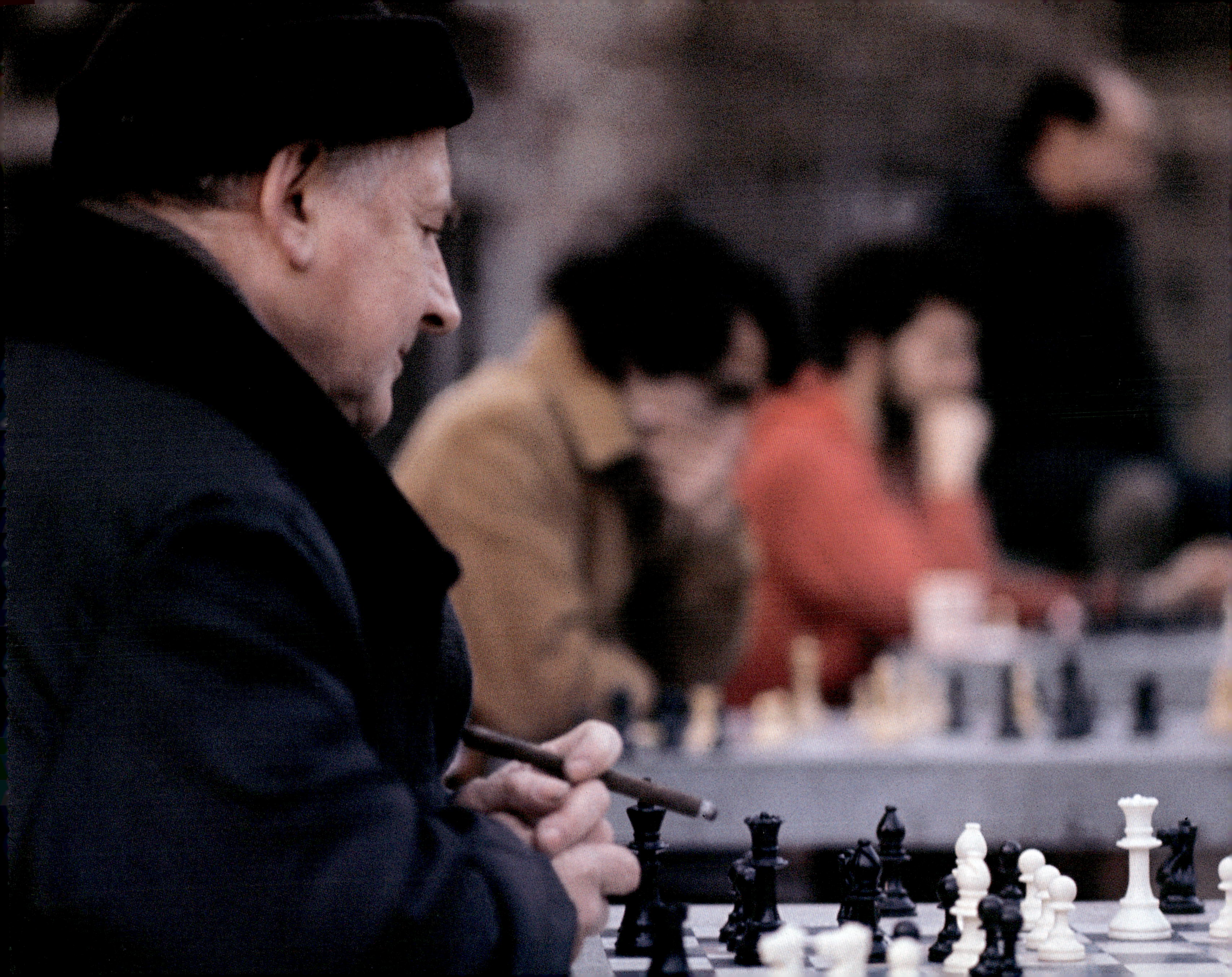

FACES

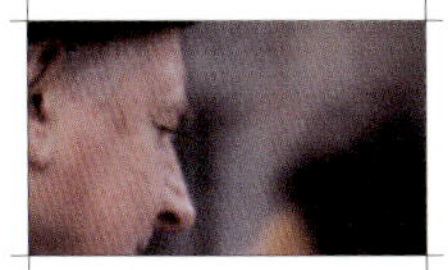

"I SEE IN THY FACE THE MAP
OF HONOR, TRUTH & LOYALTY."

— WILLIAM SHAKESPEARE'S
KING HENRY VI, PART 2, ACT 3, SCENE 1

Opposite: Old masters tutor the next generation of chess players in
New York City's Washington Square Park.

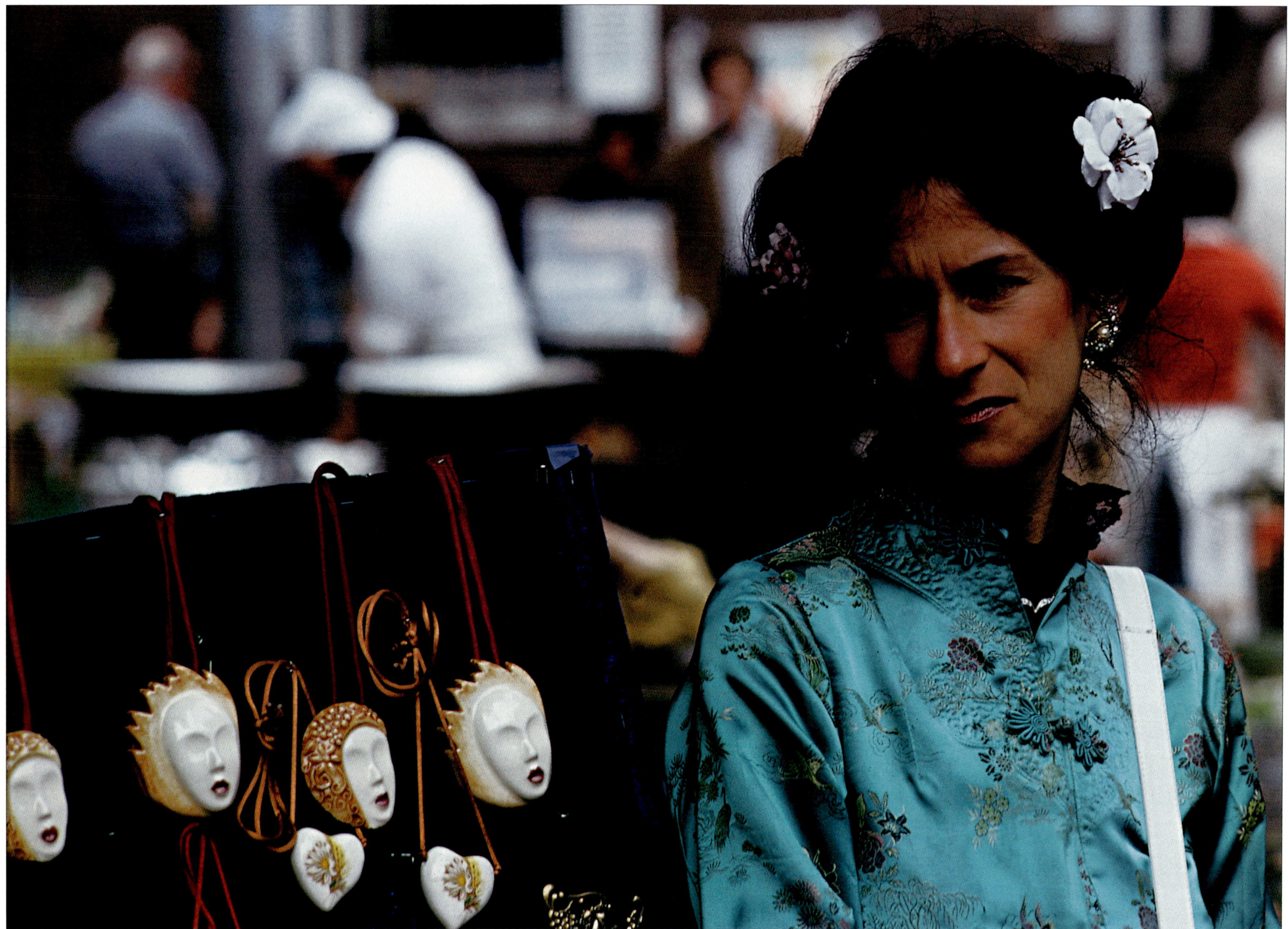

Opposite: Street vendor in Manhattan: dramatic looks characterize so many inhabitants of the "Big Apple,"—many of whom are either first generation or new immigrants, contributing new talent to an evolving country.

Right: Performers such as the pantomime actor have been for many years an integral part of the street scene of major metropolitan areas such as New York City.

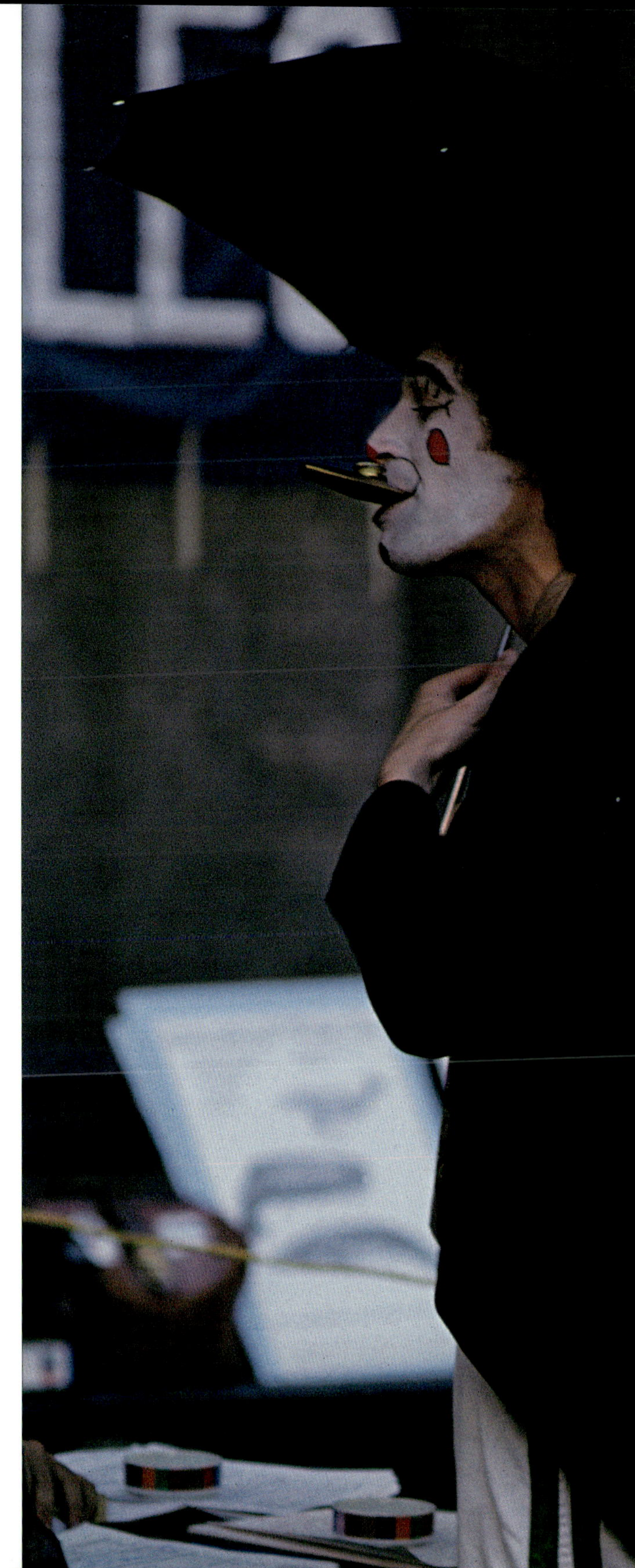

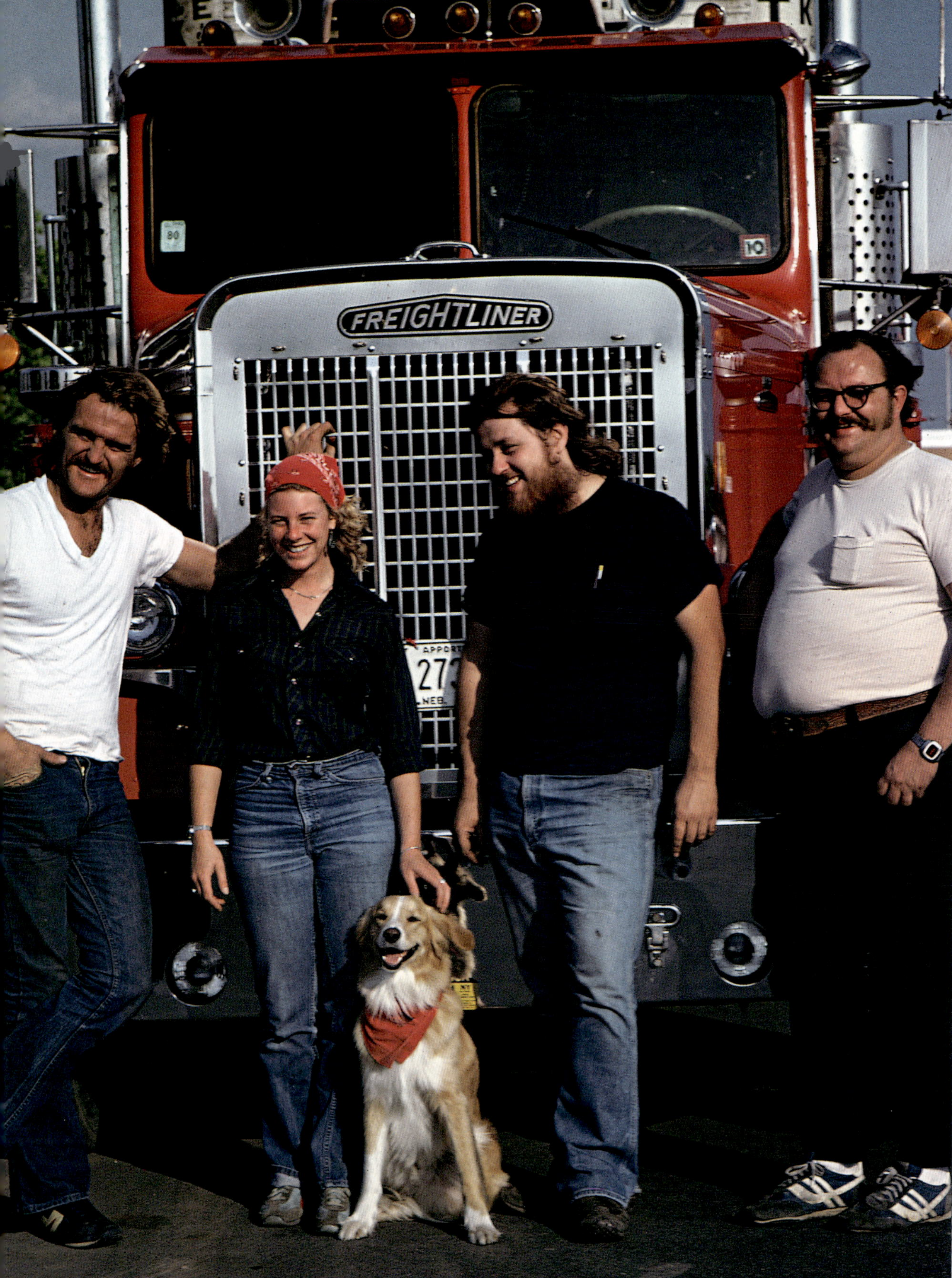

Left: Long-distance truckers are the "new" cowboys of America, criss-crossing the nation, carrying goods in their shiny "rigs."

Opposite: Long hours and risks to life and health are common for New York City's firefighters. New York's Fire Department suffered extreme losses during the attack on the World Trade Center... probably their finest hour and a clear demonstration of the credo of firefighters—to save lives no matter what.

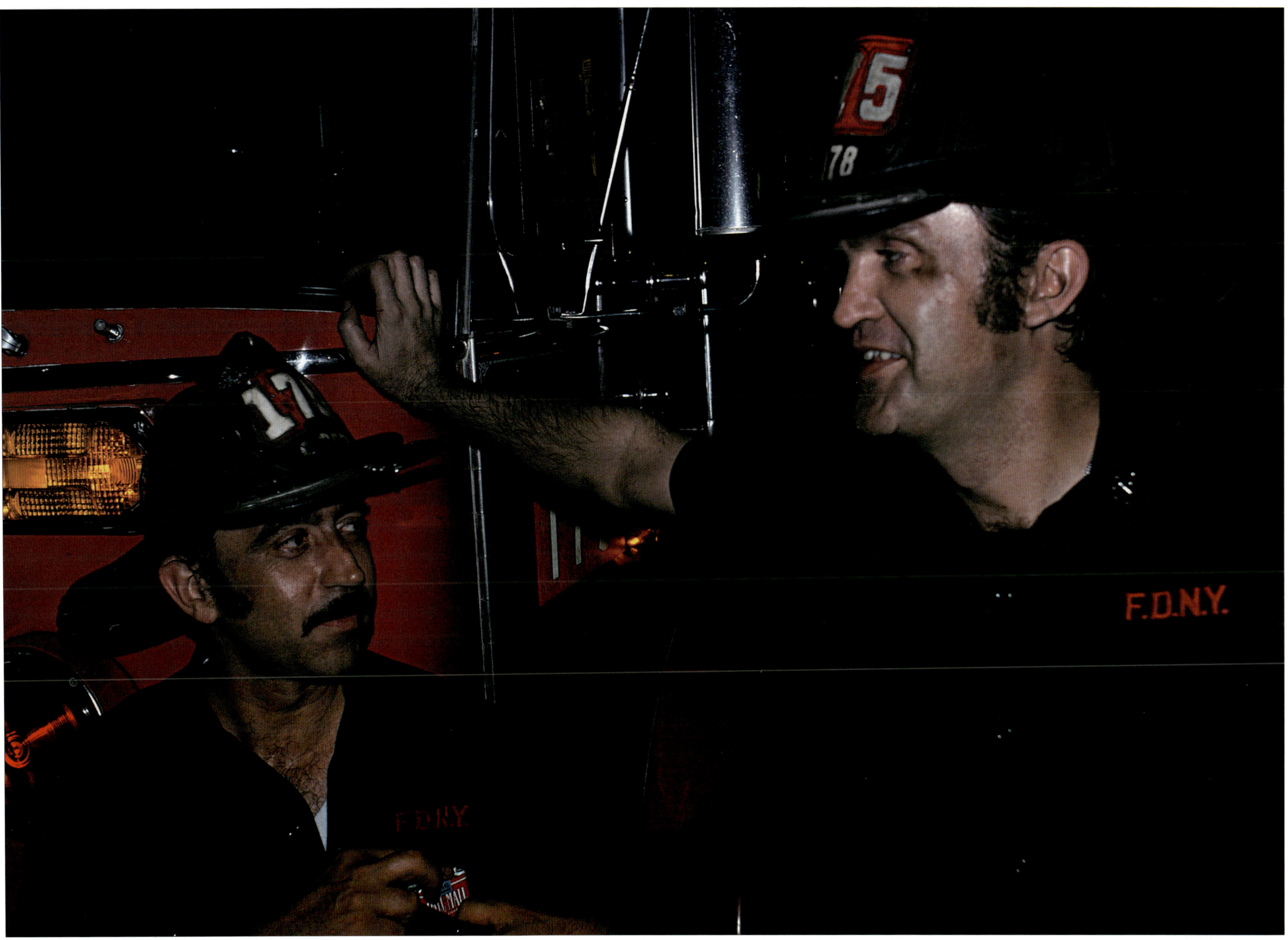

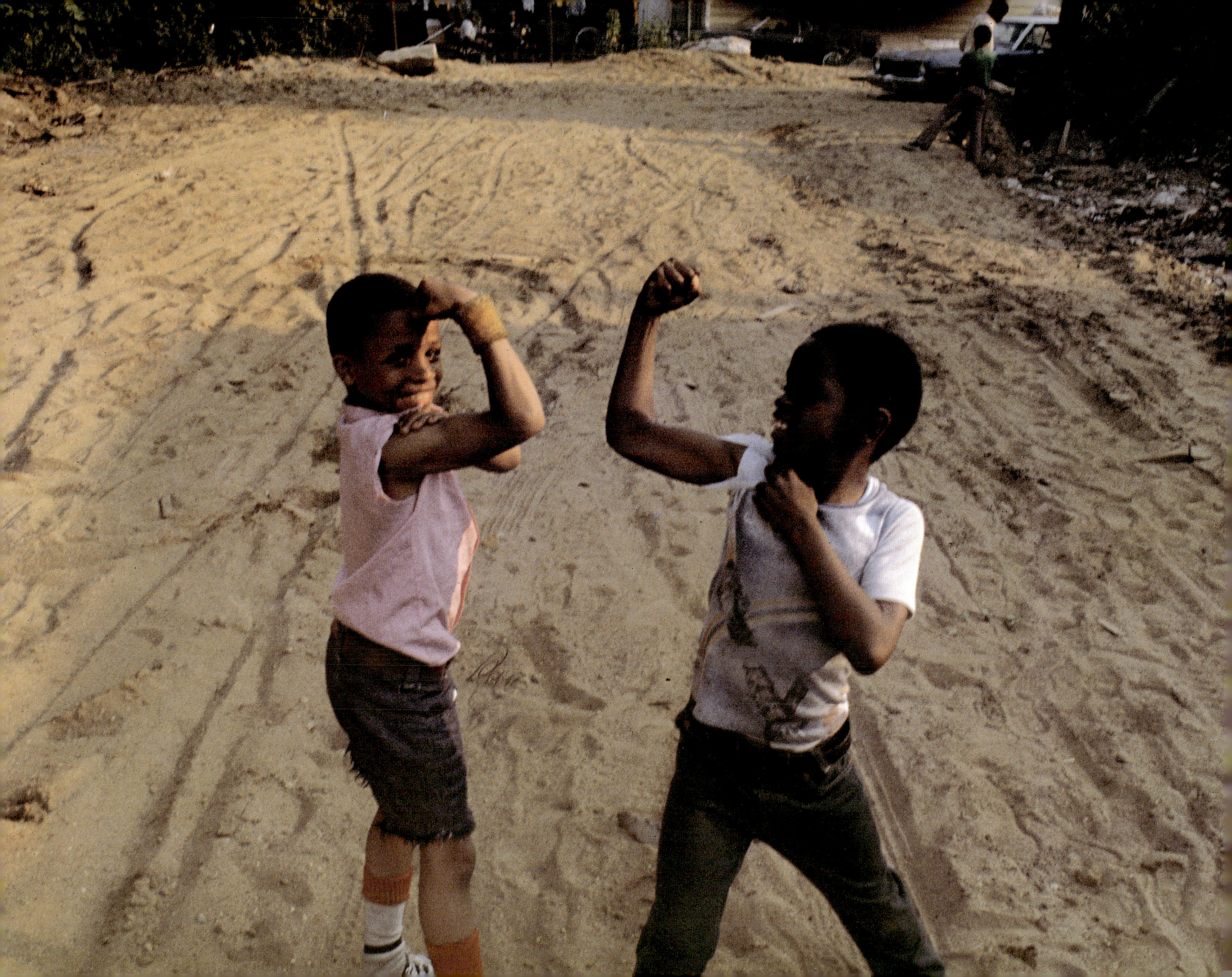

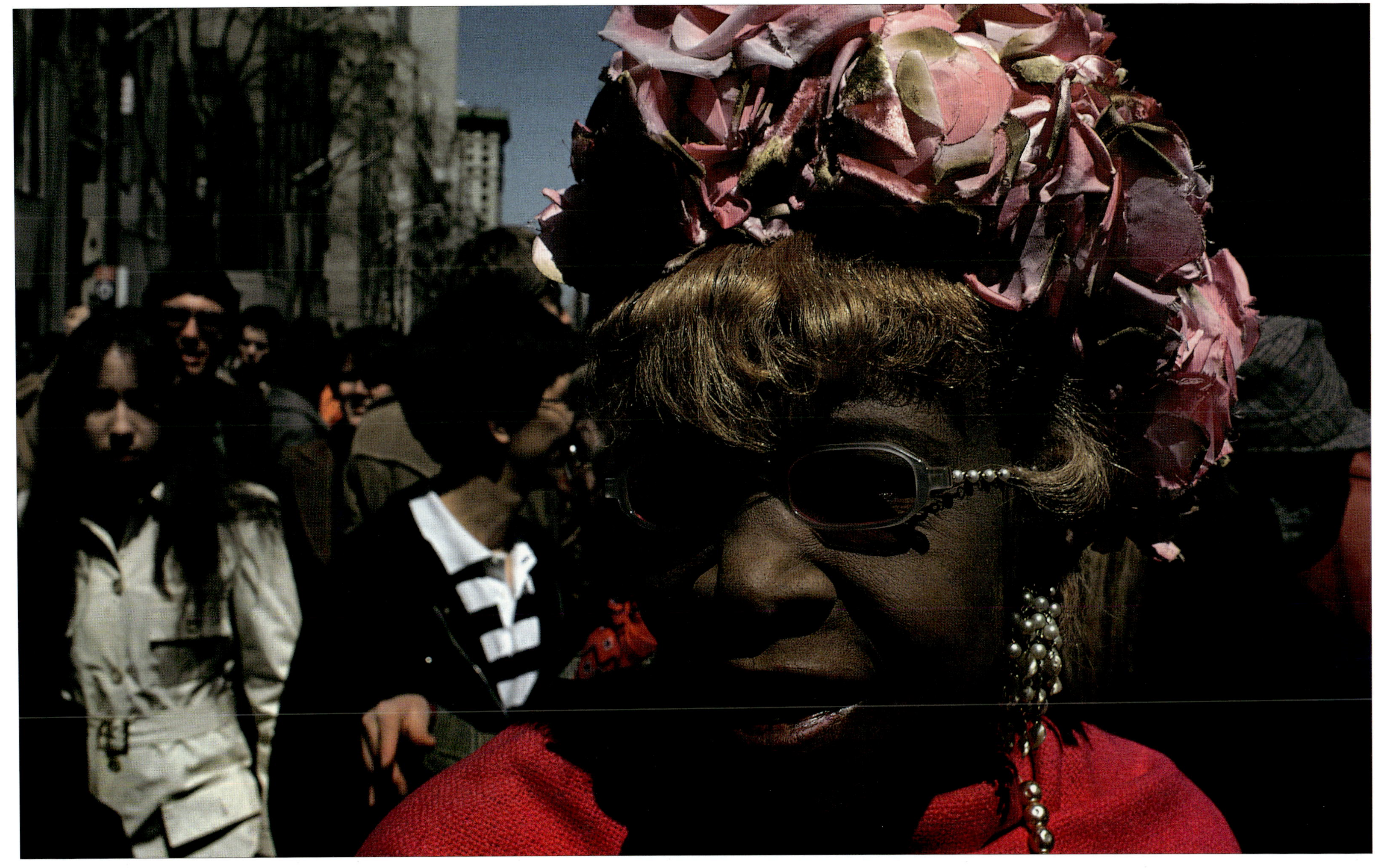

Opposite: Farm children near Wilmington, North Carolina, enjoy an early summer evening.

Above: All dressed up for the traditional Easter Day Parade on Manhattan's Fifth Avenue.

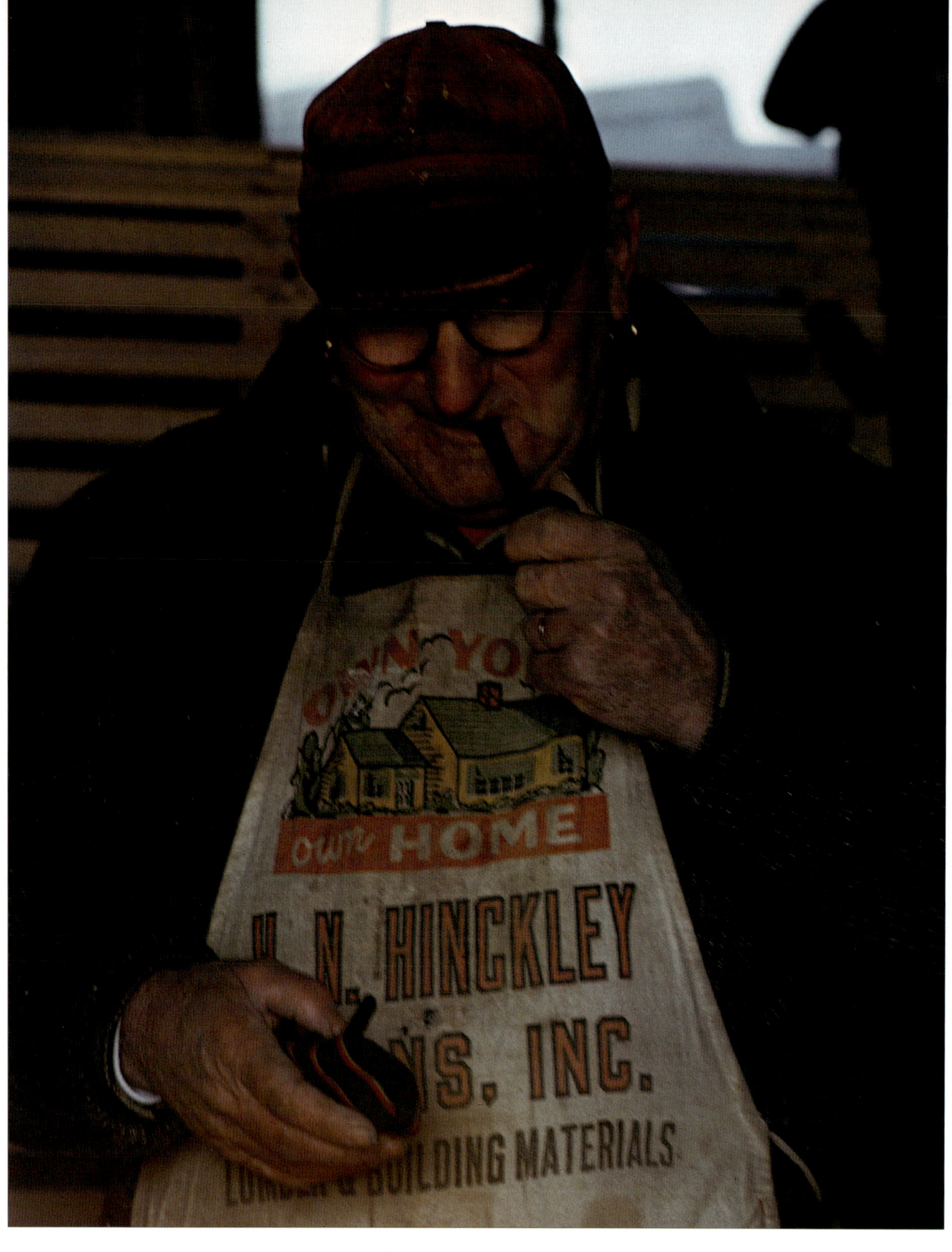

Left: Attention to detail and pride in craftsmanship are hallmarks of America, such as this venerable artist and carpenter who builds lobster pots on Martha's Vineyard, Massachusetts.

Opposite: "Pinky" Edmonds, dressed in formal fox hunting attire, monitors other fox hunters with care, drawing on several generations of knowledge of working with horses, hounds and often careless riders.

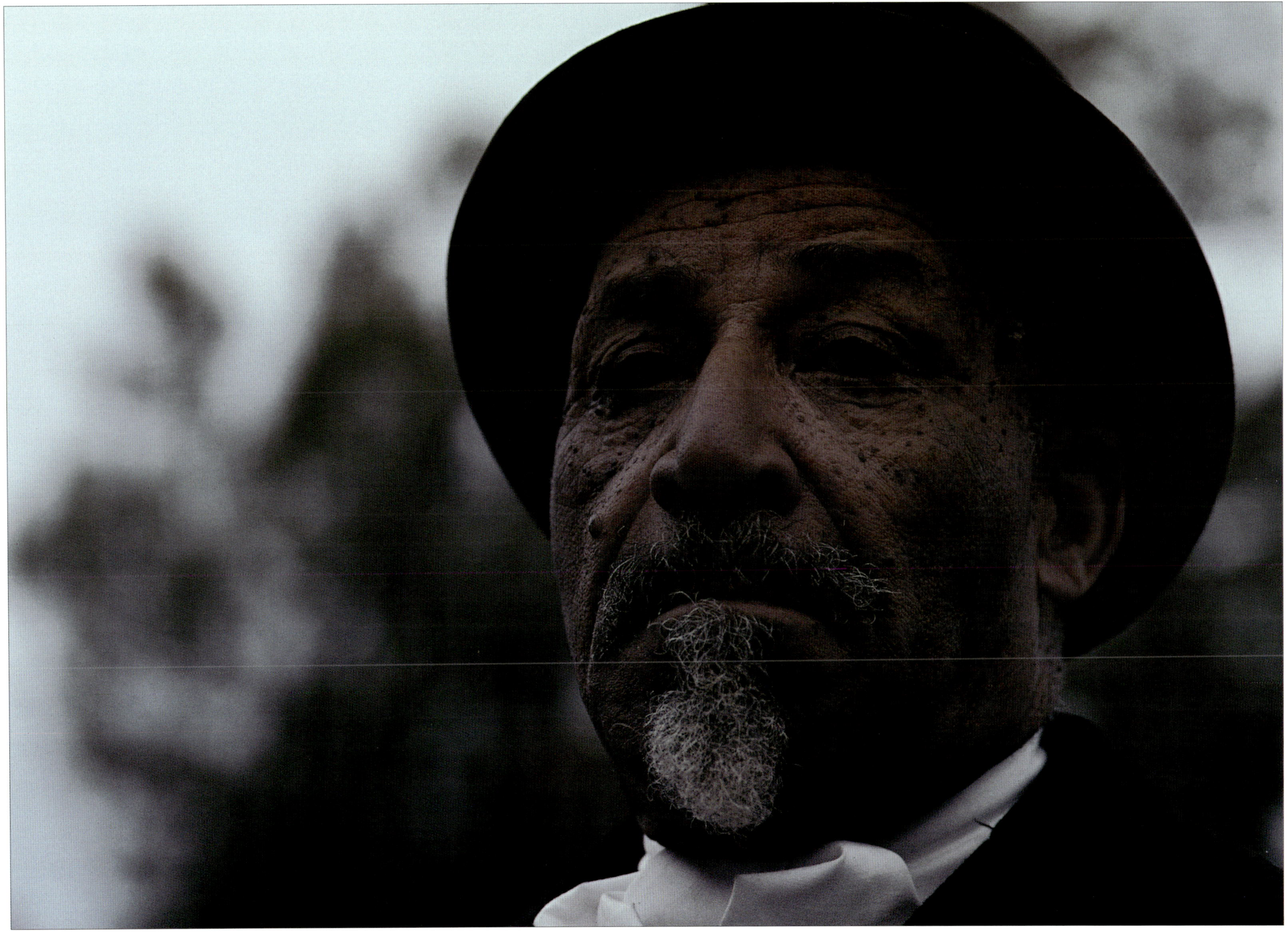

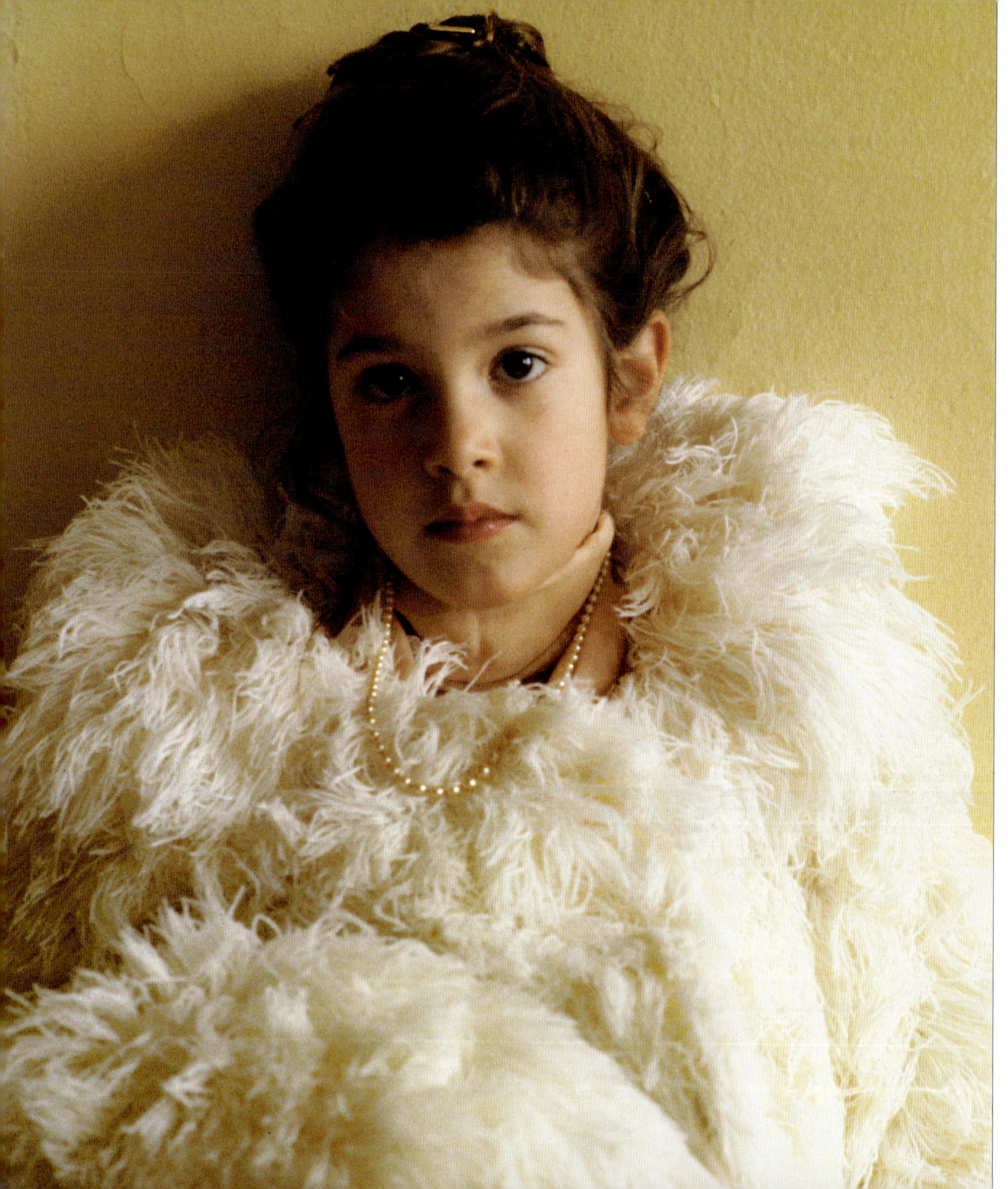

Left & Opposite: Children are America's future. On the left is young Sofiya Balta posing, as young girls are fond of doing, in her mother's jewels and boa. Young Christian Ulrich von Hassell (opposite) gets ready to compete in America's oldest horse show, held in Upperville, Virginia, each June.

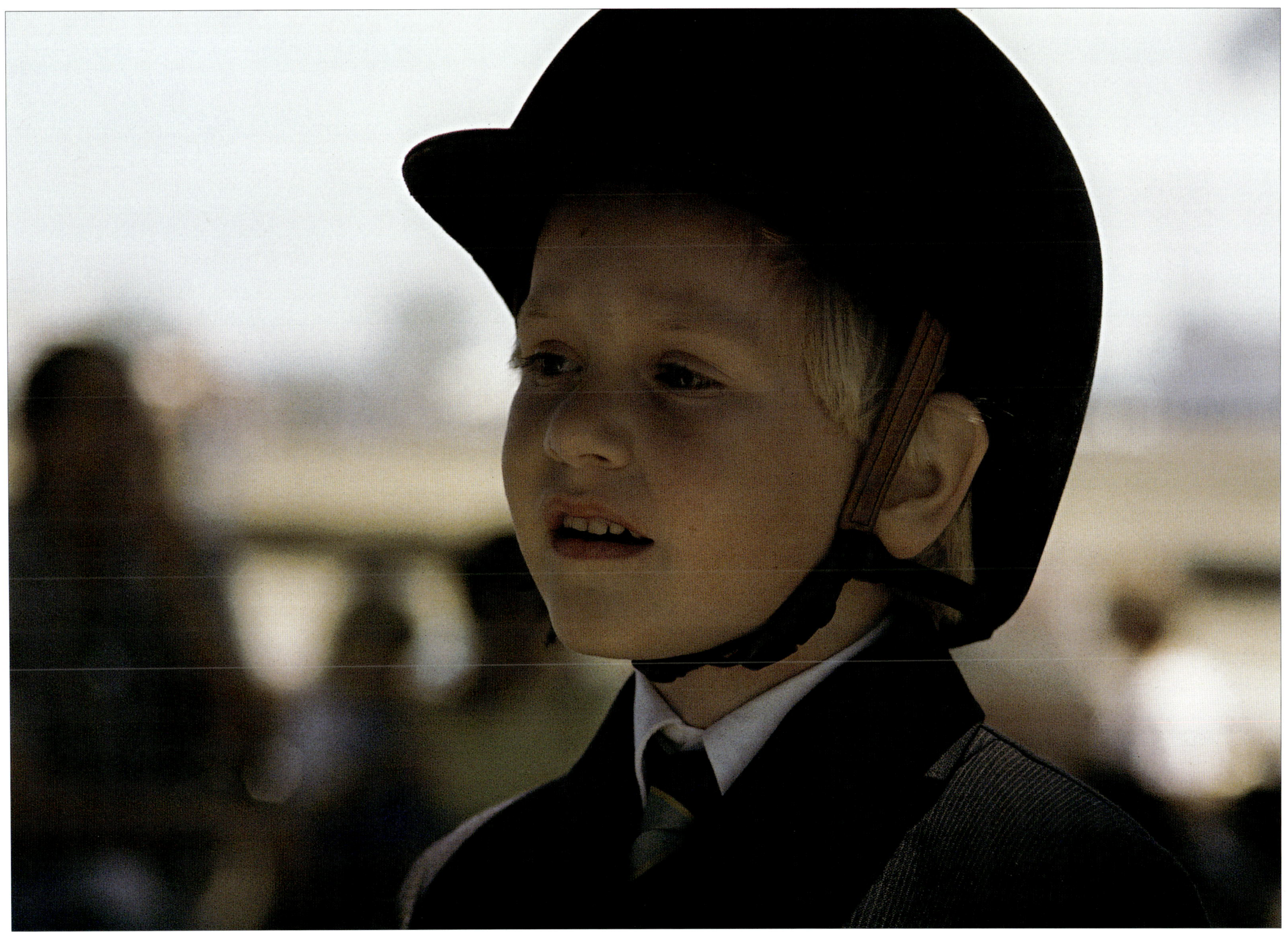

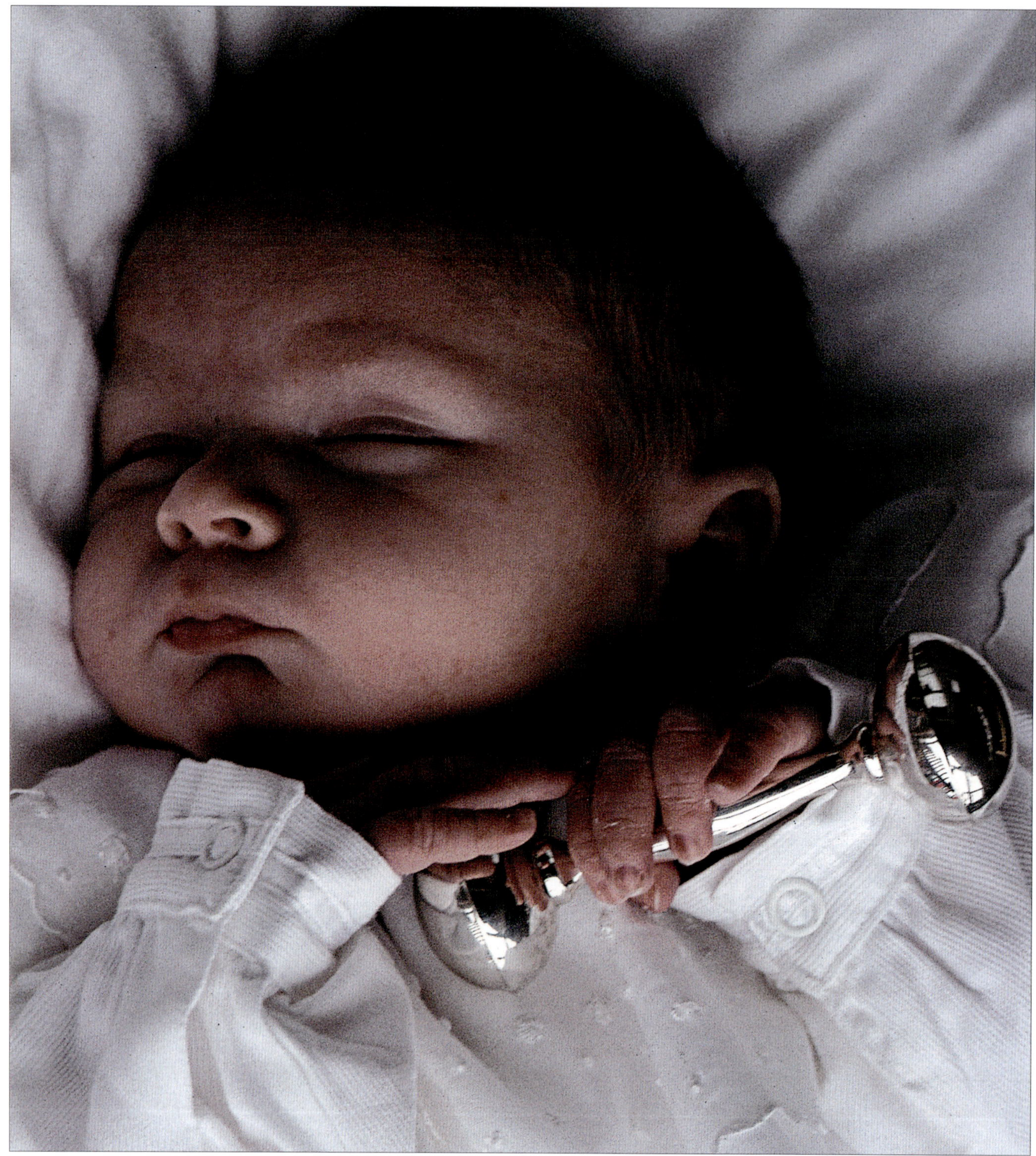

Right: What will the future hold in fast-changing America for this one-week-old baby? William Thassilo von Hassell is dressed in linens brought from Europe and worn by many generations of his ancestors.

Opposite: Famous fox hunter Madam Desireè gratefully accepts a carrot from her mistress and loyal friend, Elizabeth von Hassell. Madam Desiree started her life pulling a plow in West Virginia. She moved on to become a fancy horse and very much a grand dame, winning prizes in the most challenging competitions. She now "claims" to be a direct descendant of another famous Virginia horse, Traveller, a gray gelding that carried the hero of the Confederacy, Robert E. Lee.

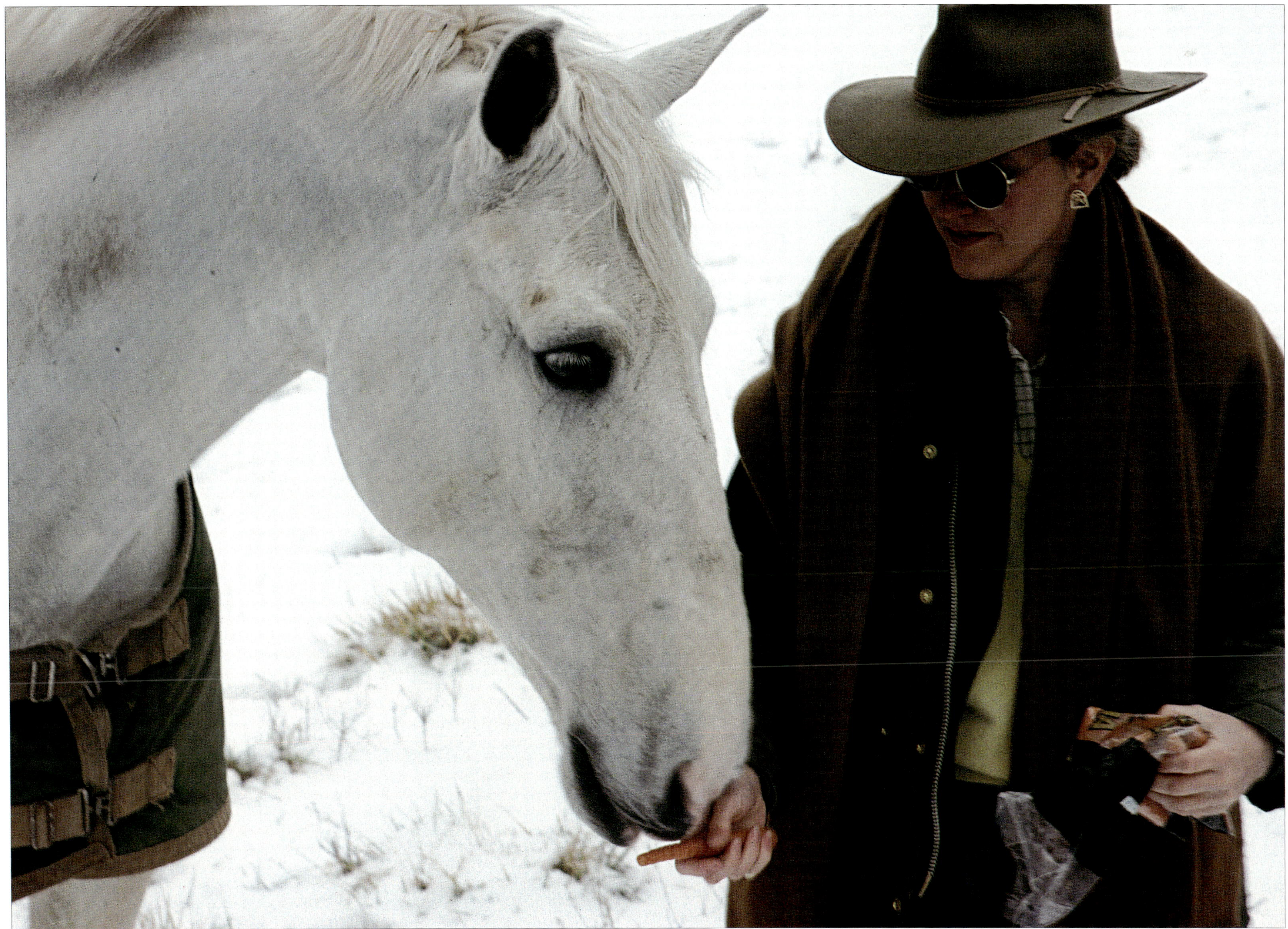

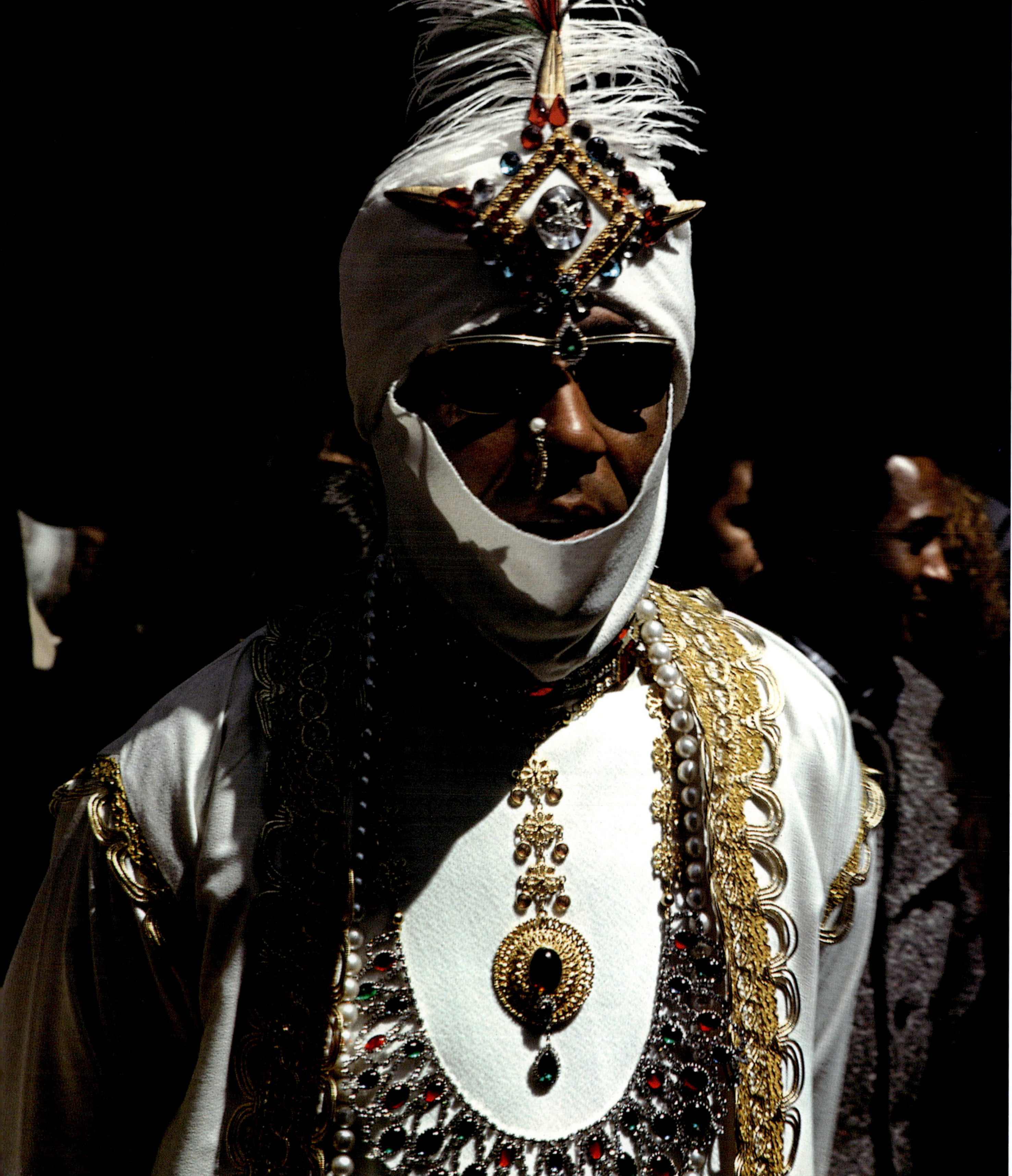

Left & Opposite: Getting dressed up in colorful costumes is a major American pastime, such as this Shriner (left) or this ice-skating Santa Claus in Rockefeller Center, New York City.

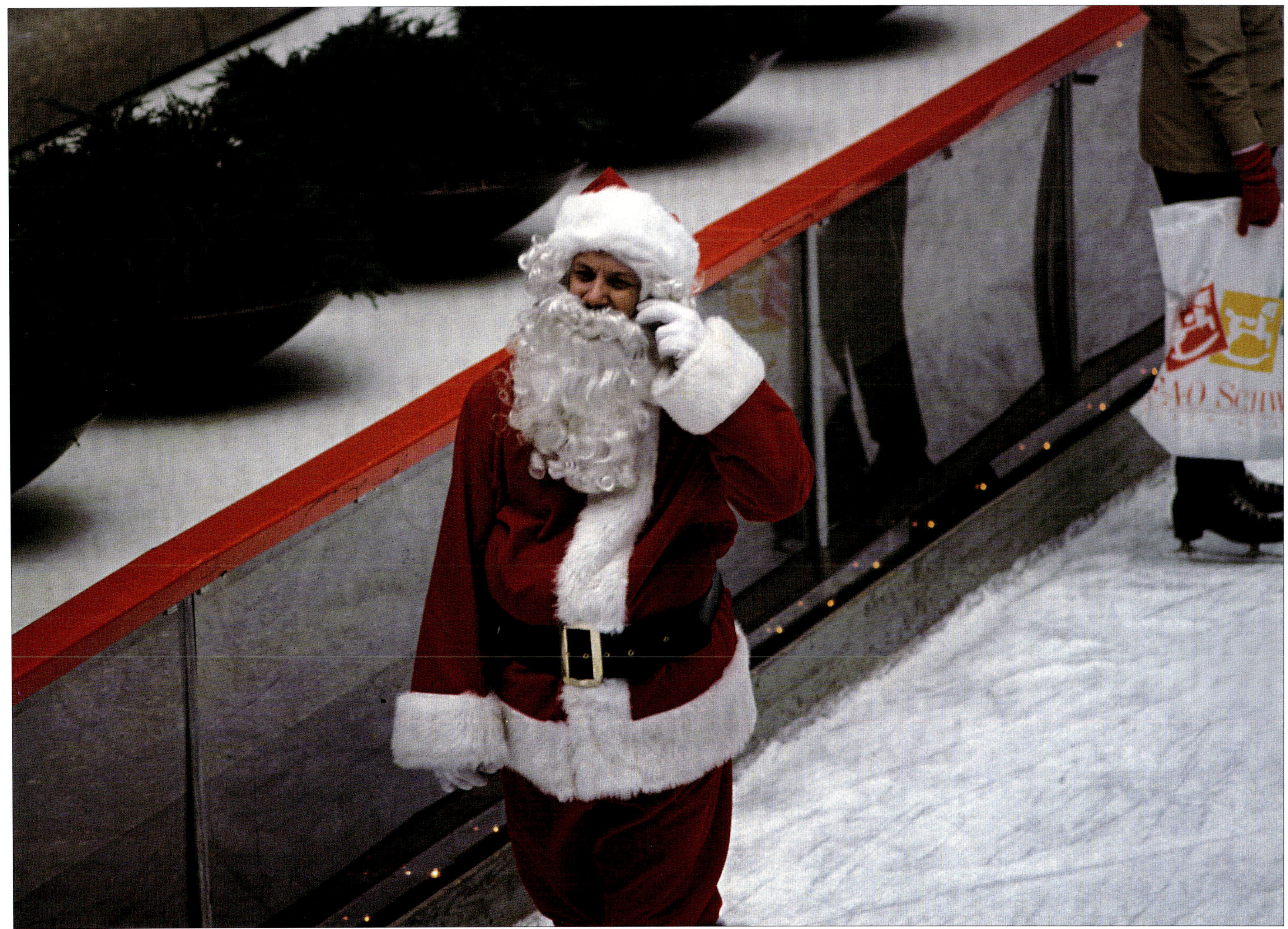

FAO Schwarz

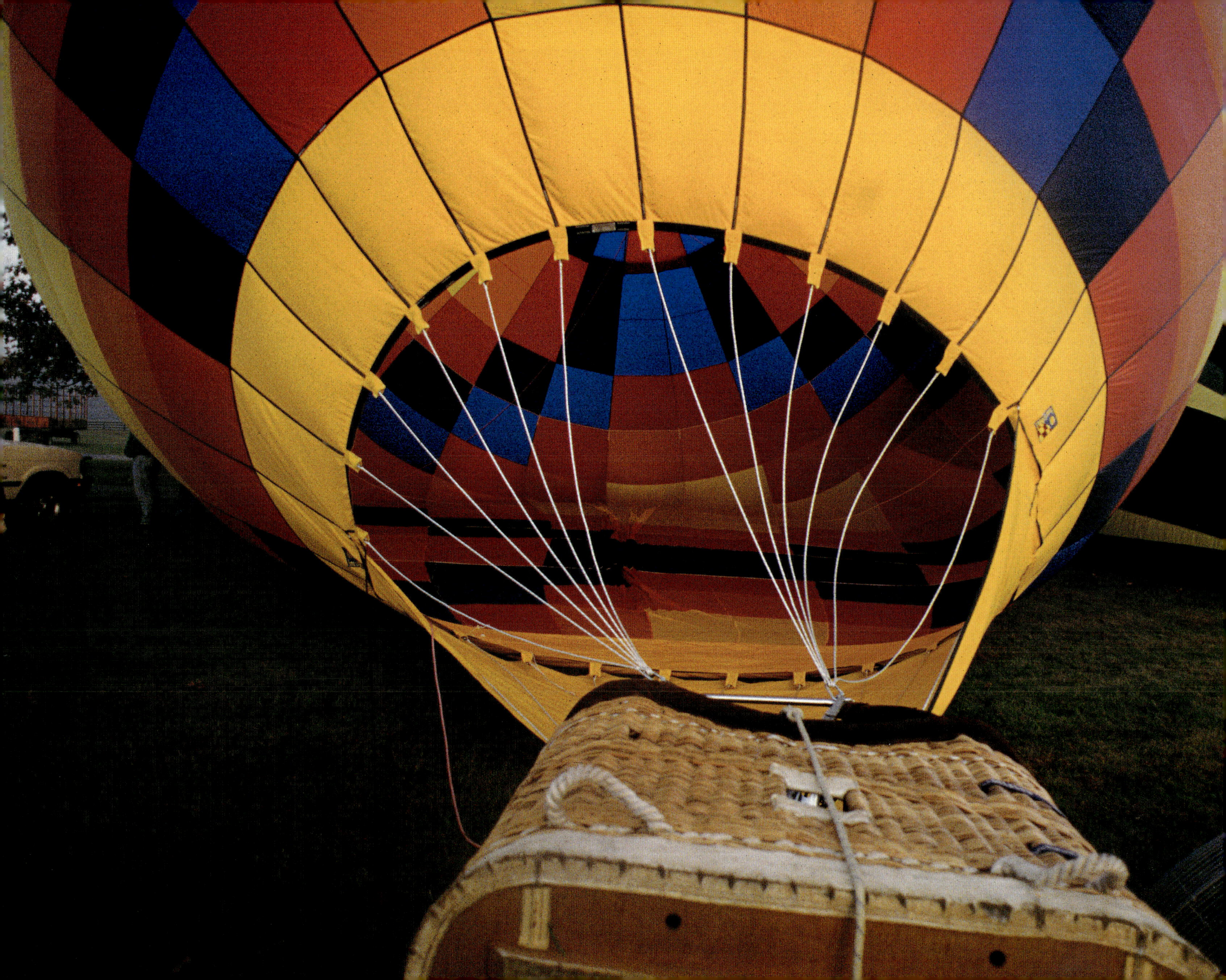

CELEBRATION

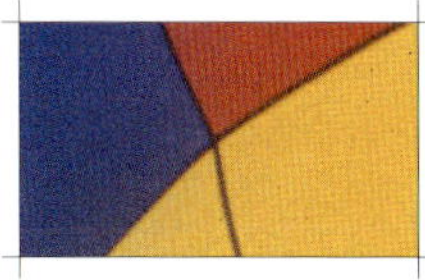

"EVERY MAN SHOULD EAT AND DRINK, AND ENJOY THE GOOD OF ALL HIS LABOUR, IT IS THE GIFT OF GOD."

— ECCLESIASTES 3:13

Opposite: Peacefully soaring high above the land in New Mexico while enjoying nature's majesty is the essence of hot air ballooning.

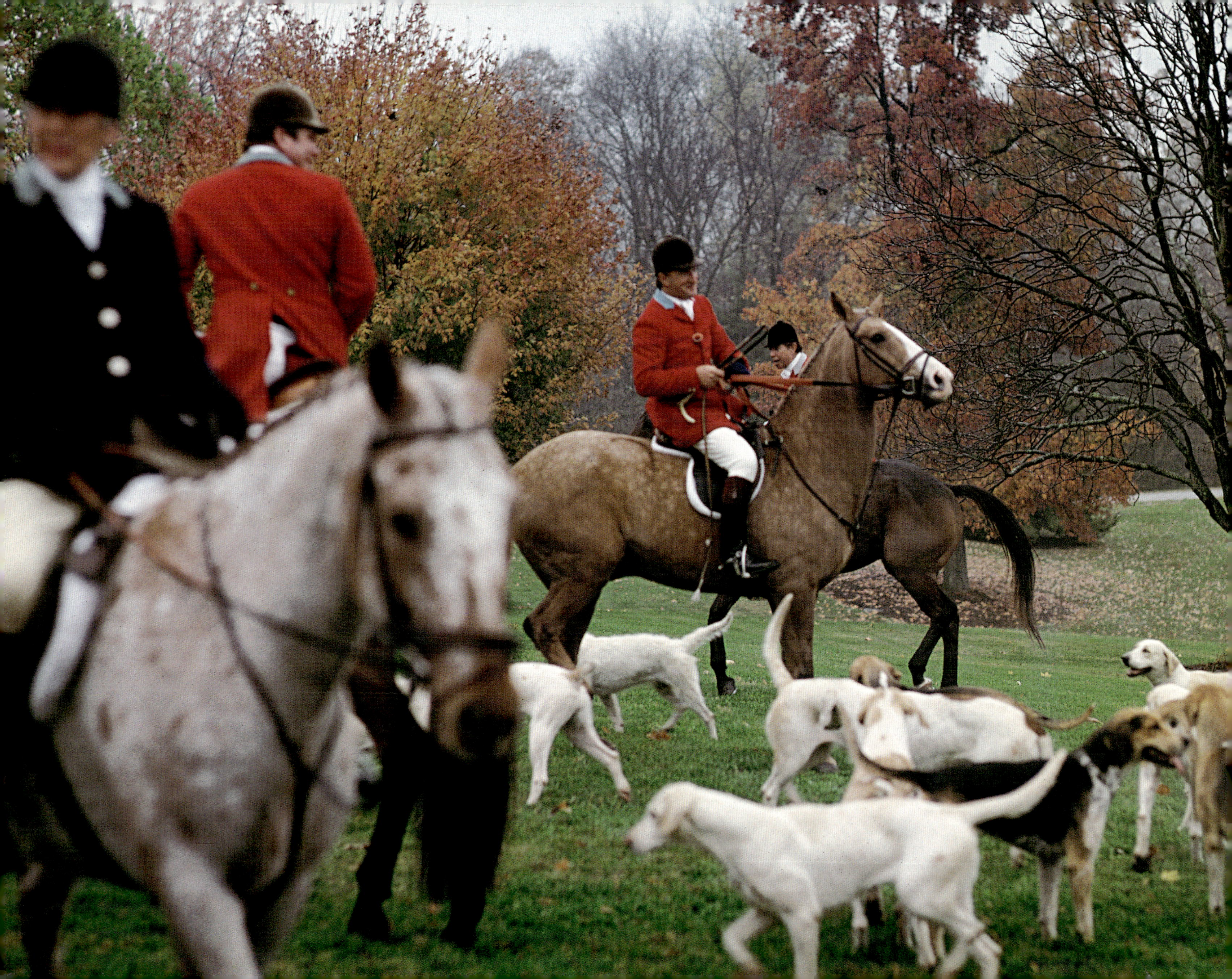

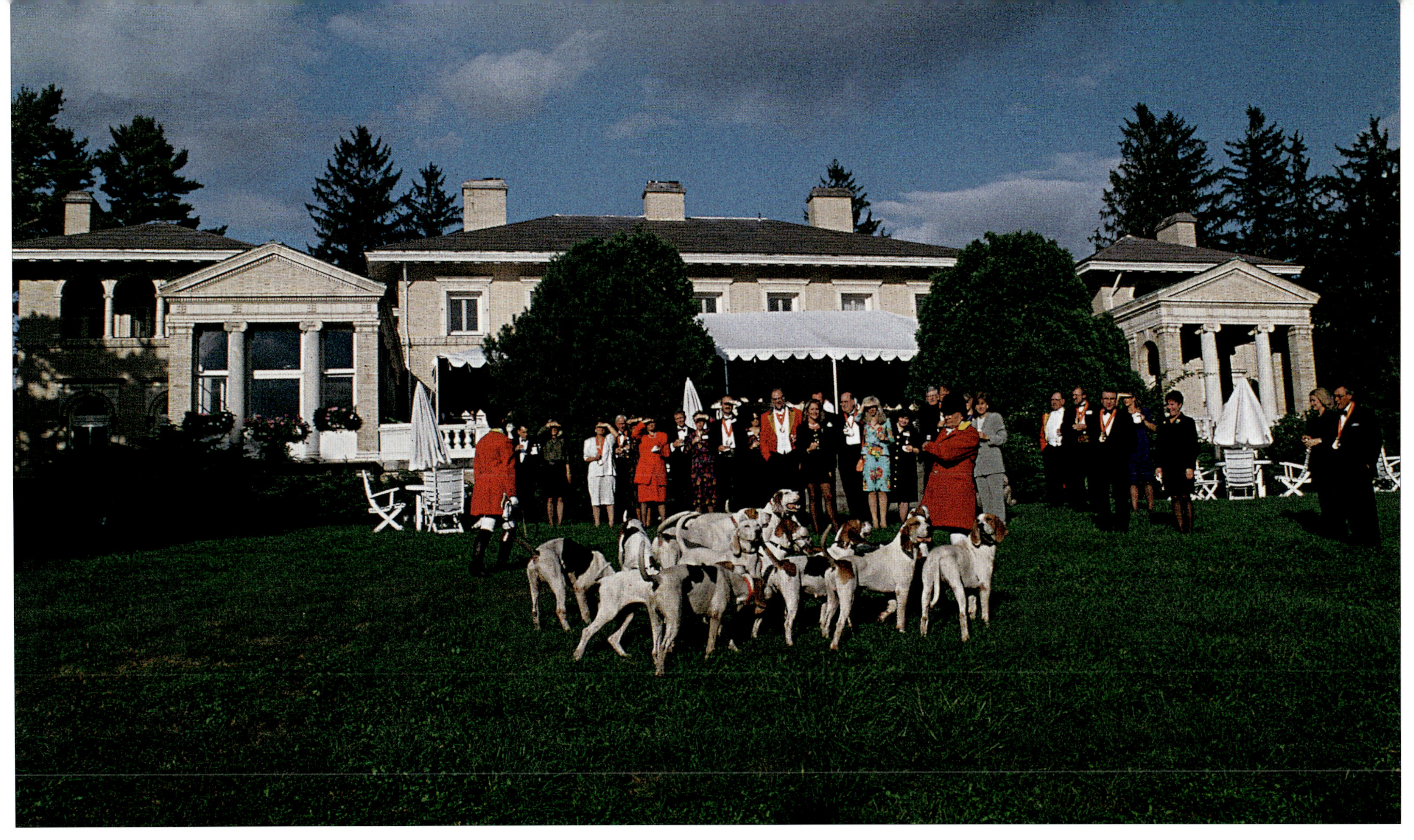

Opposite & Above: Thomas Lord Fairfax first organized fox hunting in Virginia in the 1750s. Now, bloody yet noble endeavors like the Blue Ridge Hunt in Clarke County, Virginia (opposite), have become essential to preserving open land. States all over the United States also sport a fine fox hunting culture. Above, at the Wheatleigh Hotel in the Berkshires, the hounds of the Old Chatham Hunt parade for an elegant wine society. This hotel was once an "Italianate" villa, combining the very best style of old Europe with modern American conveniences.

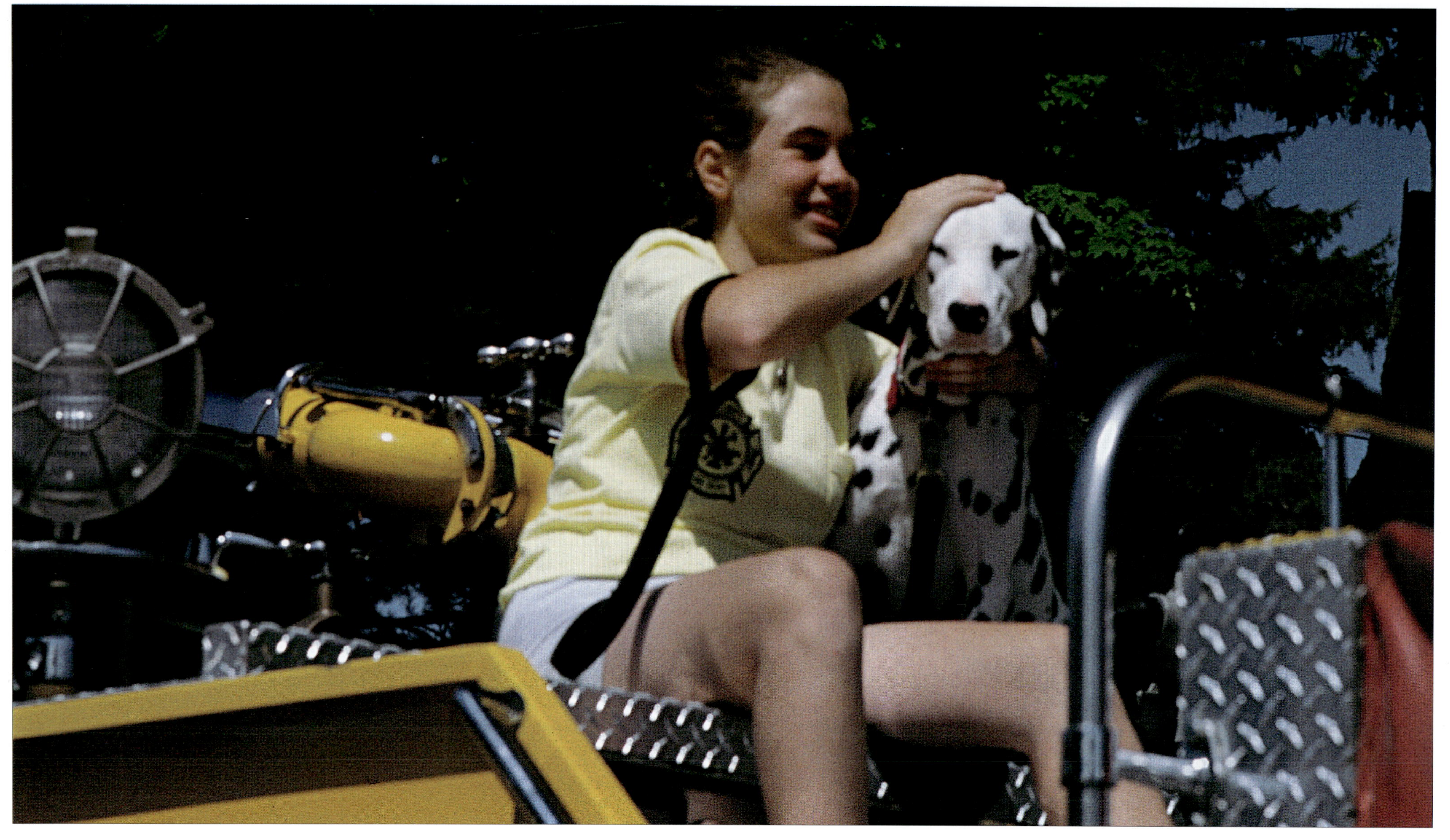

Above & Opposite: A volunteer fire department helps kick off the Columbia County, New York, County Fair by showing off the trucks, the Dalmatian (above), and the lovely Ladies Auxiliary (opposite) in the annual parade. Weimaraner Dalmatians were first used as fire dogs in London hundreds of years ago. The tradition continues today and many Dalmatians are given places of honor on board fire trucks.

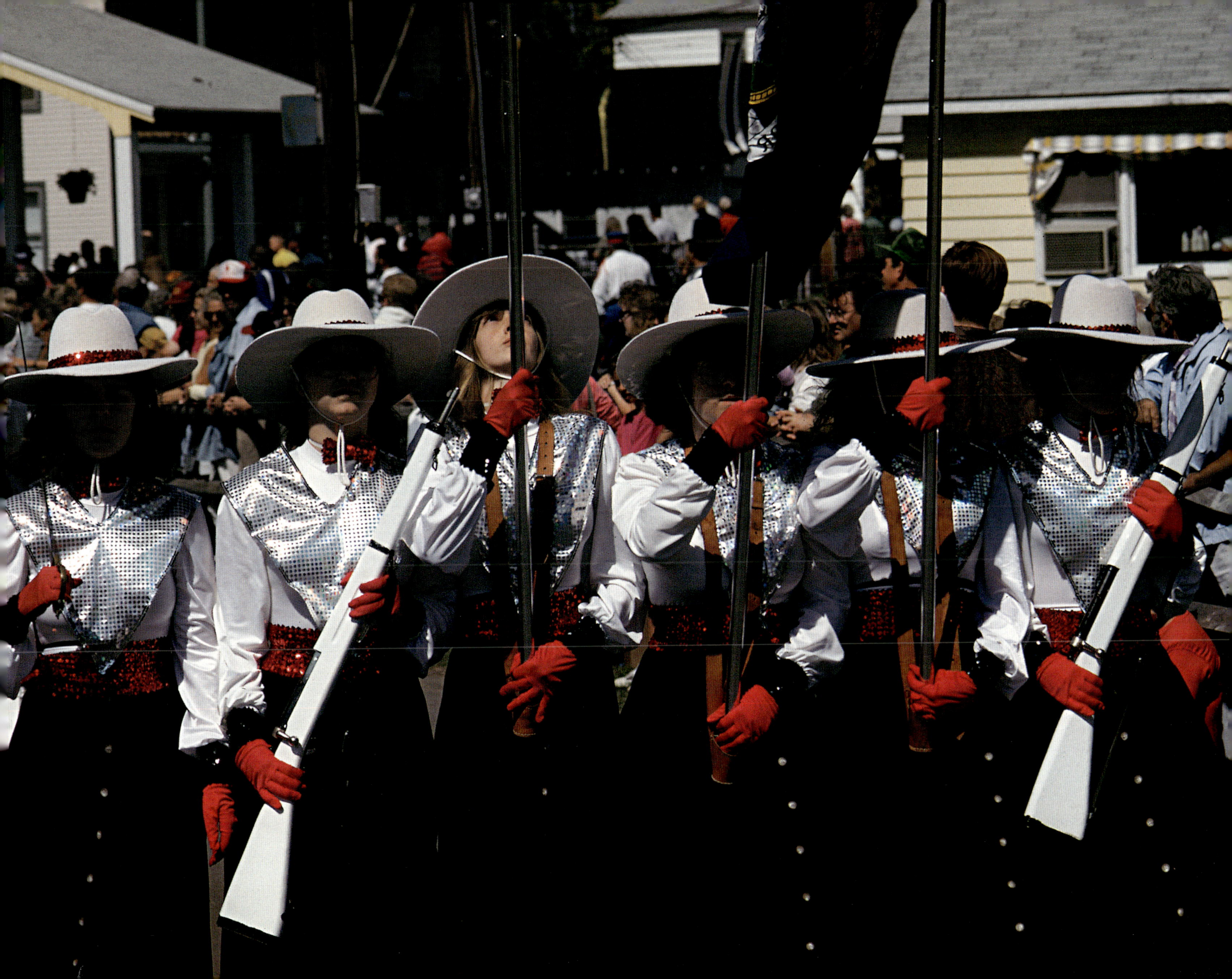

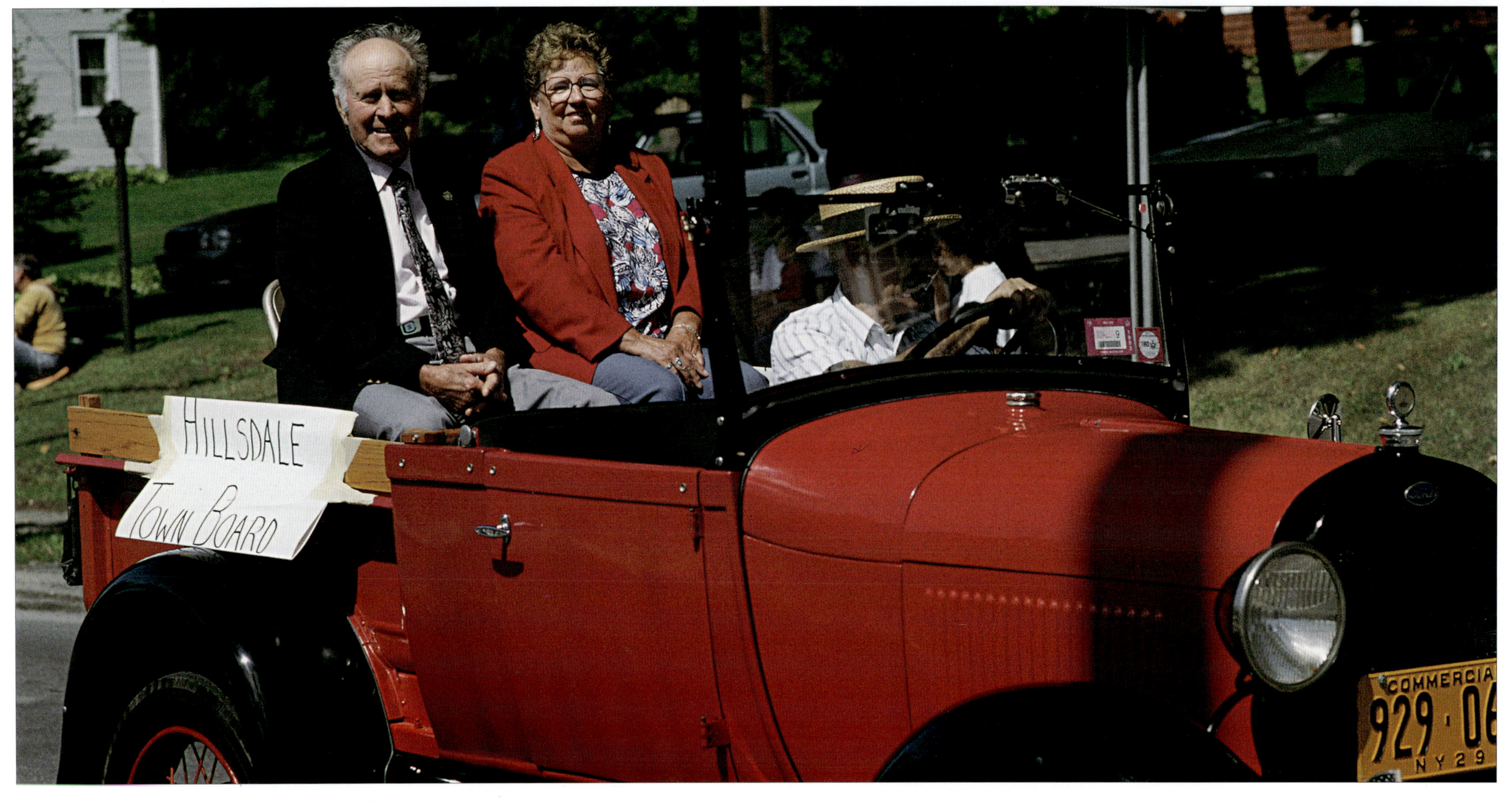

Above: Samuel W. Dawson, a second-generation dairy farmer in Columbia County, New York, rides in the annual 4th of July Parade.

Opposite: In many ways America is still recovering from the War Between the States. Reenactments honor the memories of those souls lost and teach future generations about a terrible conflict that almost tore the nation apart, but ultimately strengthened it forever. "Fervently do we pray – that this mighty scourge of war may speedily pass away," said President Abraham Lincoln in 1864.

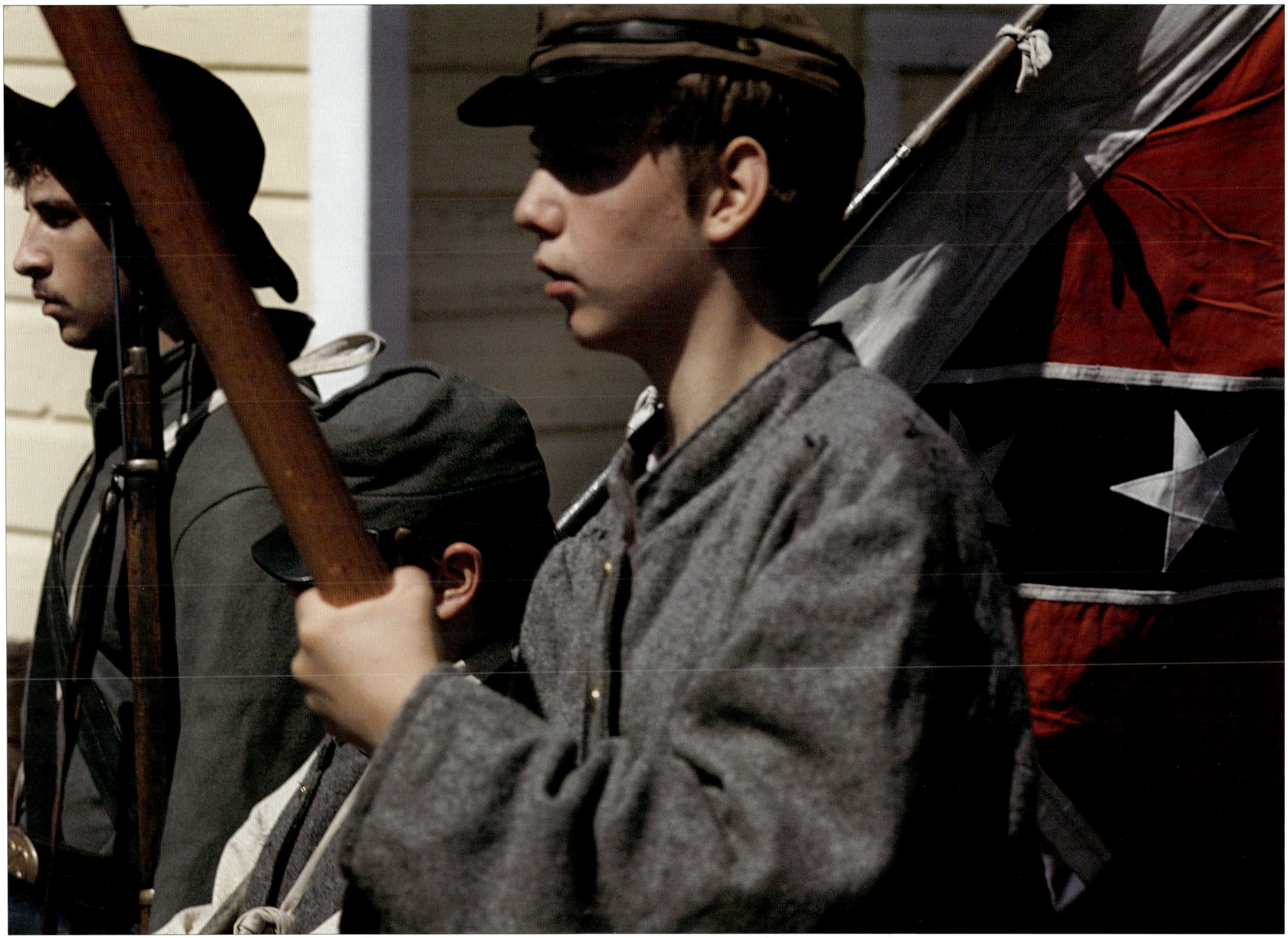

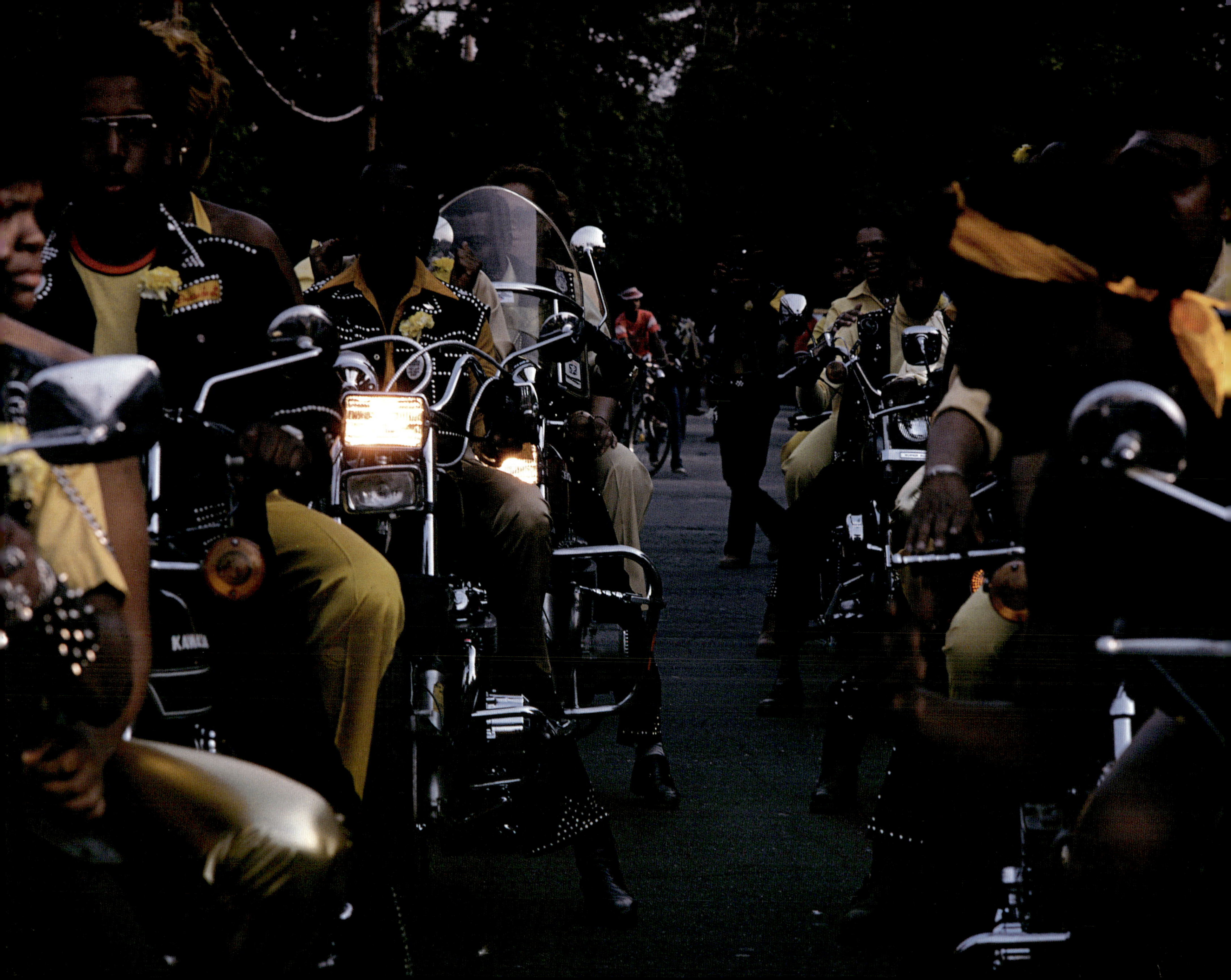

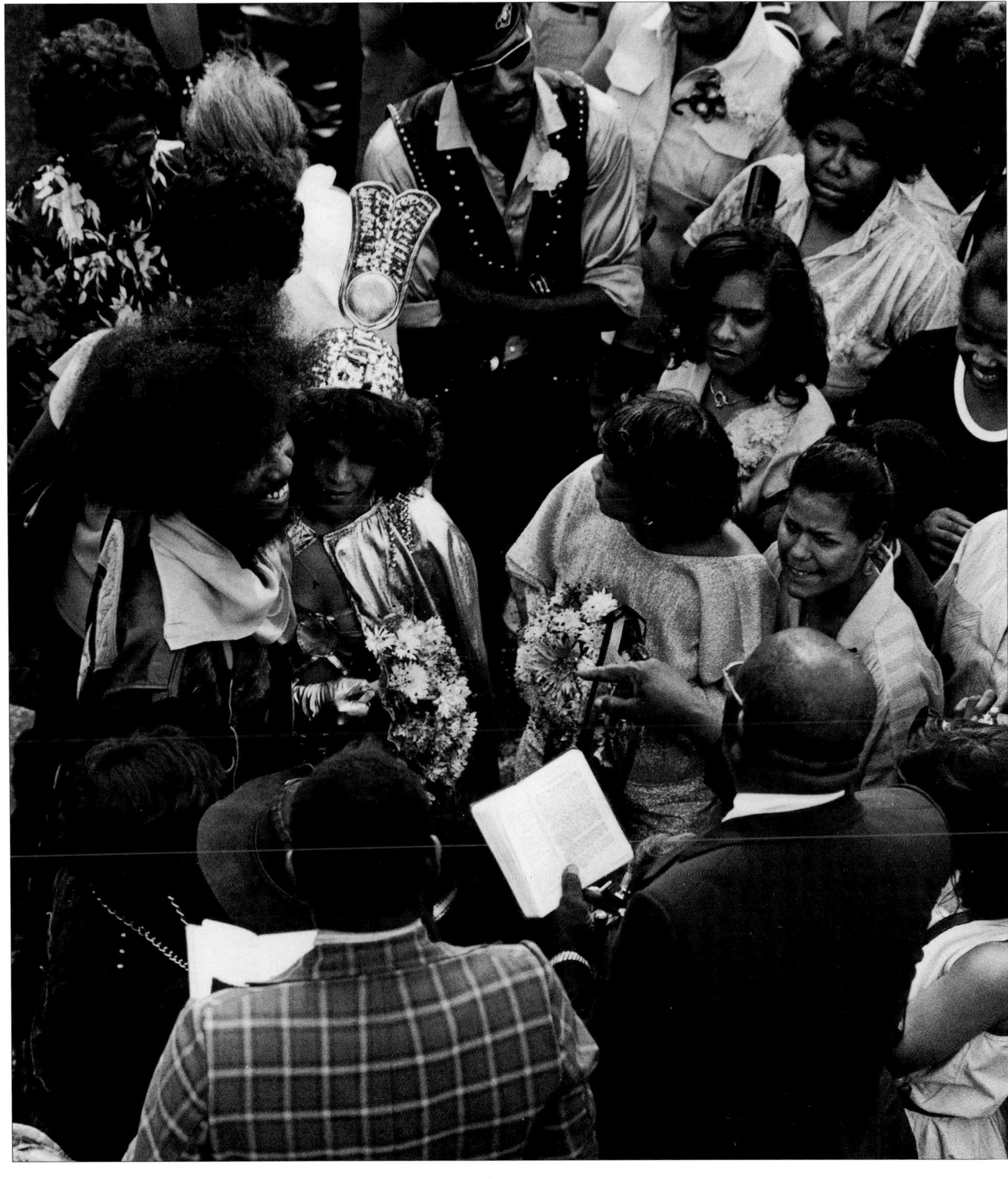

Opposite & Left: Tolerance and
racial peace are important in
holding a neighborhood together.
Locals may have feared the
wedding of two Cobra Motorcycle
Gang members one hot June
evening in Jamaica, Queens,
New York. Hundreds of gang
members took to the streets, and
the ceremony proceeded with
love and laughter, common
ground for us all.

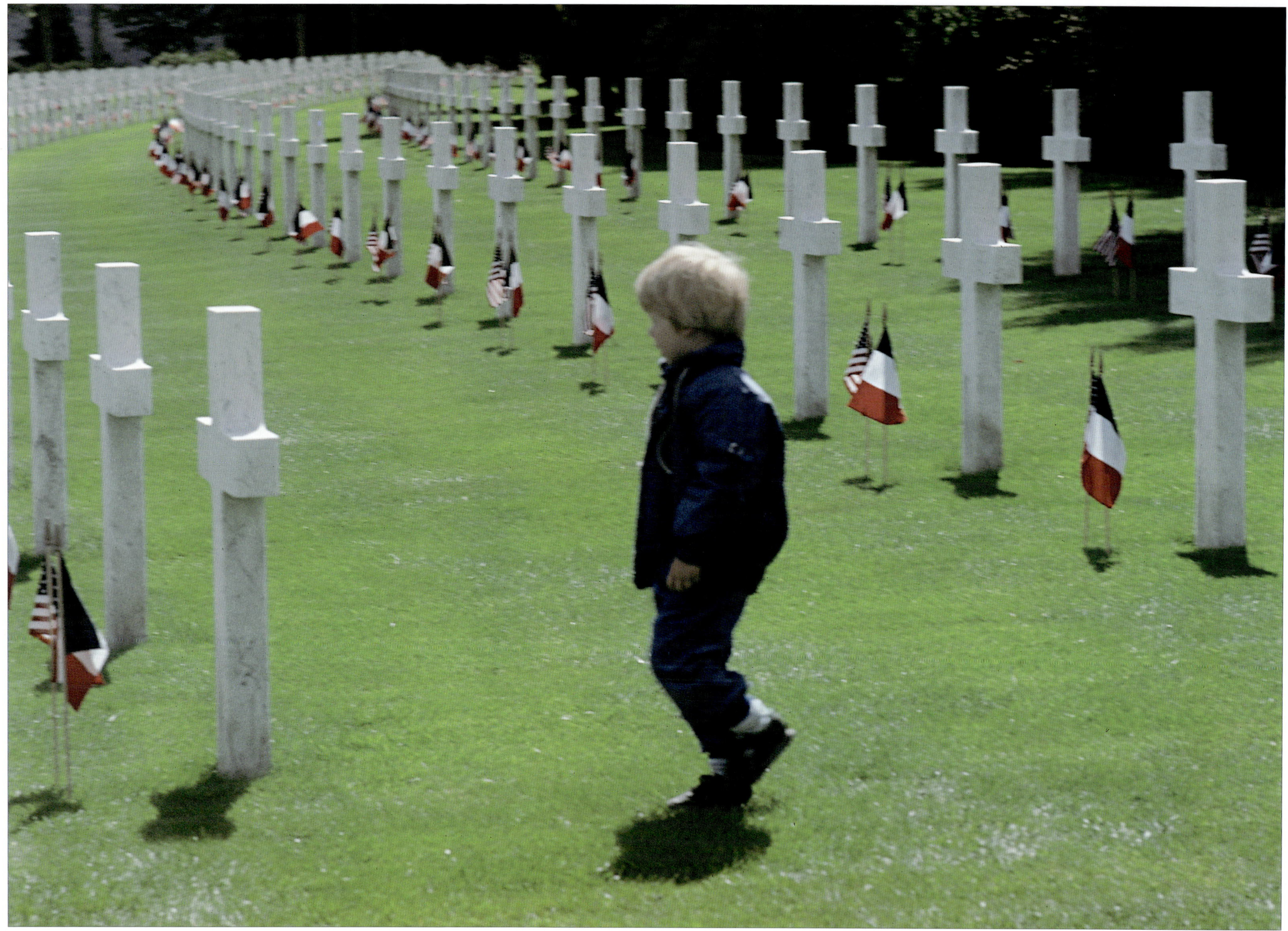

 The deep scars of the First World War still mar the lands of France and Belgium. This is the Western front, and when seen from the air, it is still clearly visible with all its trenches and fortifications. In 1918, the entry of American "Doughboys" into the war broke the stalemate and helped bring this tragic conflict to a conclusion. War cemeteries all over France attest to the heavy price the United States twice paid for peace in Europe. These images are from the famous cemetery at Belleau Wood in France (opposite) where young men from the 5th and 6th Regiments of Marines fought and died. Over 2,000 Marines are buried here, and each Memorial Day the graves are decorated with small U.S. and French flags. The monument on the right is a close-up of an imposing granite memorial to this last great battle of the Marines in the Summer of 1918.

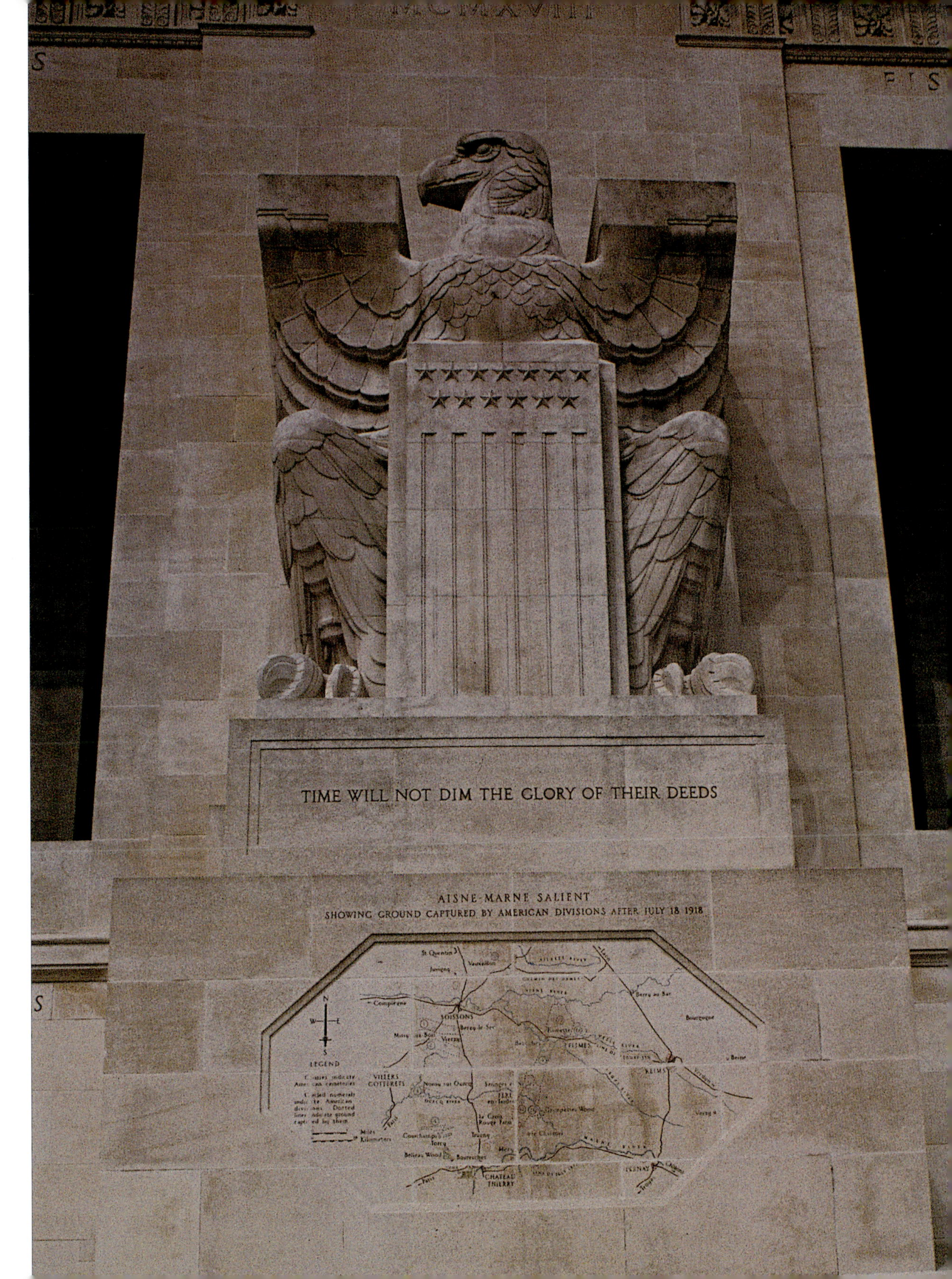

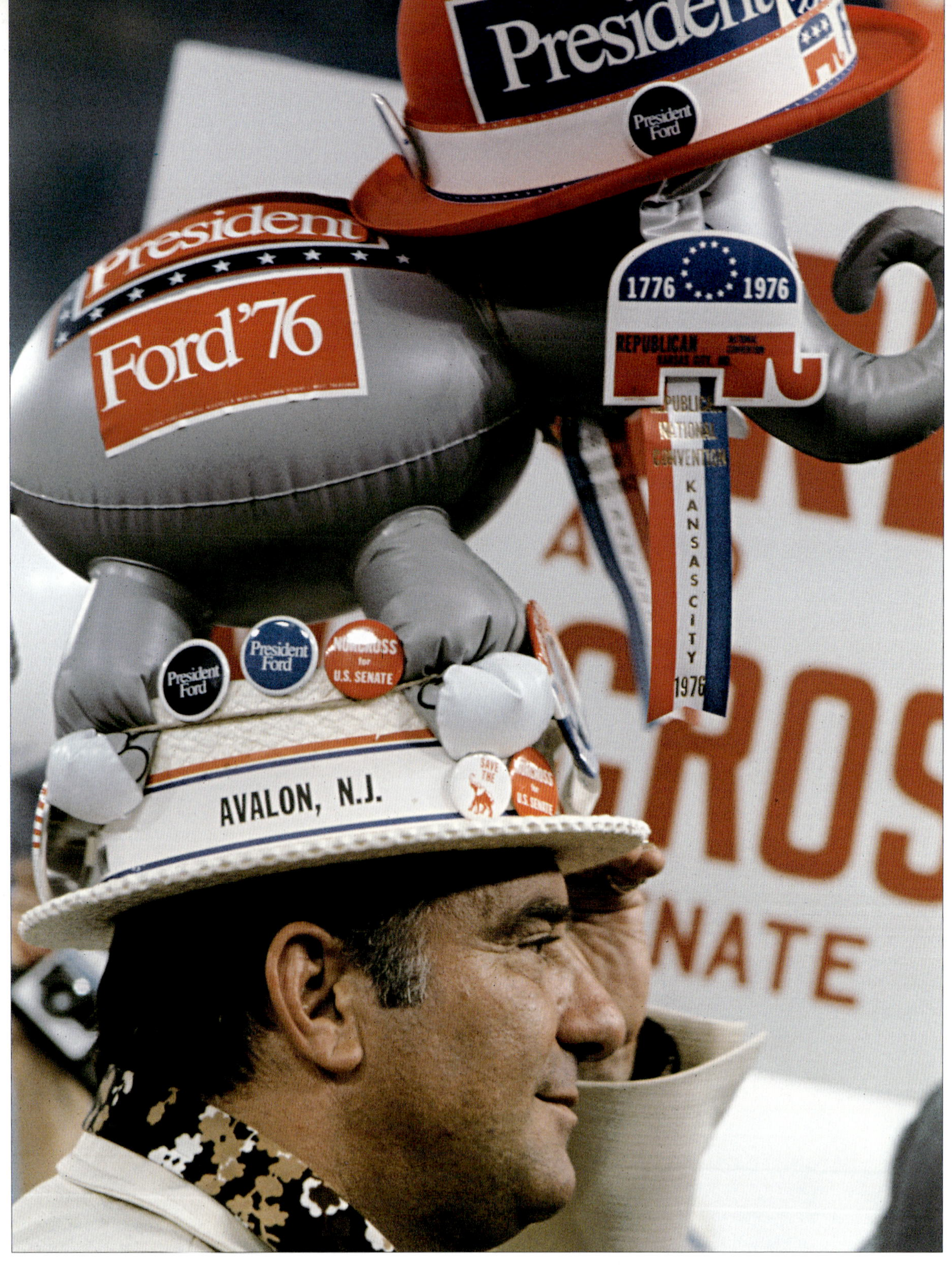

Left & Opposite: Democracy is a celebration of freedom rights. It is a celebration of our nation and our faith in this country, or as Adlai E. Stevenson, Jr., wrote: "Patriotism is not a short and frenzied outburst of emotion but the tranquil and steady dedication of a lifetime." This celebration – left and opposite – was the Republican Party Convention in 1976 in Kansas City, Kansas, complete with massive signs and weird hats. Patriotism does come in many colors.

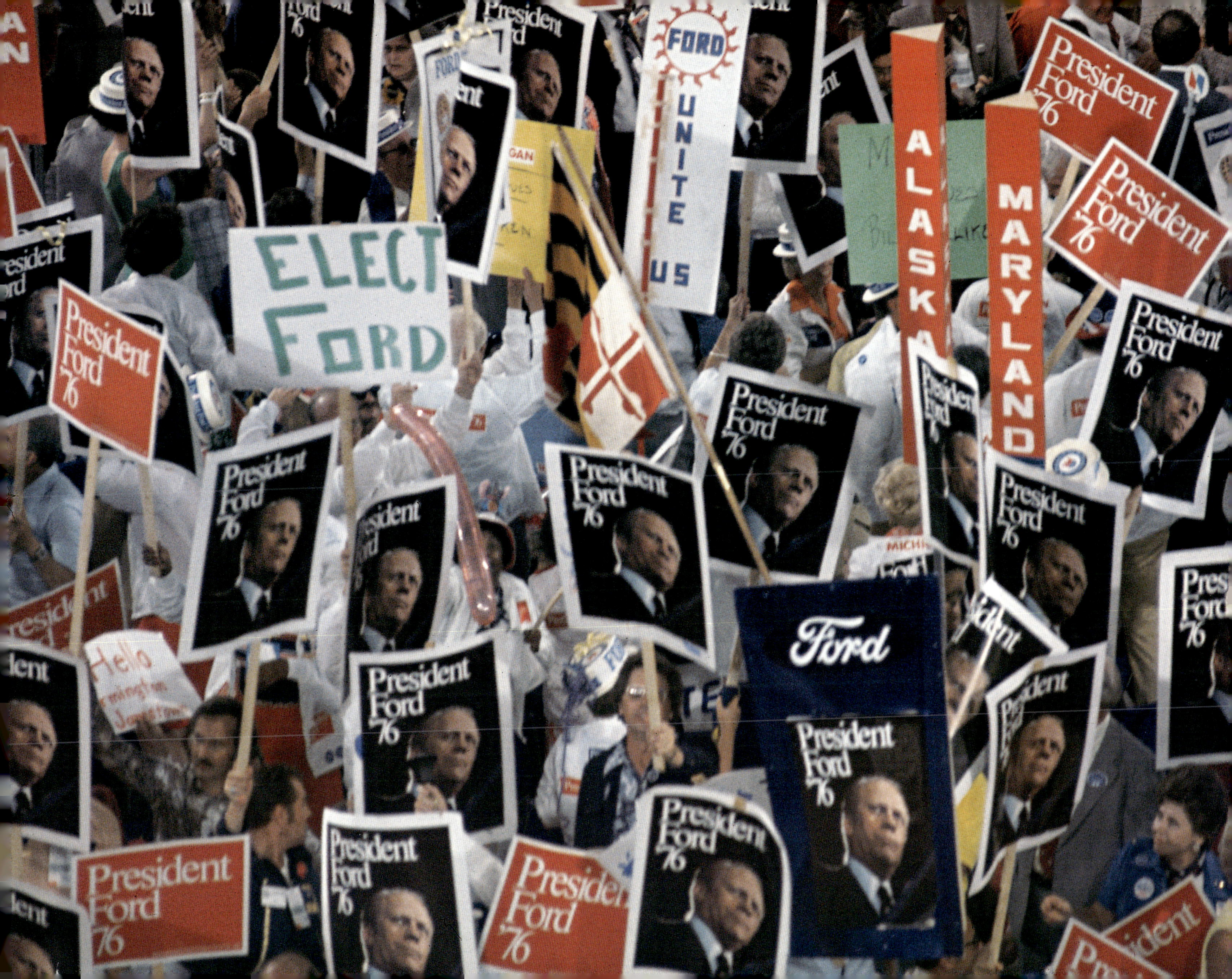

President Ford '76
President Ford '76
Elect Ford
FORD UNITE US
ALASKA
MARYLAND
Ford
Hello

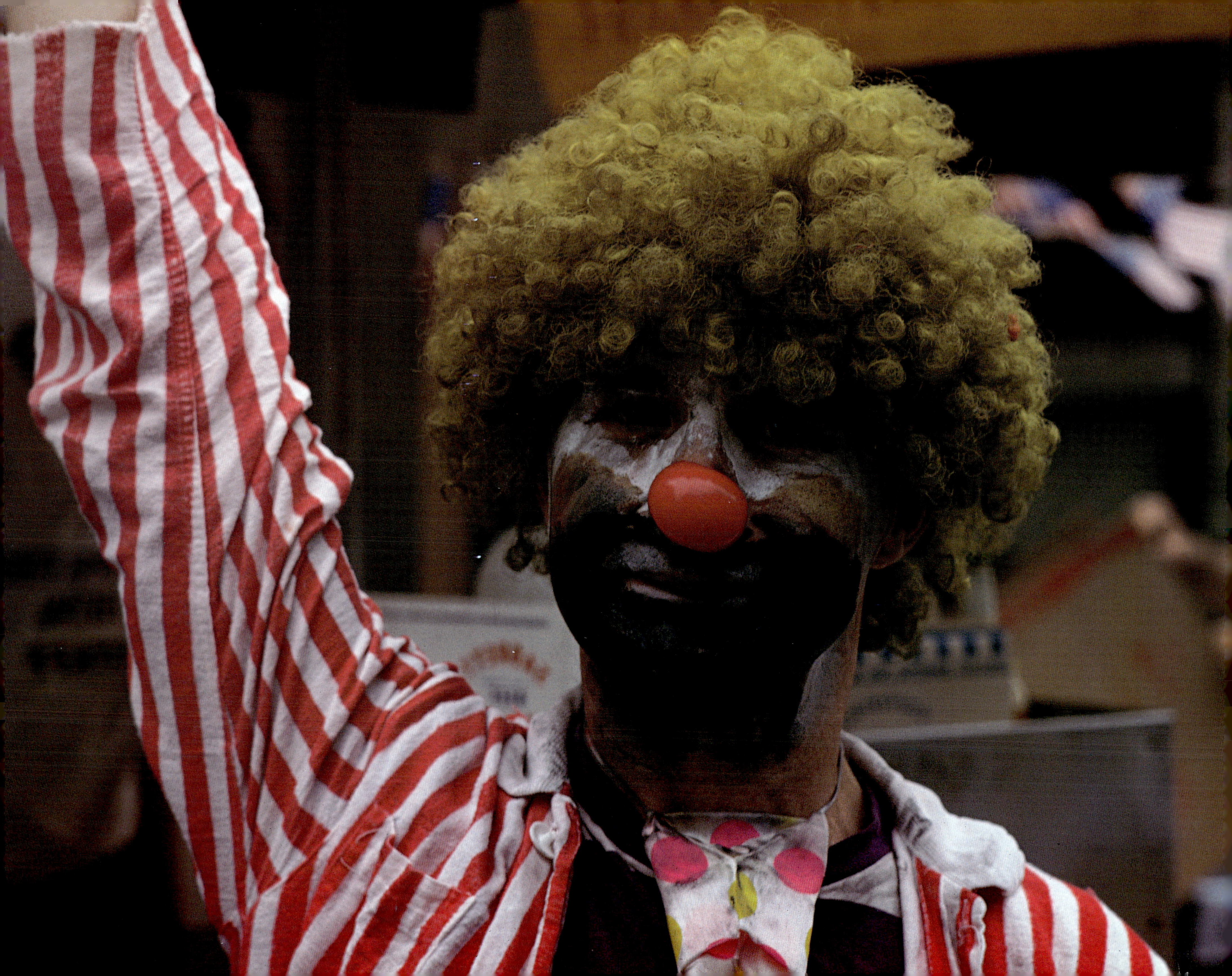

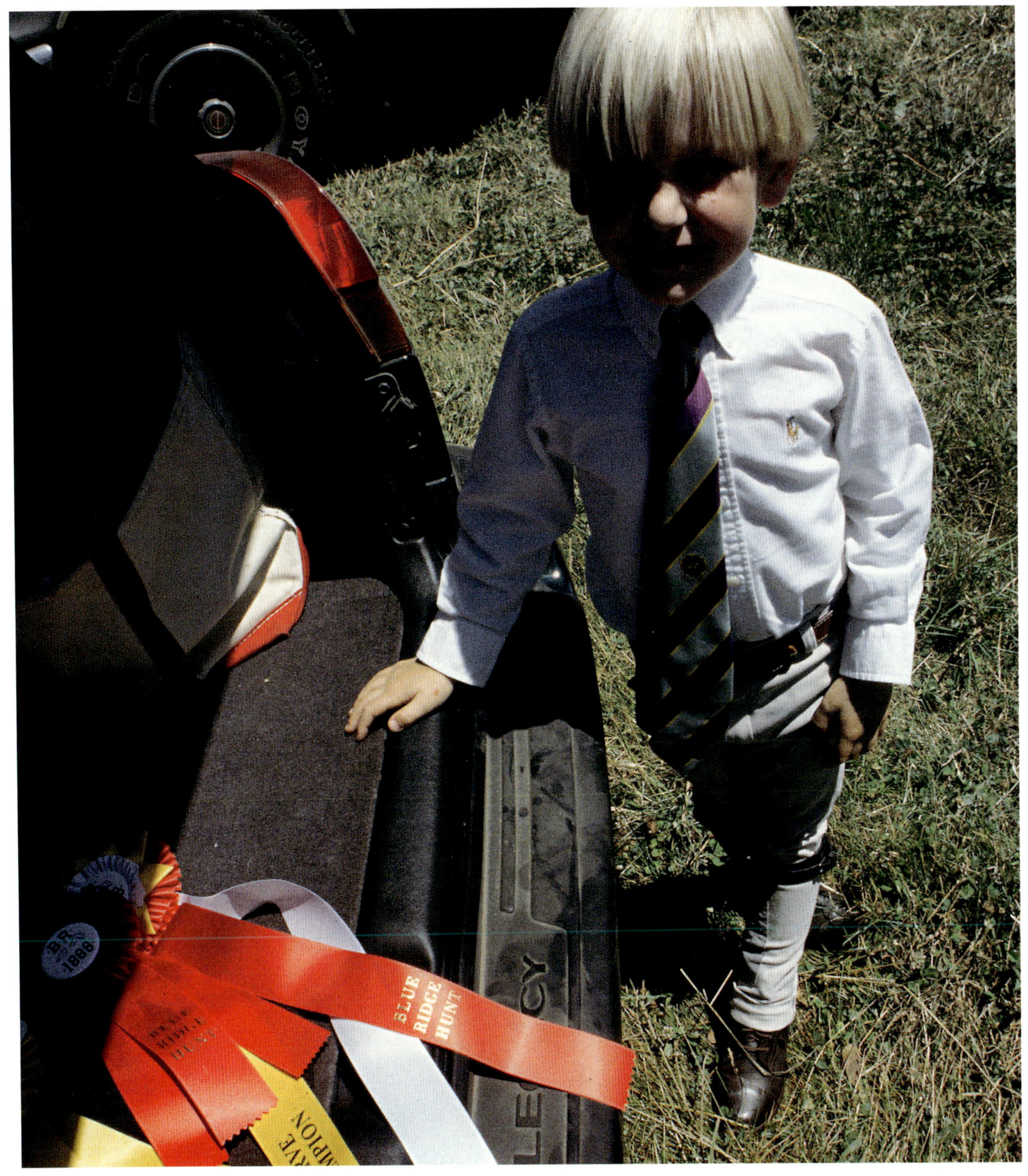

Opposite: "Be you clown or be you king, still your singing is the thing," wrote Laura Elizabeth Richards in 1930, well applicable to this all-American clown.

Left: Young Christian Ulrich von Hassell is fortunate to have grown up with horses, in a tradition of his forefathers who bred and rode horses in Hanover and Prussia for hundreds of years. Horsemanship was essential for their service in the cream of the military: the cavalry. Key to this learning "at the cannon's mouth" is attendance at an early age at horse shows.

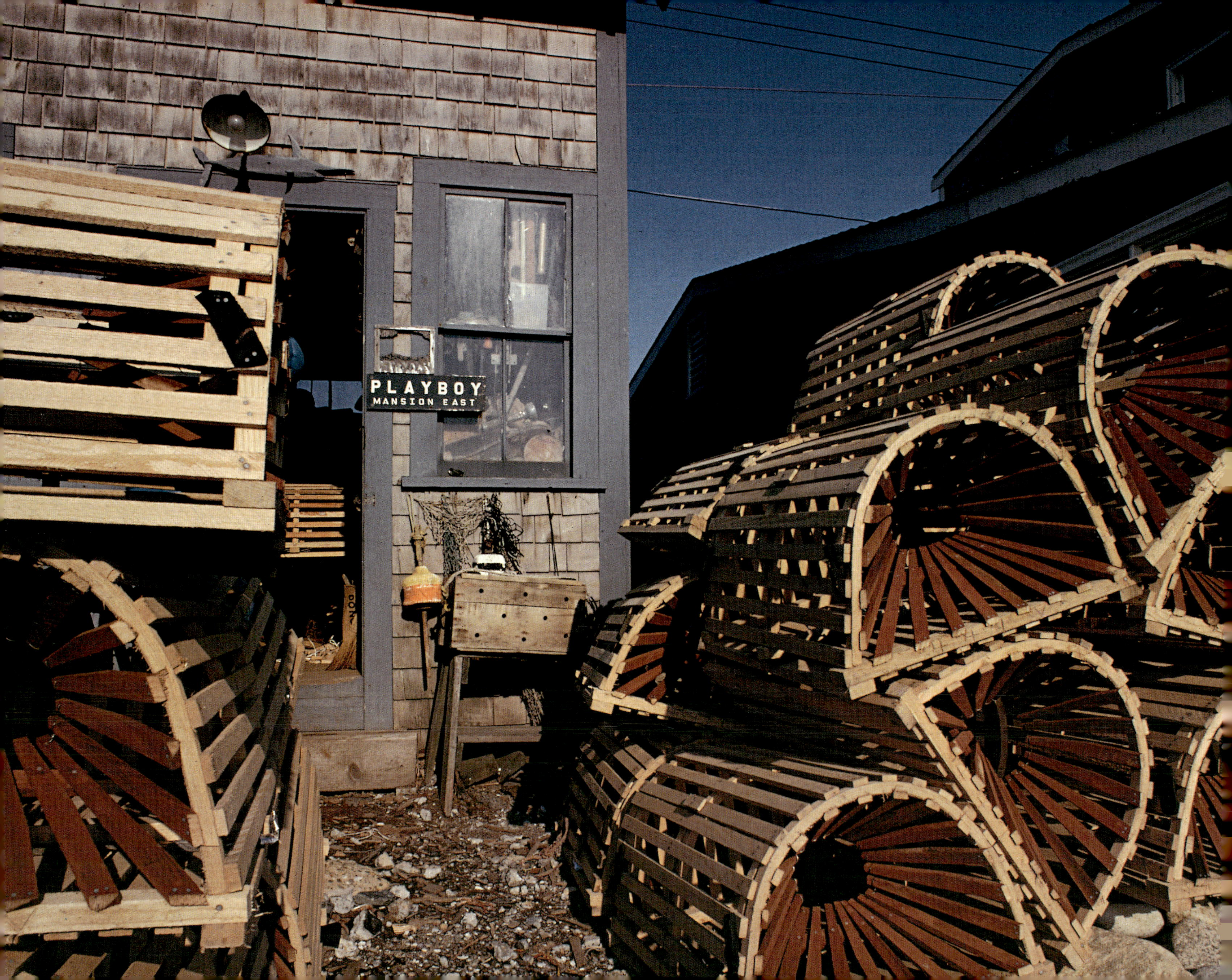
PLAYBOY
MANSION EAST

PLACES

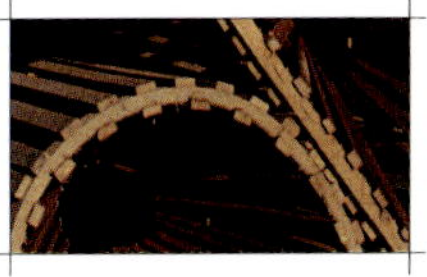

AMERICA'S LOCAL CHARMS
RANGE FROM TIGHTLY KNIT COMMUNITIES
OF A FEW HUNDRED PEOPLE TO SPRAWLING
SUBURBS TO GLITZY CITIES HOUSING MILLIONS.
THERE IS SOMETHING FOR EVERYONE.

Opposite: Fishing for lobster is hard work, and stout-hearted New Englanders are world famous for their catches. These lobster pots, carefully made by hand during the long, cold winters, are on Martha's Vineyard in Massachusetts.

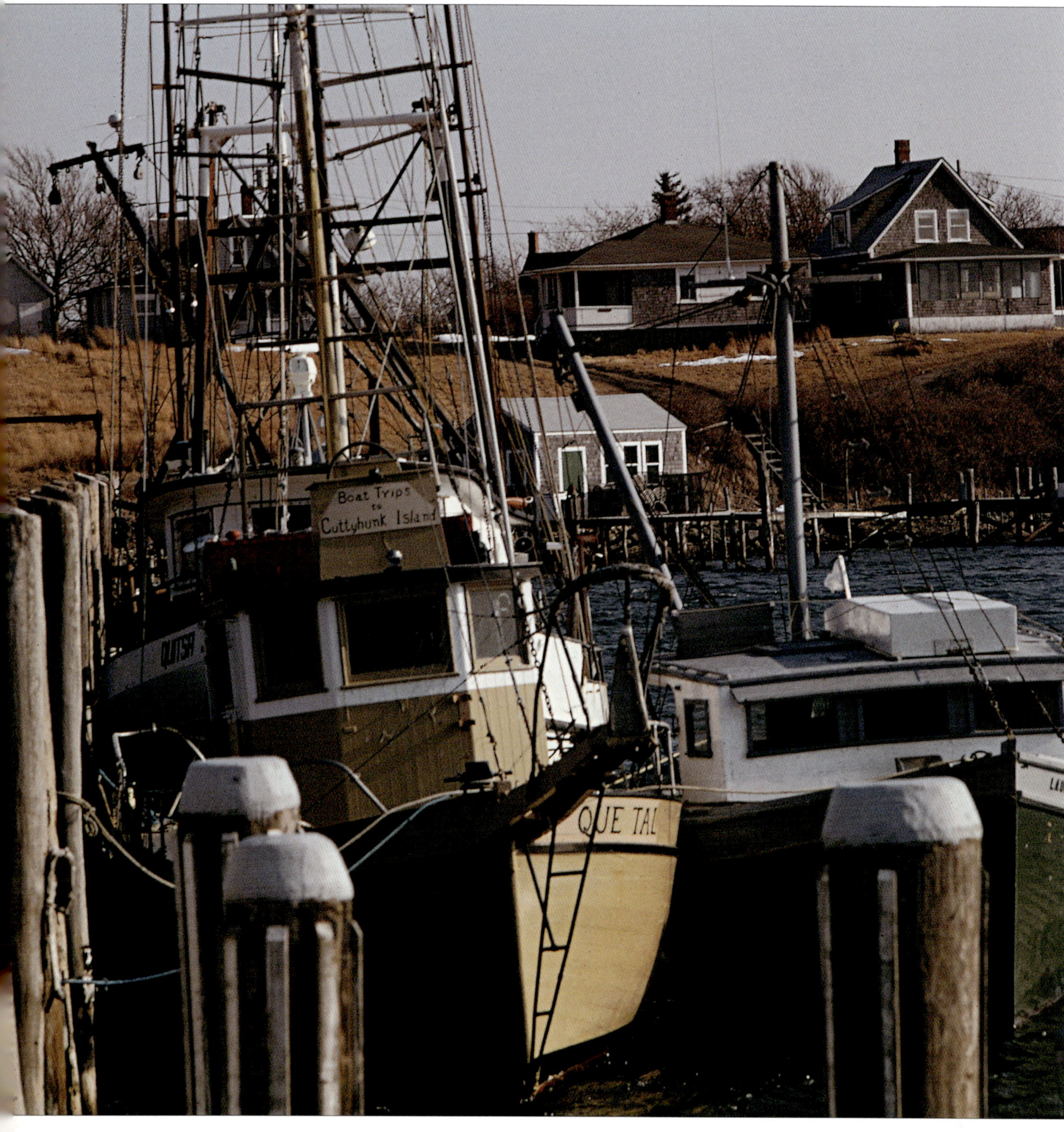

Left & Opposite: Fishing was one of the very first true "industries" of the colonies and later of the young United States. Plentiful fish up and down the East Coast were seen as part of the bounty of America. Recent over-fishing and severe cost pressures have brought a sense of crisis to fishermen from Maine to Florida.

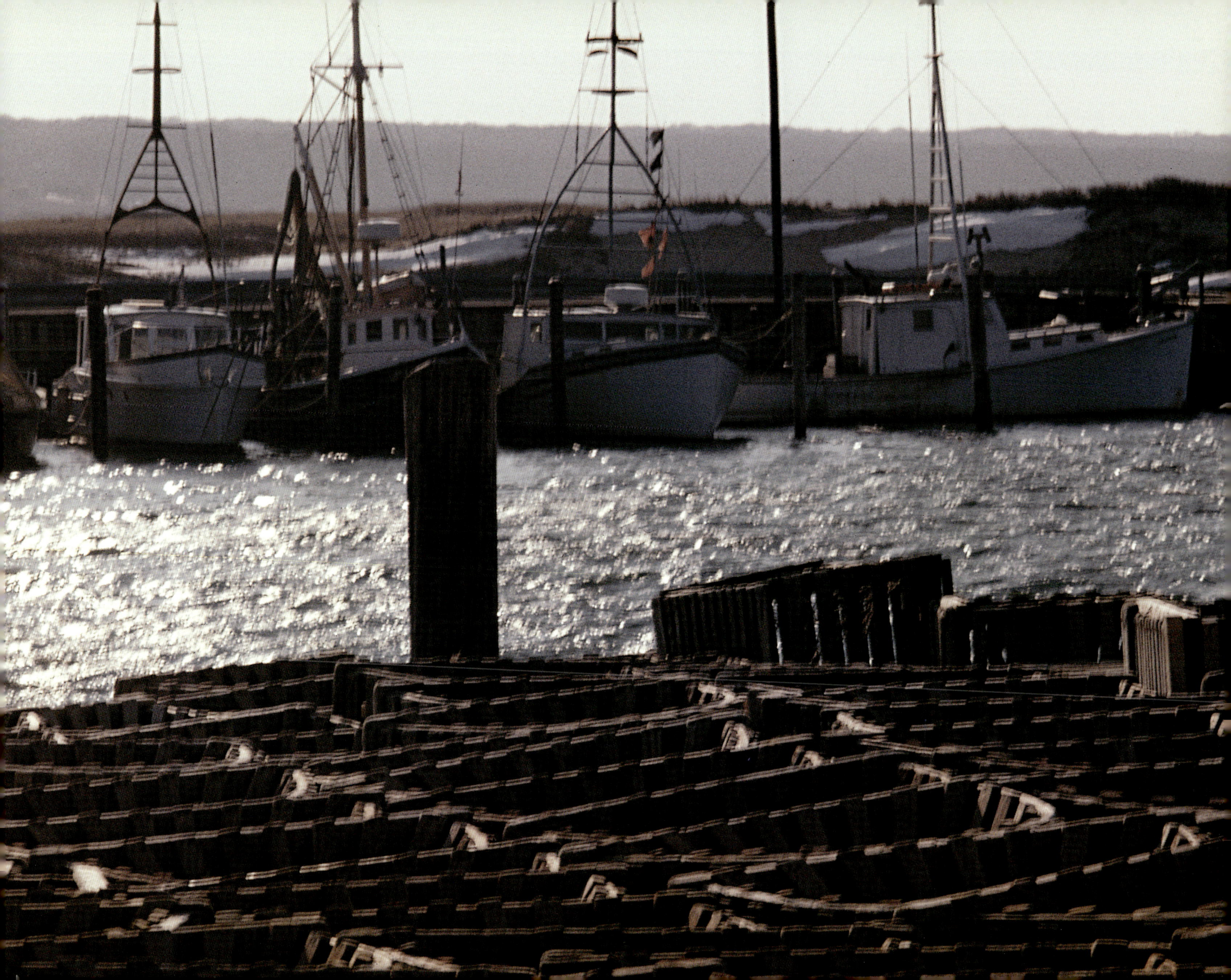

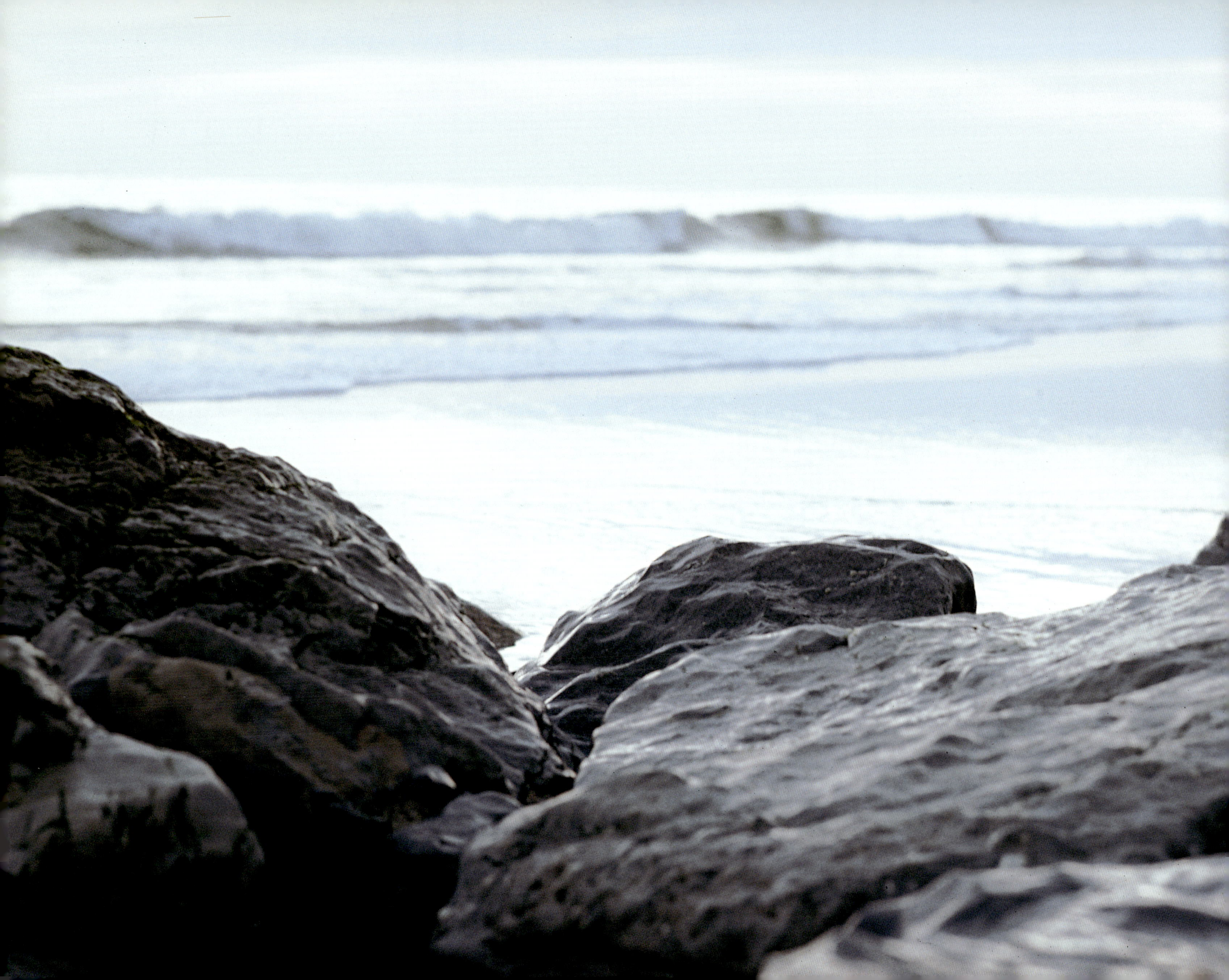

Opposite: On a clear day one can see almost all the way from the rocks of Connecticut's shores to distant Europe.

Right: It takes more than rain to dampen spirits along the boardwalk in Atlantic City, New Jersey. Much of this old boardwalk has been destroyed due to rapid development.

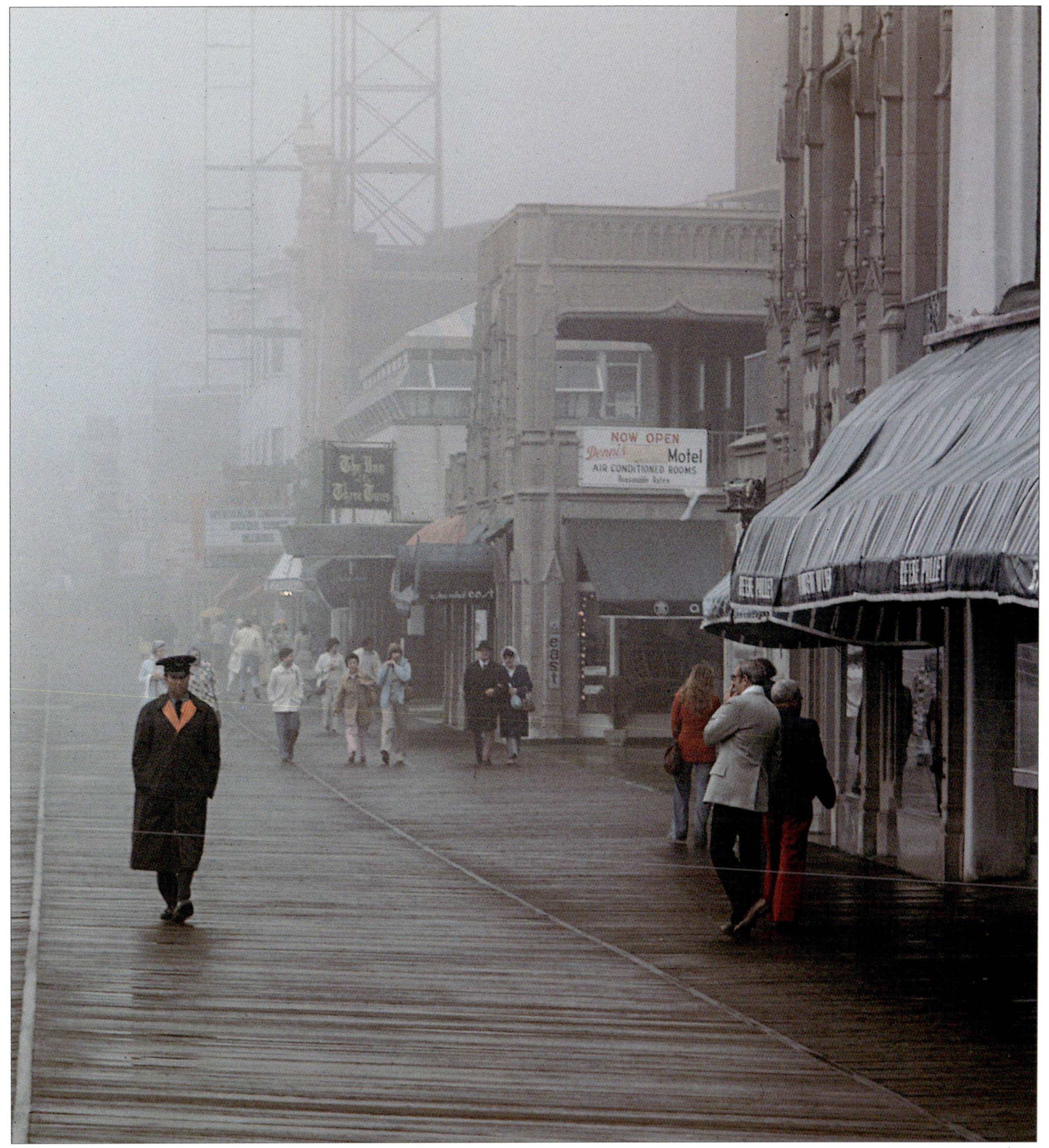

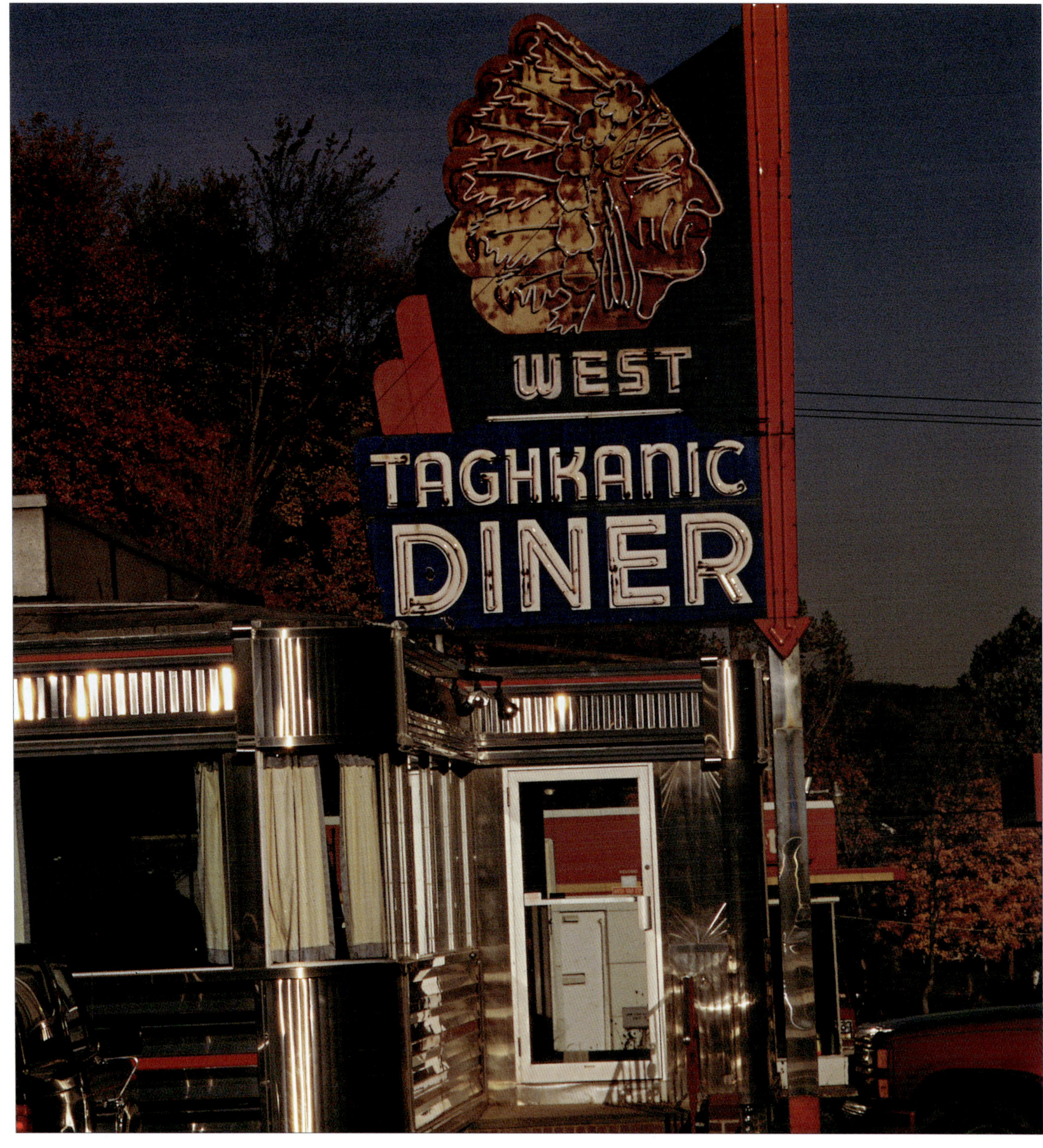

Left: Diners are truly amazing places that have survived the introduction of fast food and fancy food. Home-style cooking, steaming hot coffee and locally baked pies are mainstay diner fare from coast to coast. This diner is in Columbia County, New York, evoking an Indian tribe long lost.

Opposite: Firefighting boats demonstrate their power and beauty in New York harbor escorting a pride of the U.S. Navy, an attack submarine.

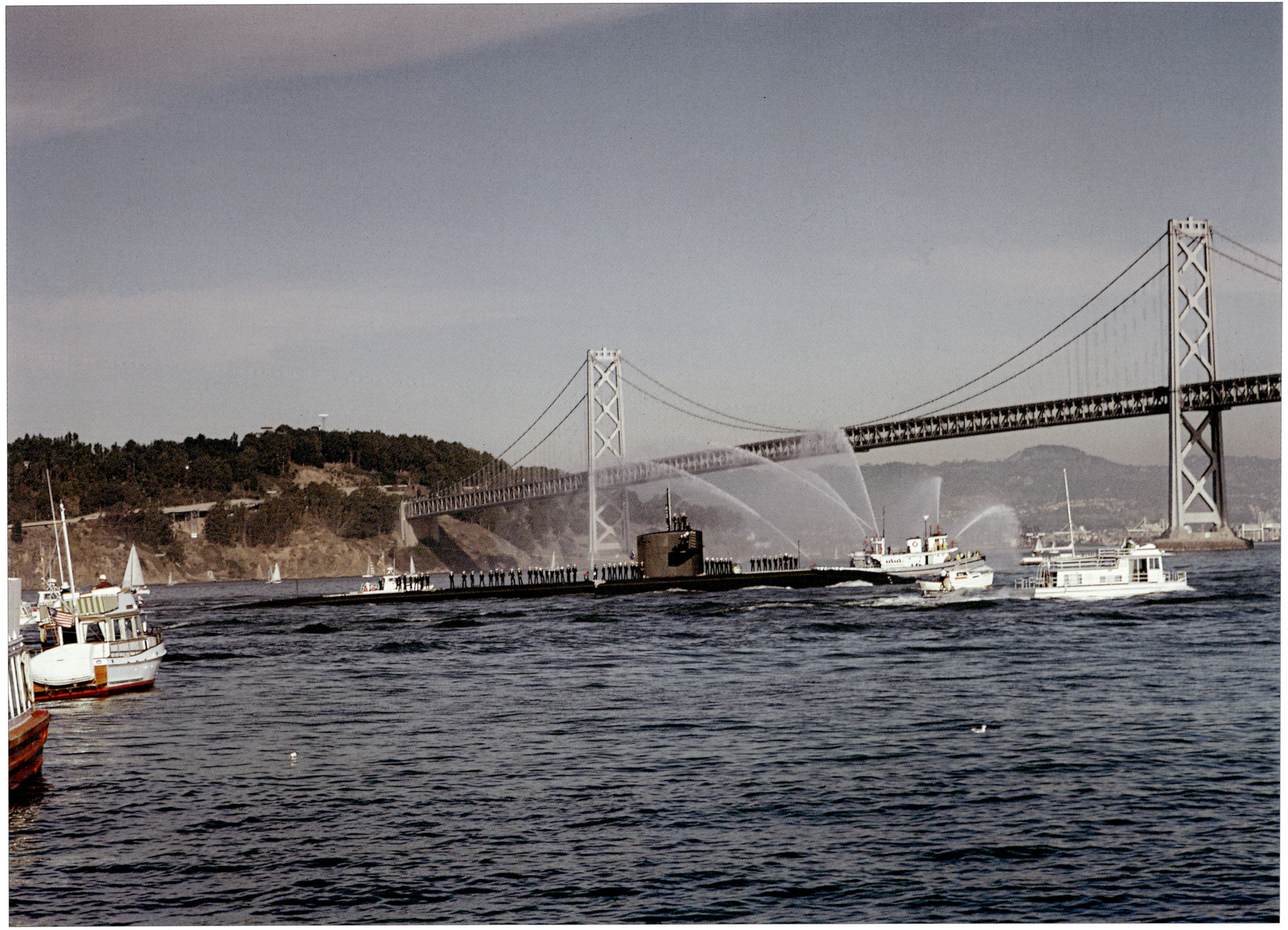

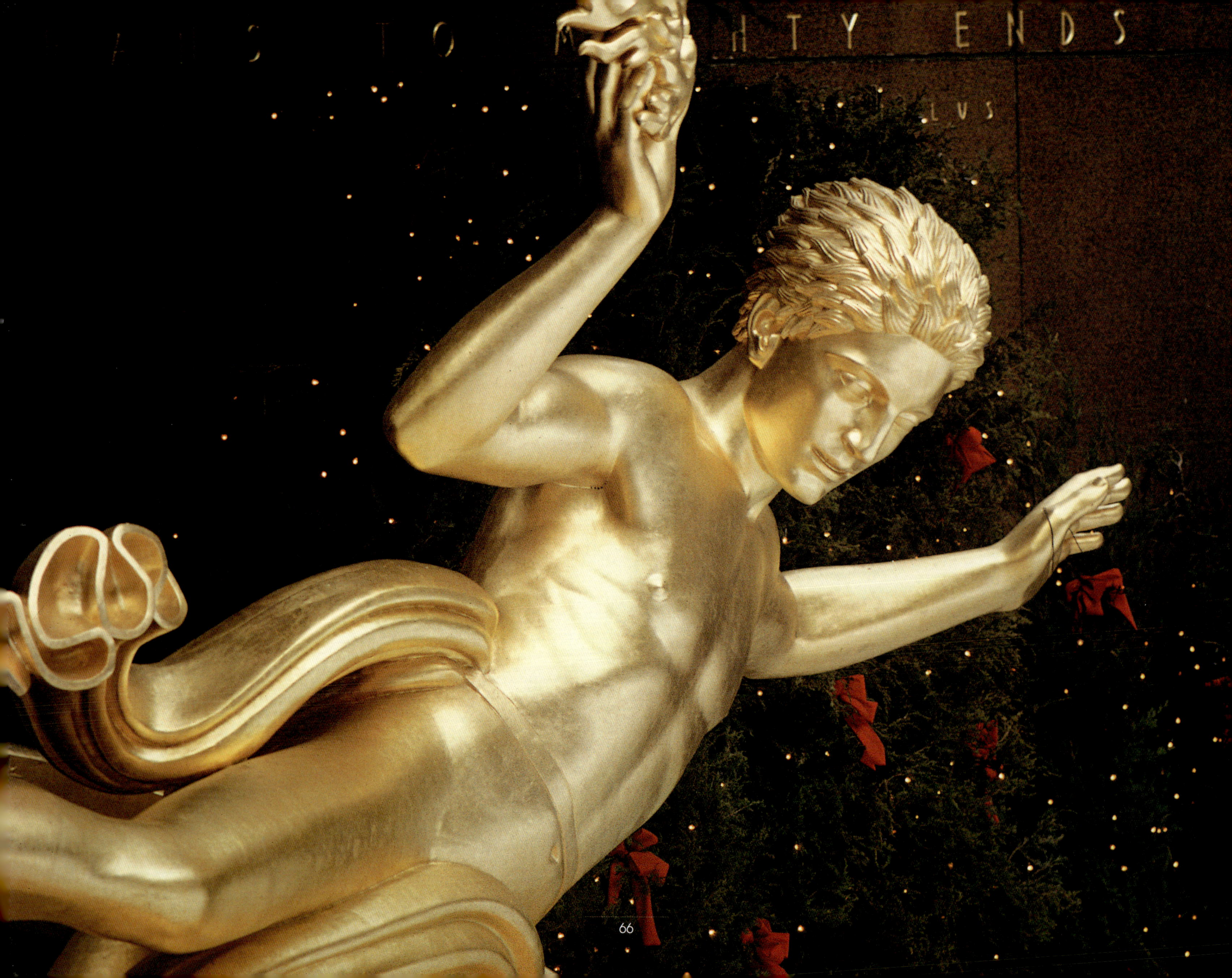
TO
TY ENDS
LUS

Opposite & Right: Ice skating in front of the Christmas tree in New York's Rockefeller Center is a holiday treat for tourists and locals alike. Few remember now that the first stones were laid during the height of the Great Depression, bringing hope to a battered city and a downtrodden nation.

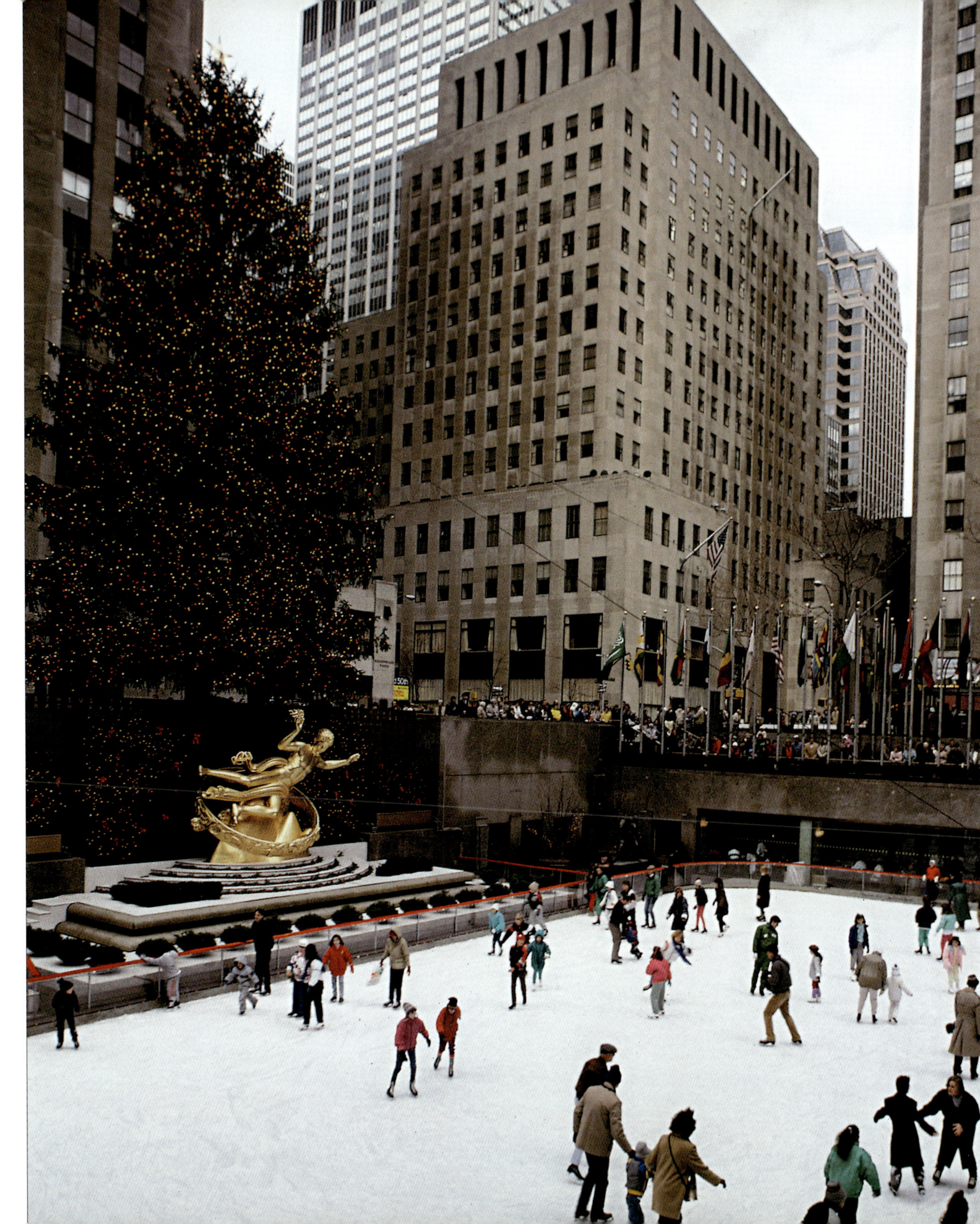

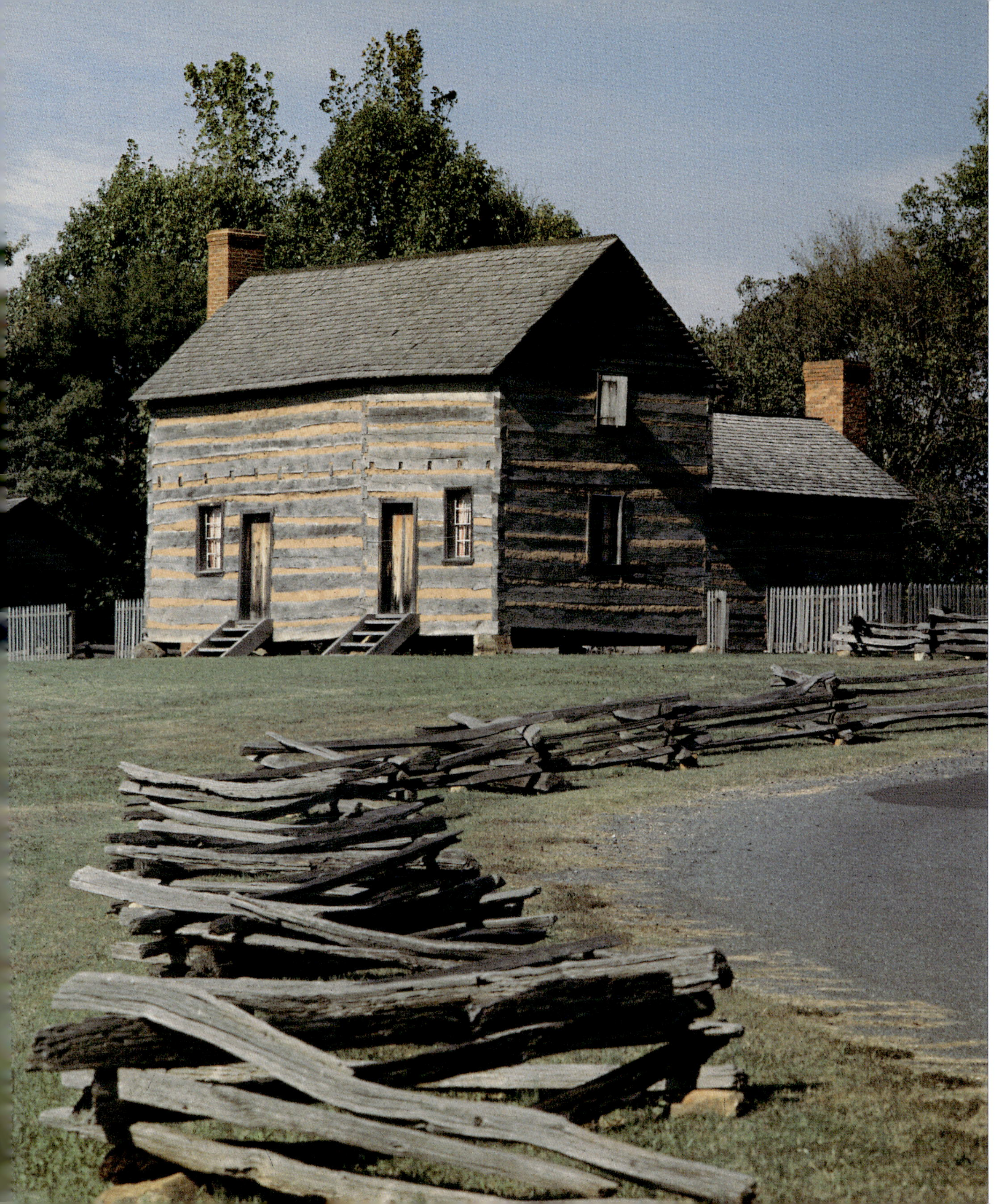

Left: Split-log homes such as this echo the adventure of the American frontier.

Opposite: Miles from the nearest neighbor, it can be tough going on this farm in Colorado as winter's wind cuts across the plains.

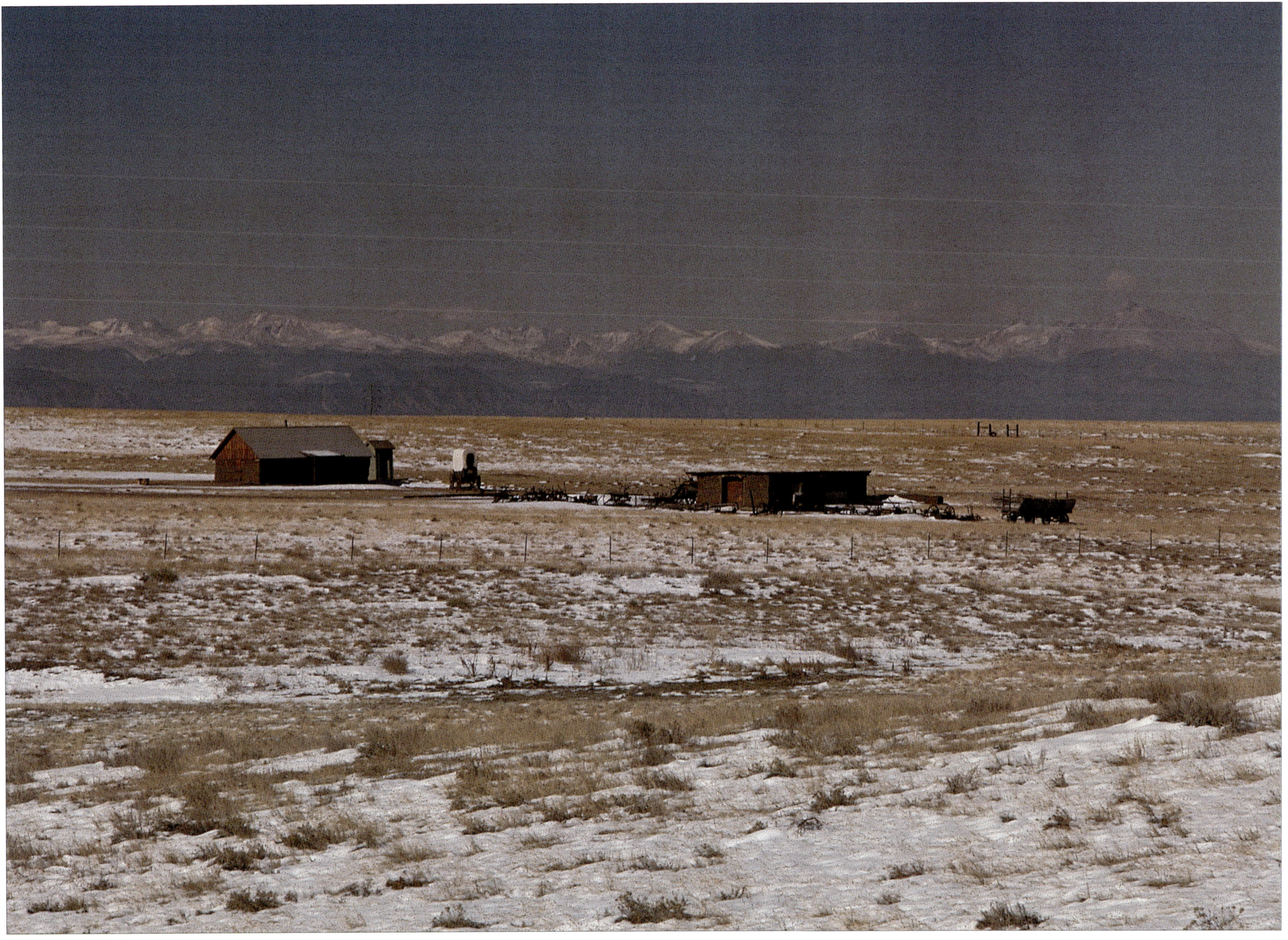

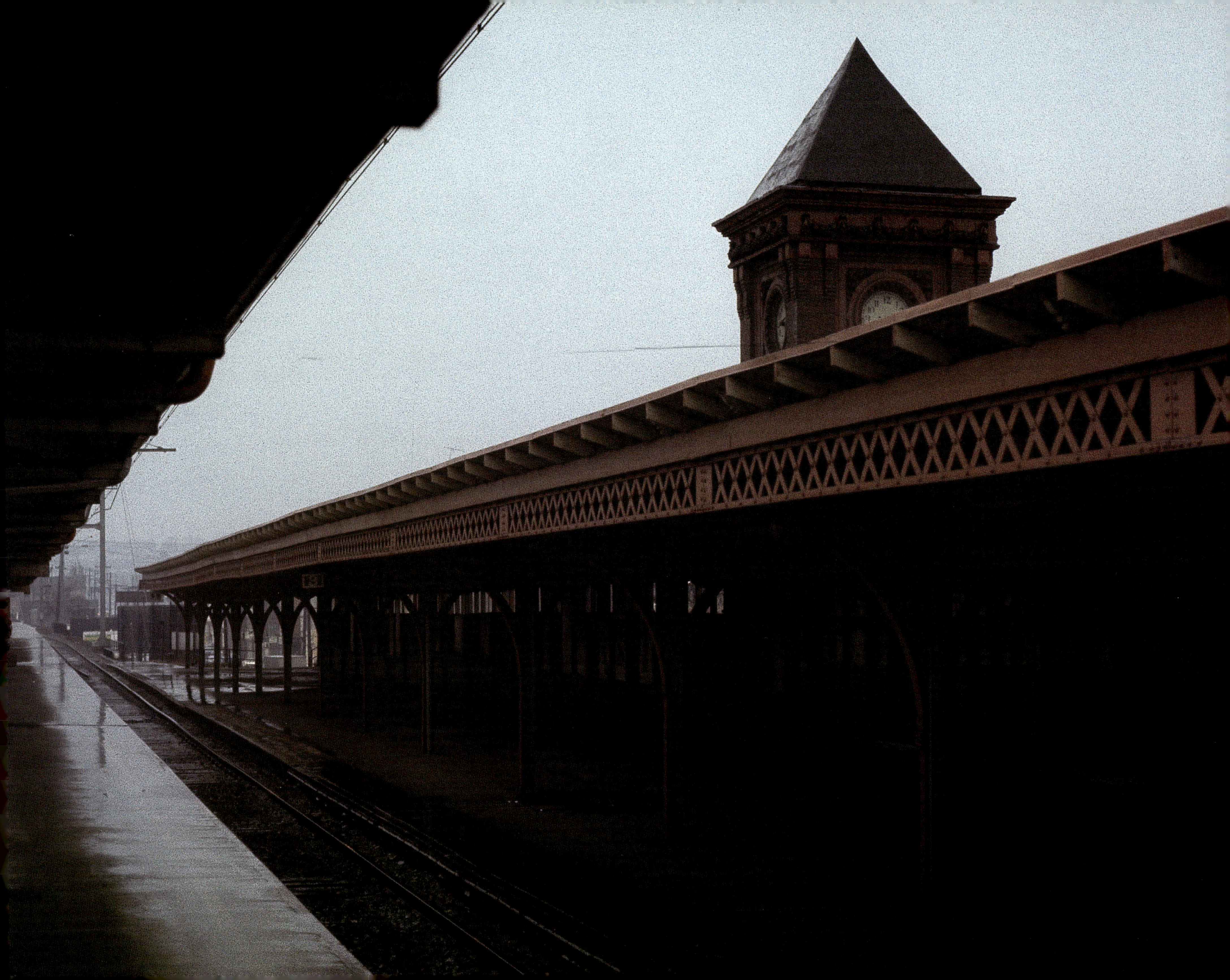

Opposite: At the turn of the century America boasted more miles of train track than paved road. Railroads are still a vital mode of transportation for people, mail and freight. Typical of the grand old days of railroads is this finely restored rail station in Wilmington, Delaware.

Right: Hurray for Hollywood whose movie magic has brought glamorous visions to people around the globe. To this day Hollywood and California attract people throughout the world, trying to live a dream.

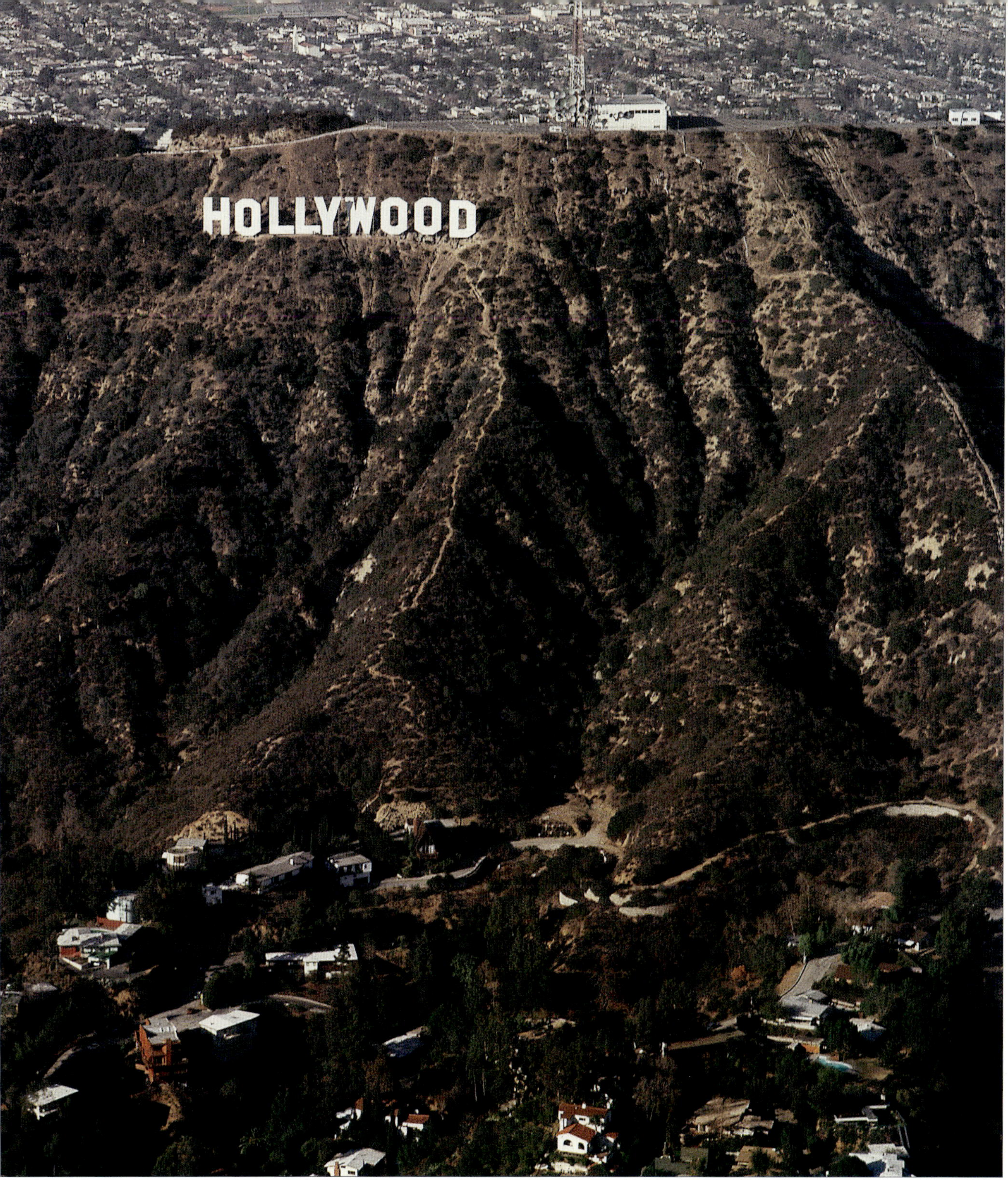
HOLLYWOOD

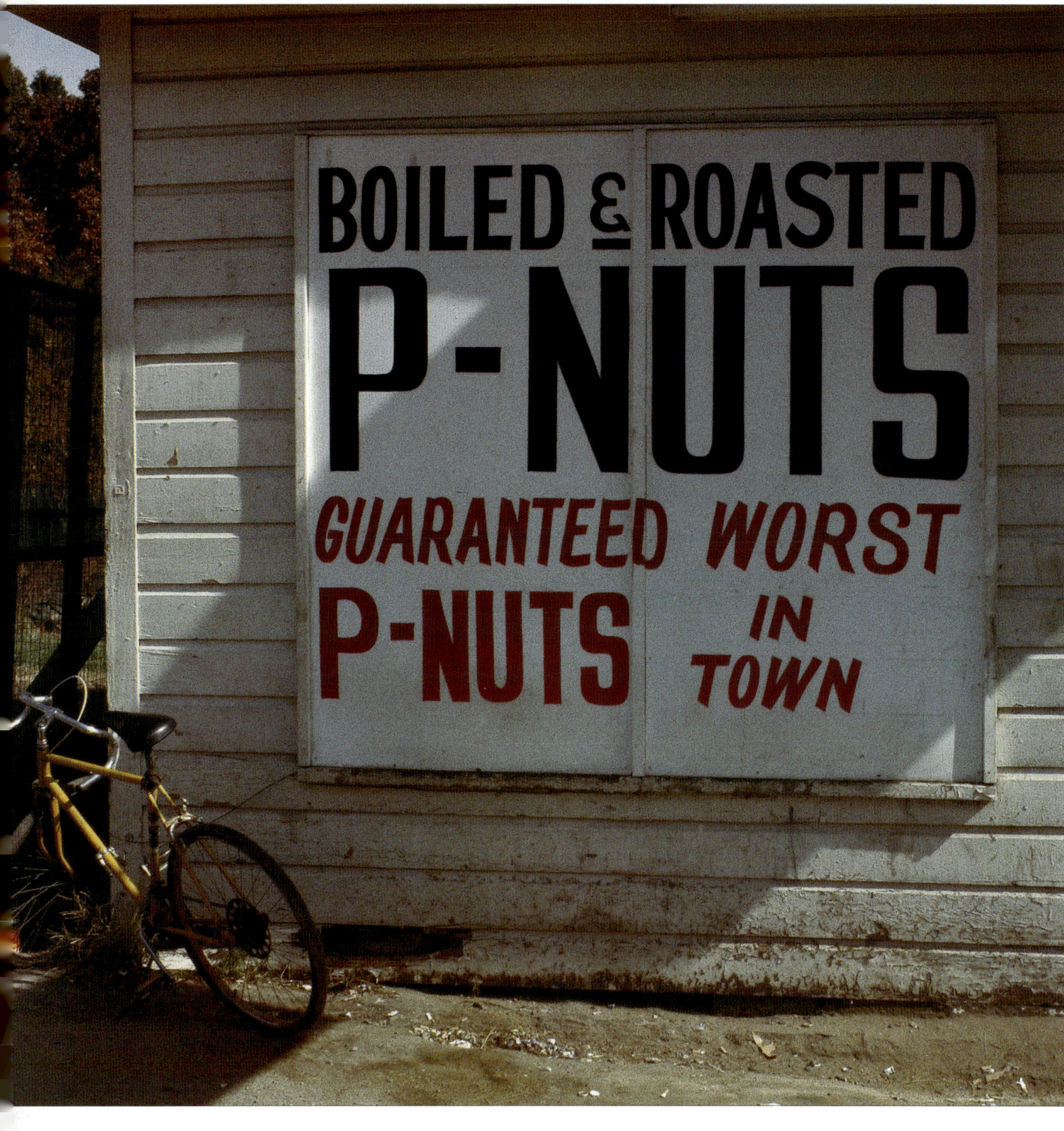

Left: Truth in advertising? Actually this tiny store in rural Georgia sells superb peanuts. Boiled peanuts are a uniquely Southern delicacy, virtually unknown north of the Carolinas. Occasionally in New York you hear of Southerners who have managed to obtain large bags of raw peanuts, which they boil for a taste of home.

Right: Everything that's fit to print and then some. This multiethnic neighborhood in New York's Little Italy supplies newspapers in a variety of languages. It is part of America's culture to support an ever-evolving plethora of publications. Freedom of expression, freedom of the press – they are part of America's birthright.

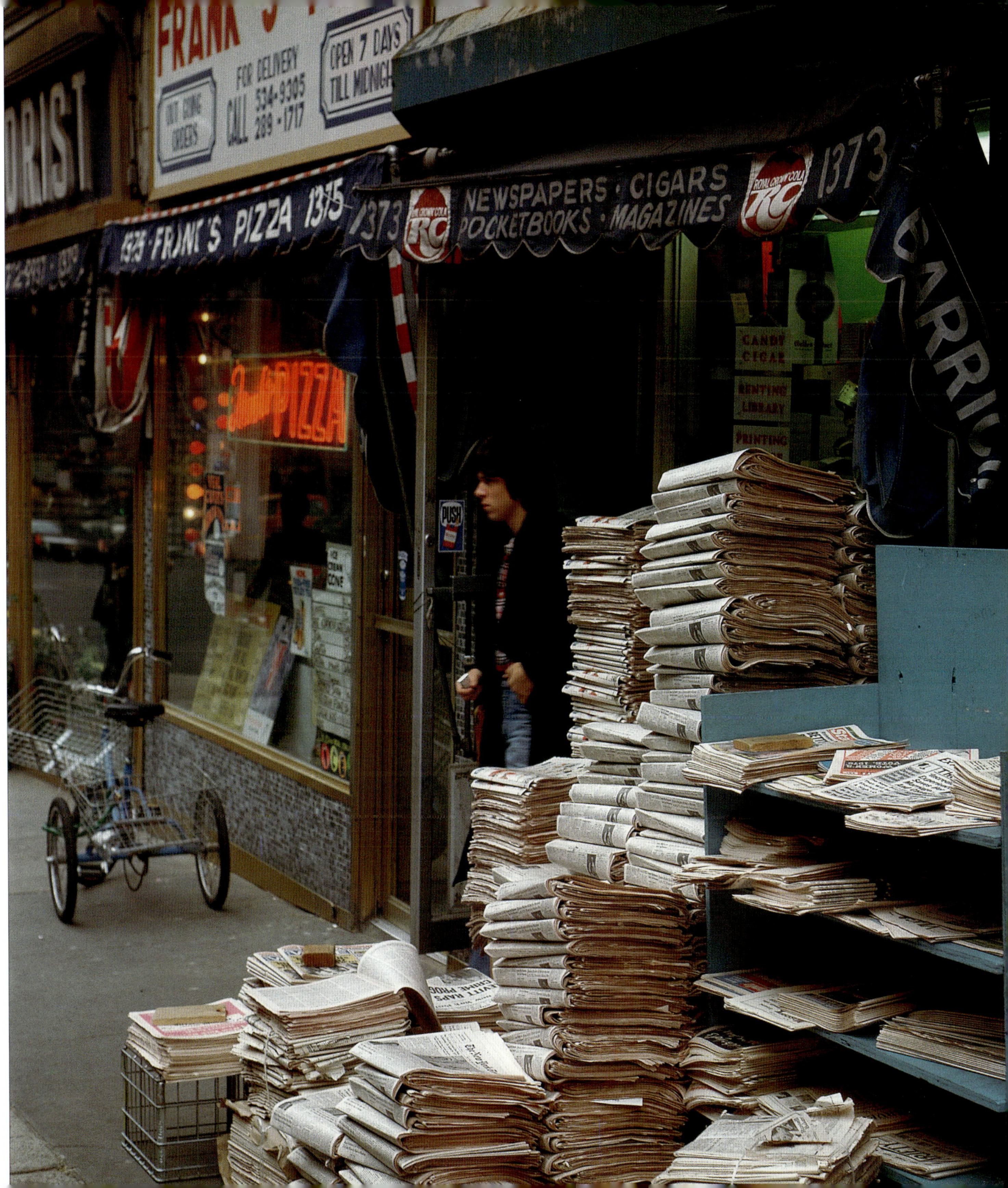

Right: It wouldn't be a carnival without the sweet tastes of caramel apples and cotton candy.

Opposite: This combination flower shop and ice cream parlor provides treats for the eyes and the palate.

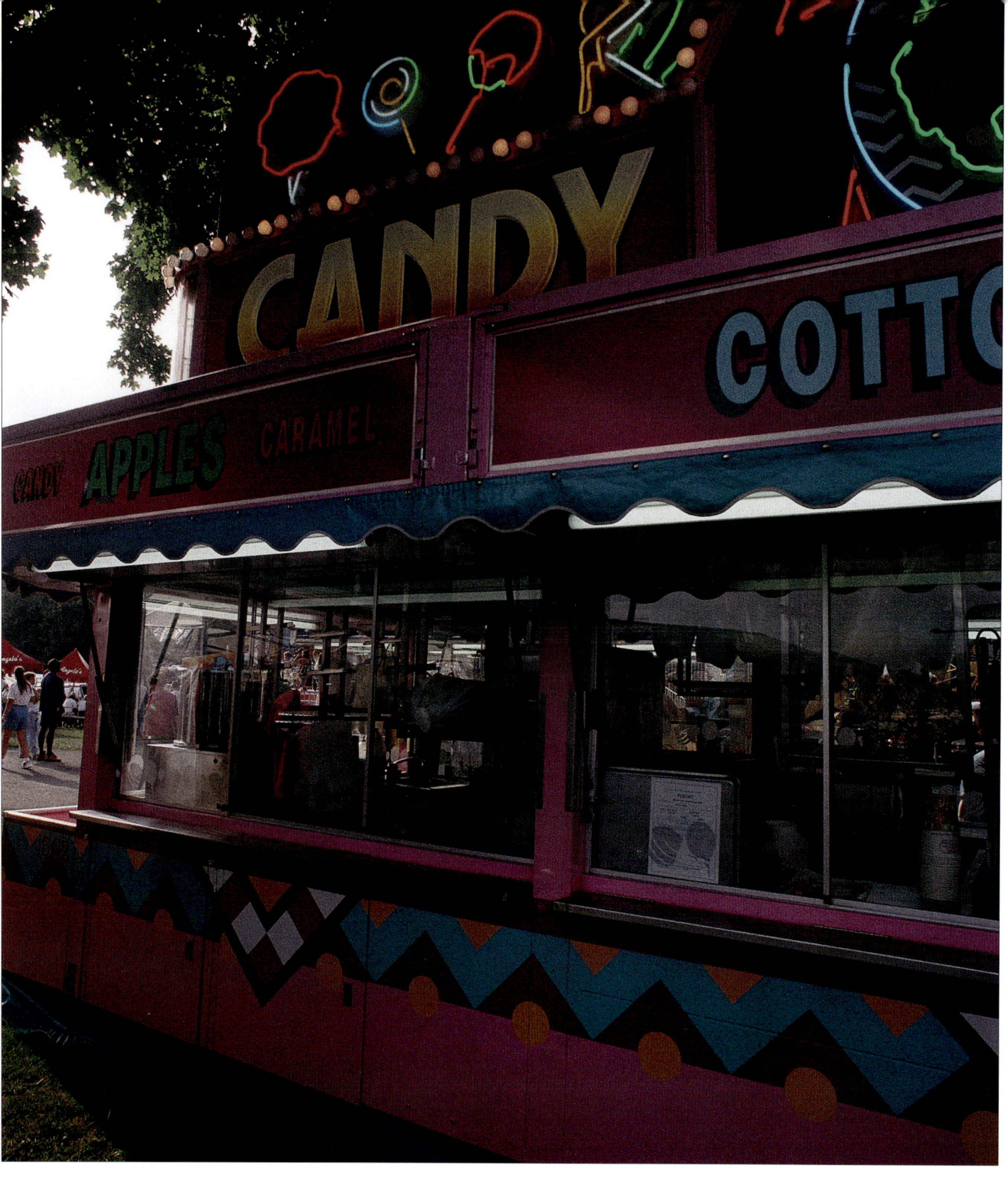

CANDY
COTTO
CANDY APPLES CARAMEL

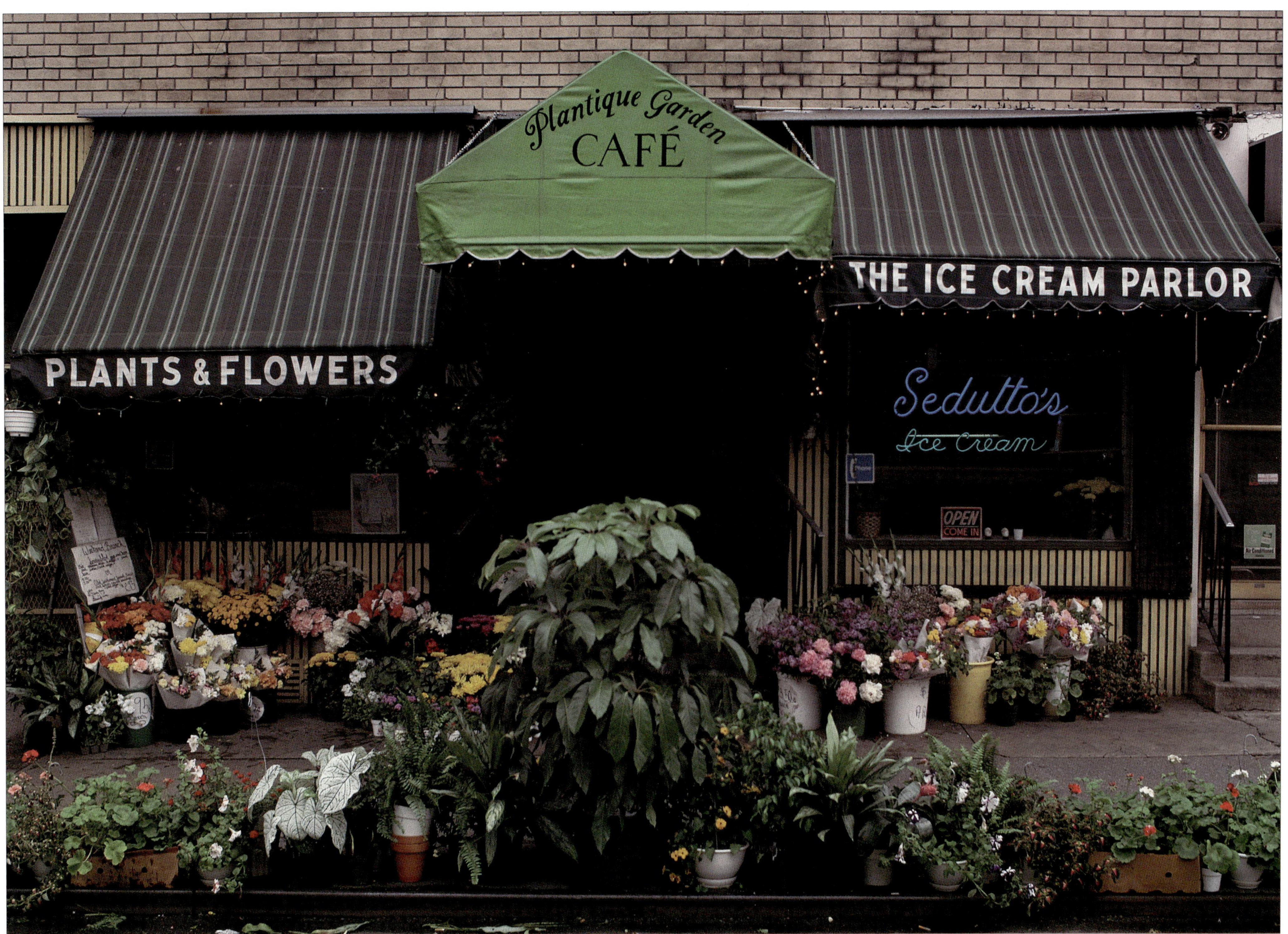

Plantique Garden CAFÉ
THE ICE CREAM PARLOR
PLANTS & FLOWERS
Sedutto's
Ice Cream
OPEN COME IN

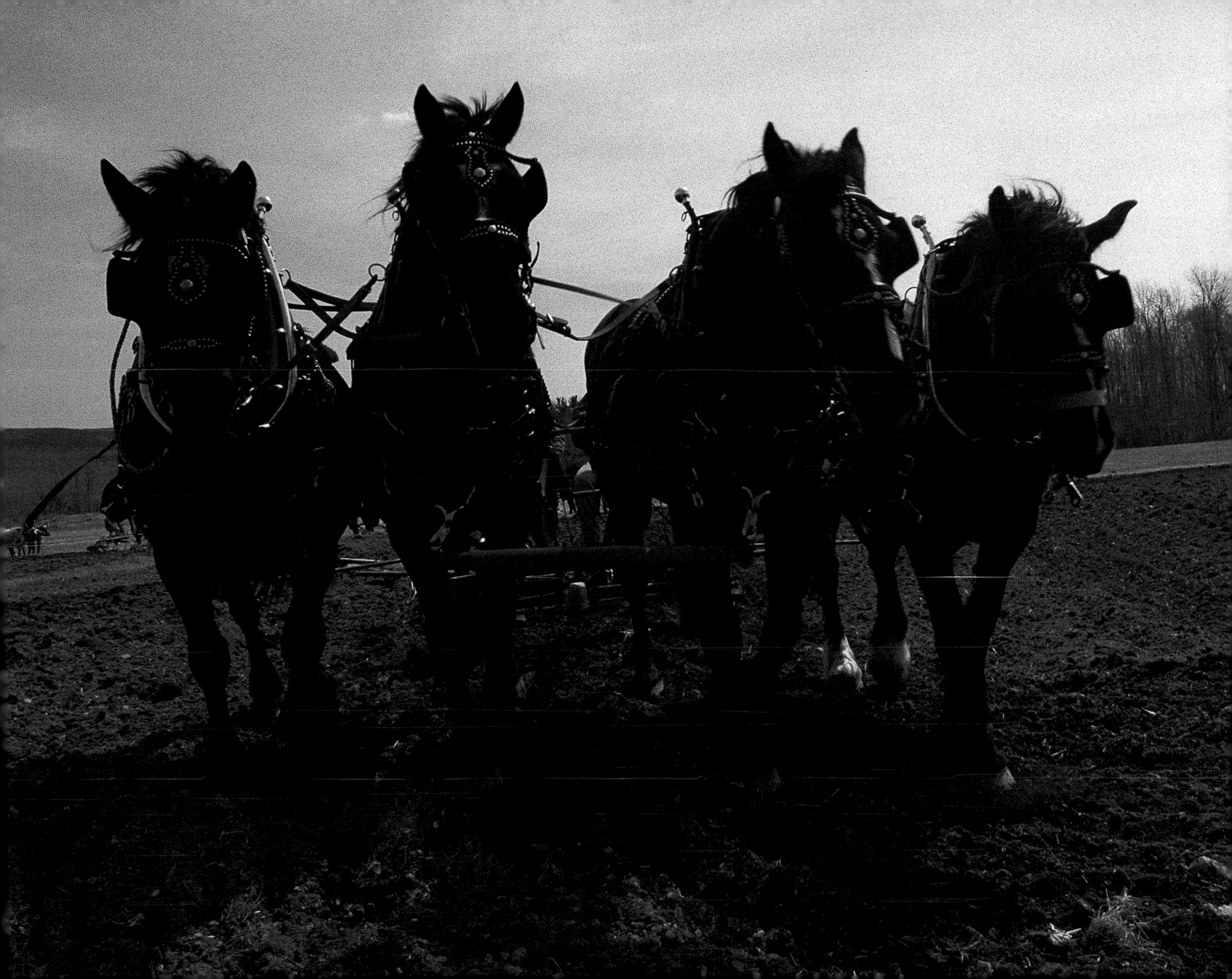

ANIMALS

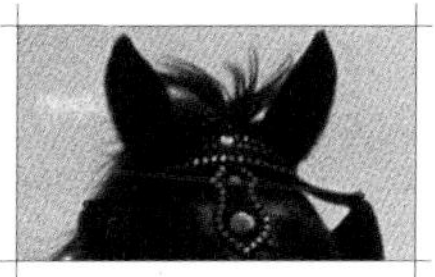

BE THEY FOR WORK, FOR PLAY OR FOR FOOD, ANIMALS ARE AN INTEGRAL PART OF OUR DAILY LIVES.

Opposite: Four heavy draft horses plow a field in Massachusetts, keeping alive the farming traditions of the age before mechanical power. Even though highly mechanized farming has taken over most homesteads in the United States, some pockets of the country, such as Amish communities, continue with old-style farming. The Amish are typical of small groups that have prospered with the freedom America grants.

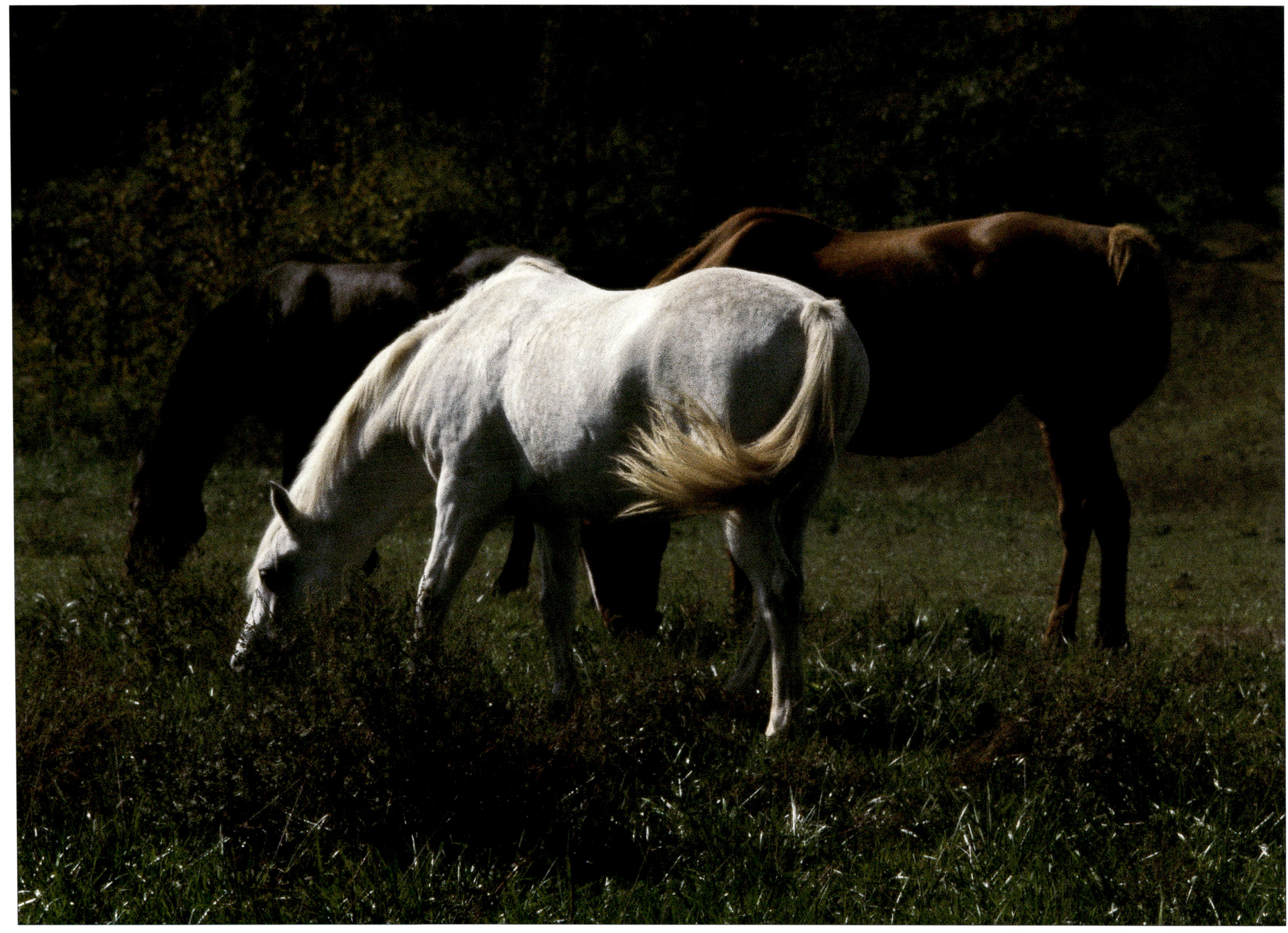

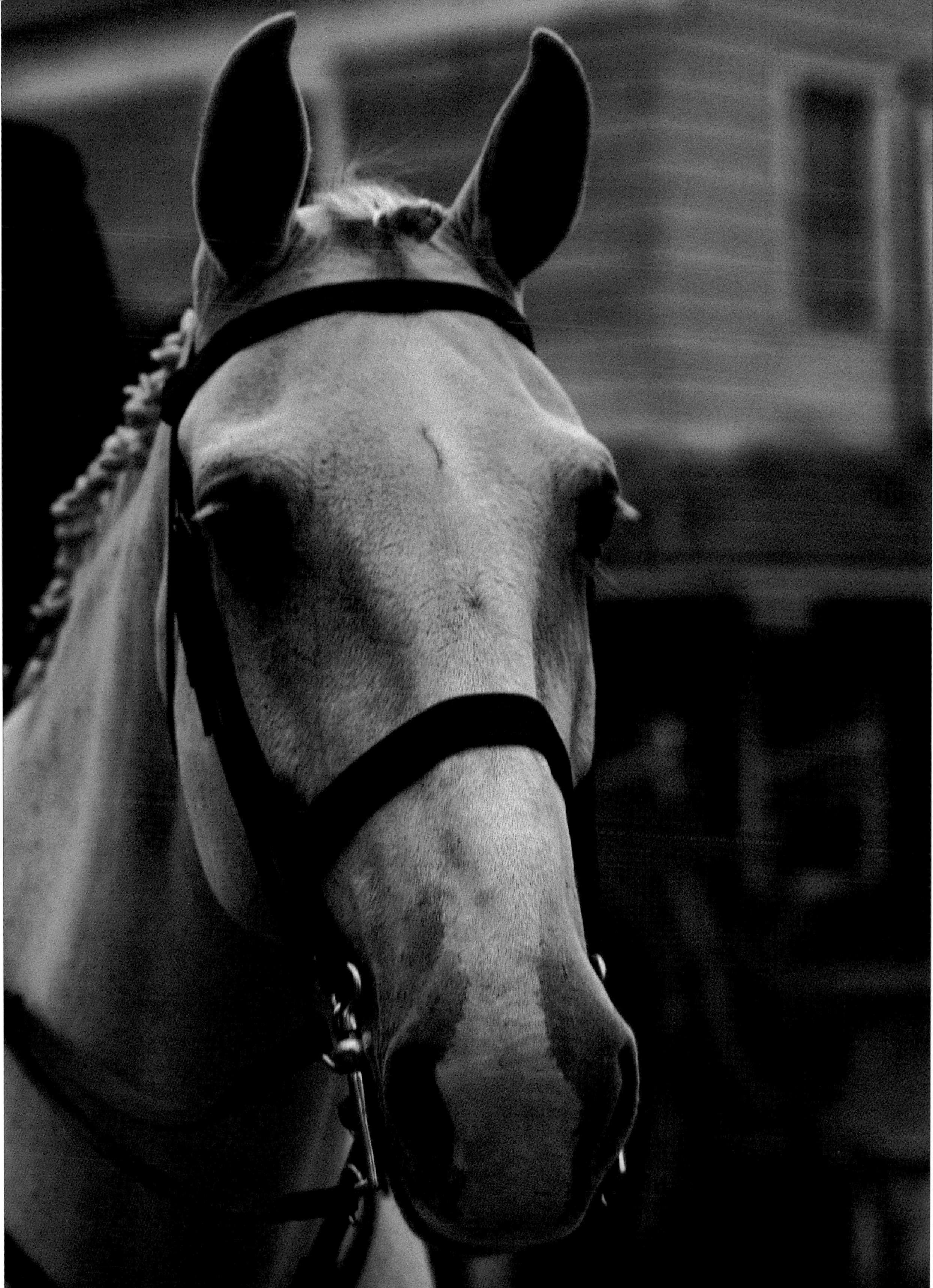

Opposite: Horses are at their happiest feeding, grazing and just hanging out, doing as little work as possible. These animals are quite adept at hiding if they see riding clothes and other "implements" that suggest work.

Left: Fully dressed in fancy tack and all cleaned up, a horse becomes a performer and a star, carrying the rider and being in full control at all times. Many horses love the competition, love the work and love the praise.

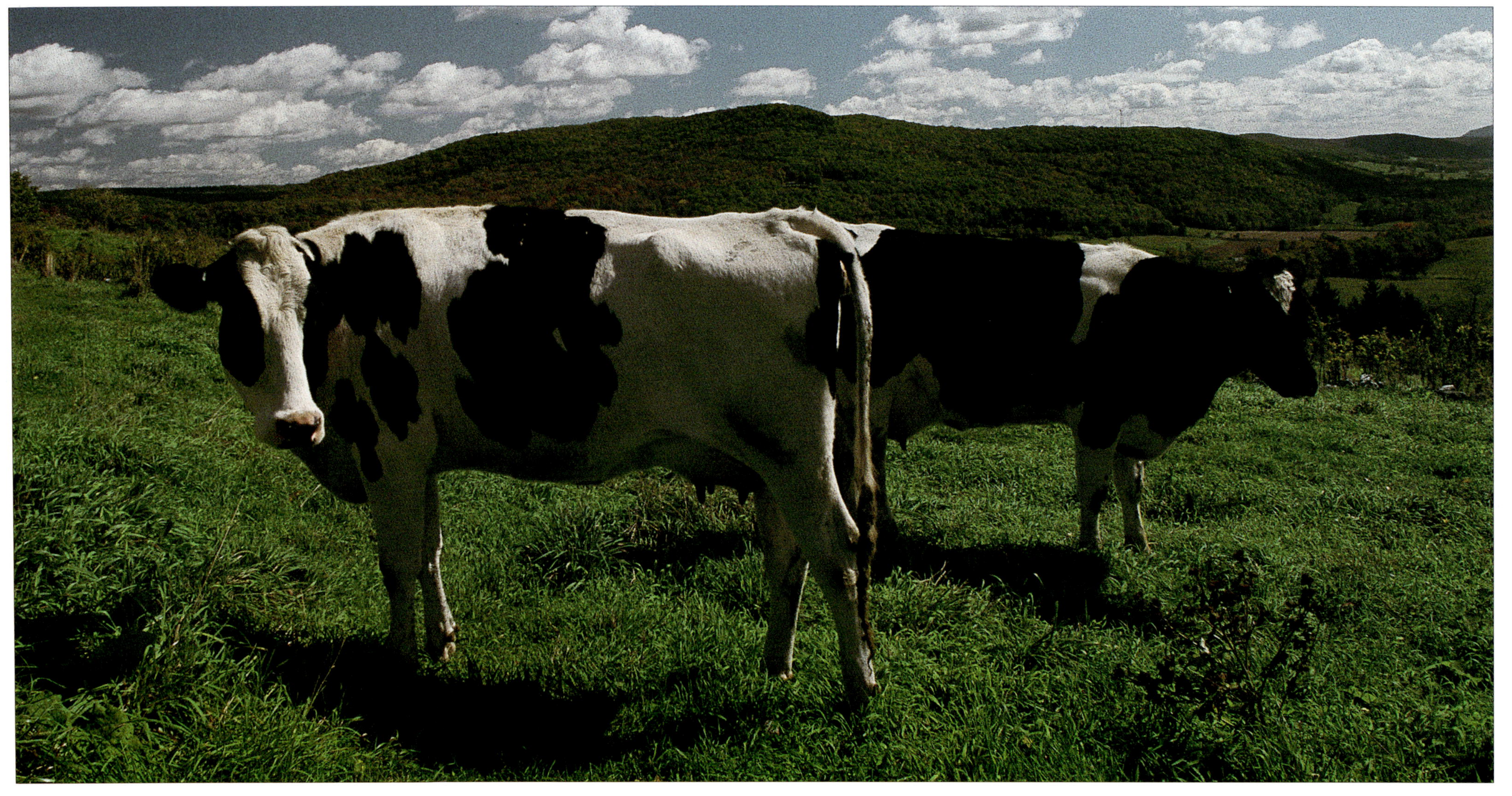

Above: Holstein dairy cows graze happily in upstate New York. Their milk is used for all kinds of food products including healthy country cheeses. One sign of rural revival in America has been the recent emergence of handmade quality cheeses from Oregon to Vermont to Louisiana. They put those square, yellow, processed "cheese food" slices (so oily they have to explain that it's food) to utter shame.

Opposite: Young dairy cows, just a few months old, are curious and eager like all children, watching intently and learning about their new world.

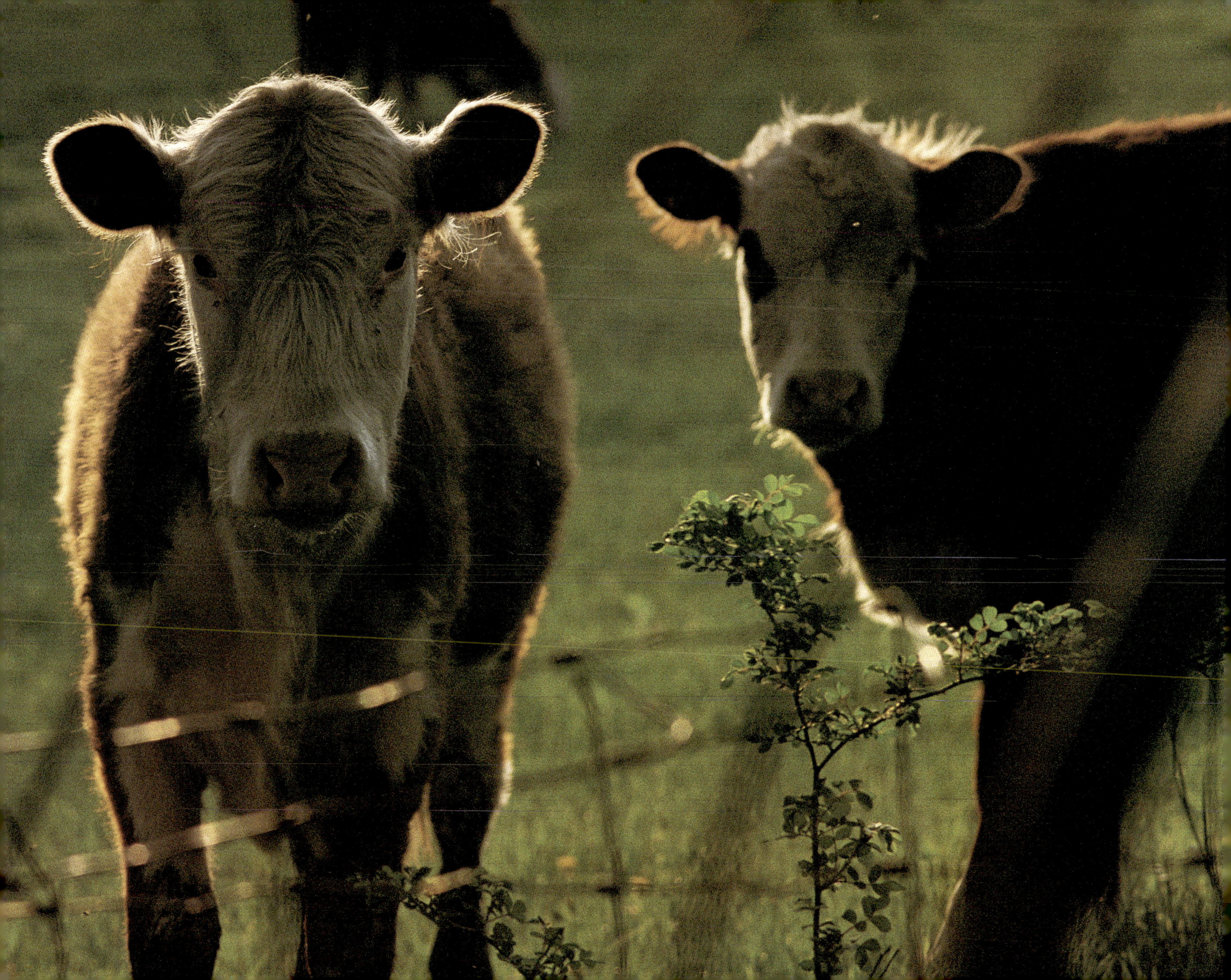

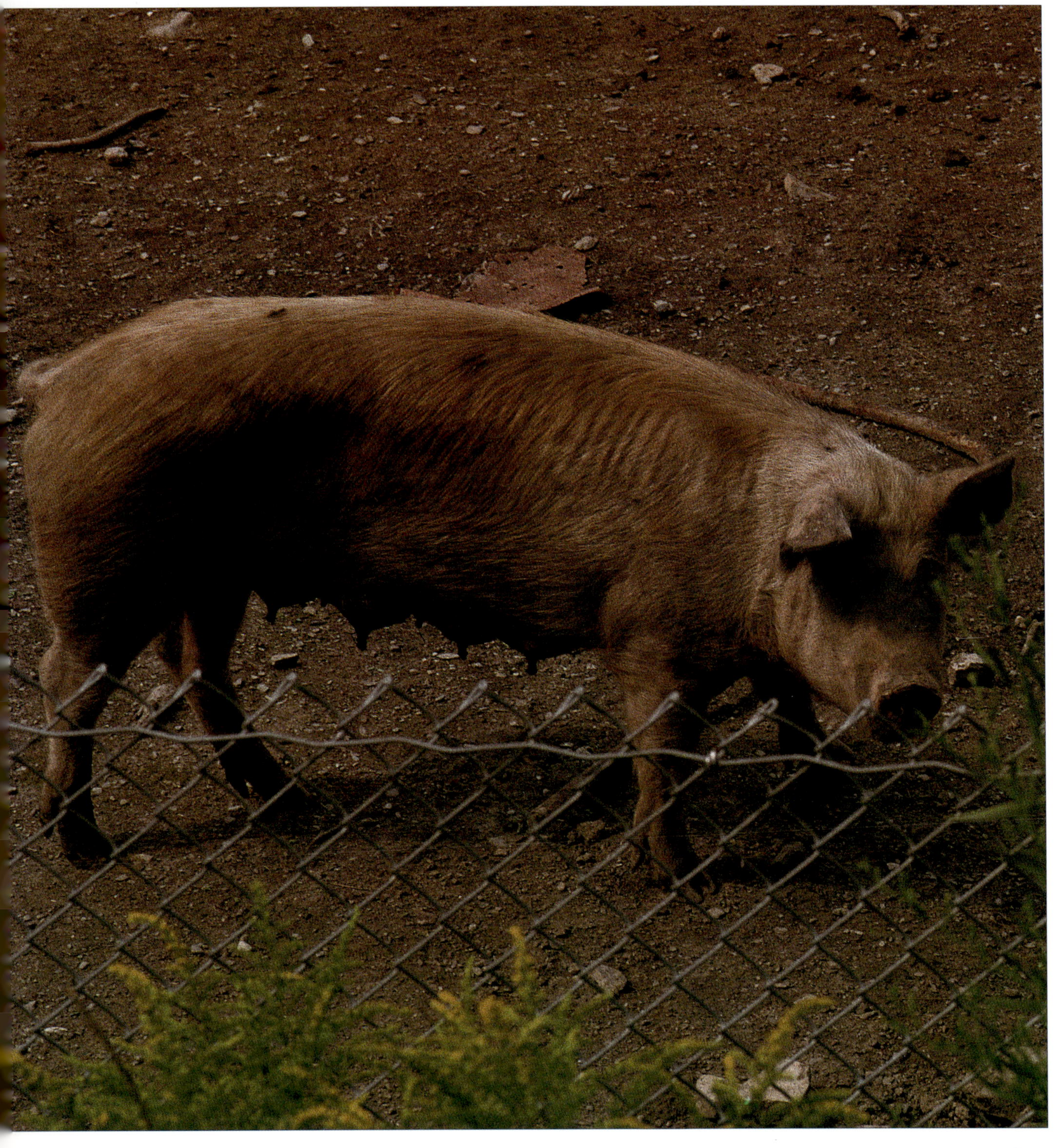

Left: The hog, the pig: the main meat staple of the South. This South Carolina hog probably ended up as the main course at a succulent barbecue. Barbecue is a native Southern cuisine that combines the many splendors of the region such as plentiful oysters, fresh corn, grits, and unique rice. Best of all it combines traditions that go back to Africa, the Ukraine, England, Vietnam, France, Iran – everywhere Southern immigrants have come from.

Opposite: County fairs are annual rituals in farming communities across the United States.

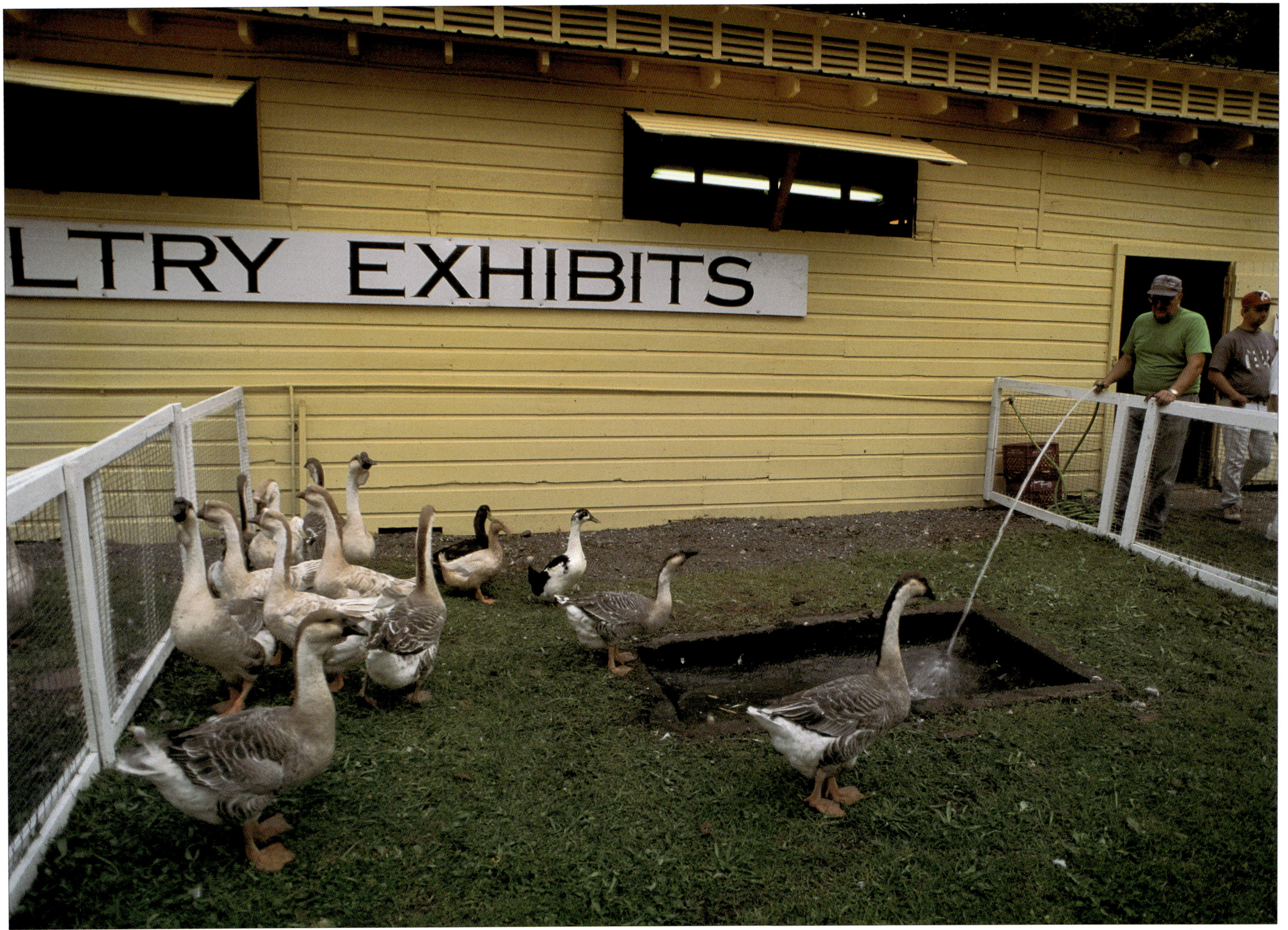
LTRY EXHIBITS

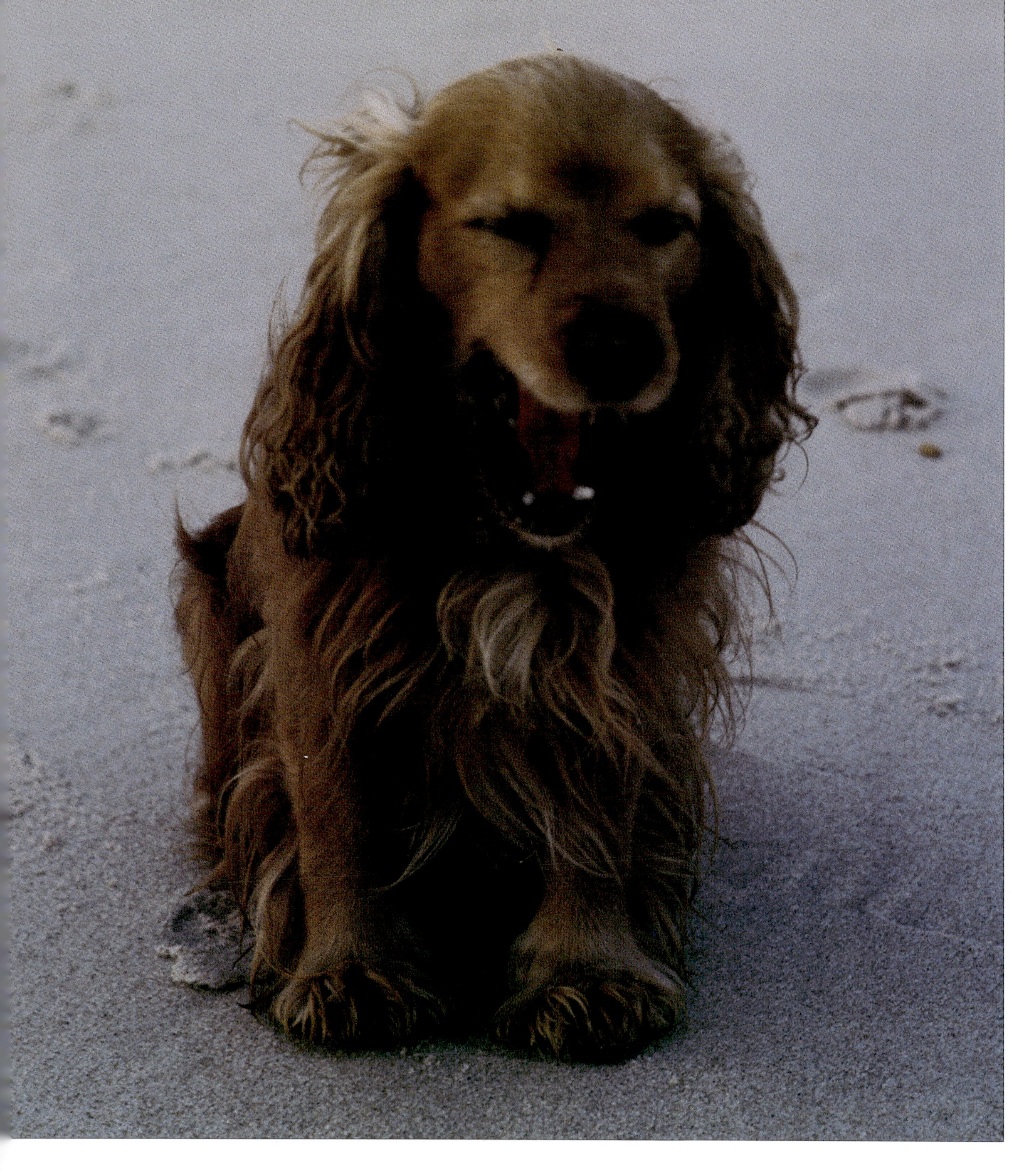

Left: This small cocker spaniel named Bayard enjoys the beach and the water. He is courageous, tenaciously trying to capture sticks from the ocean.

Opposite: Even naptime can't separate a boy from his dog. "Taco" Maria, a beagle mutt, is living the good life, sharing a bed with young William von Hassell.

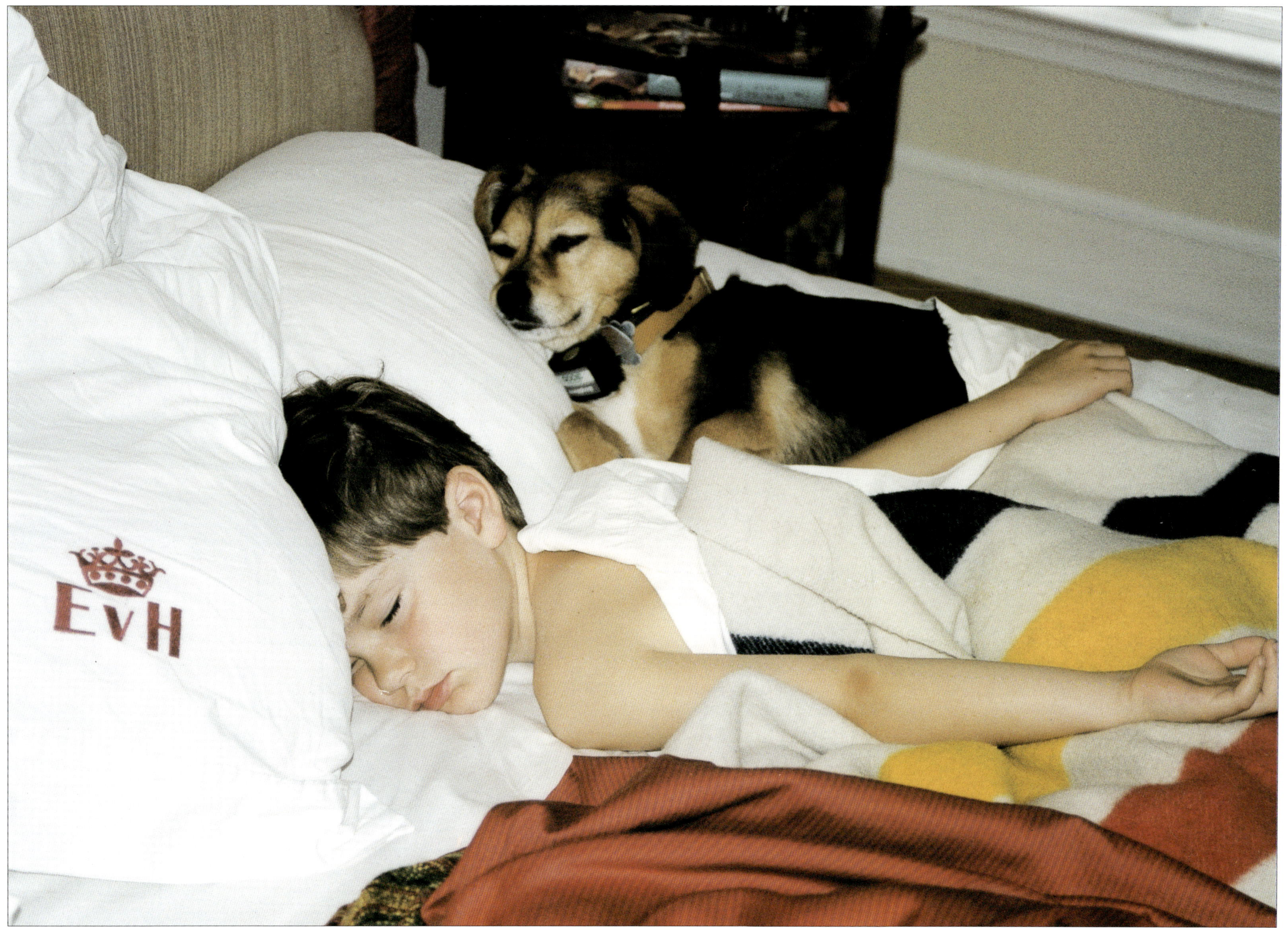

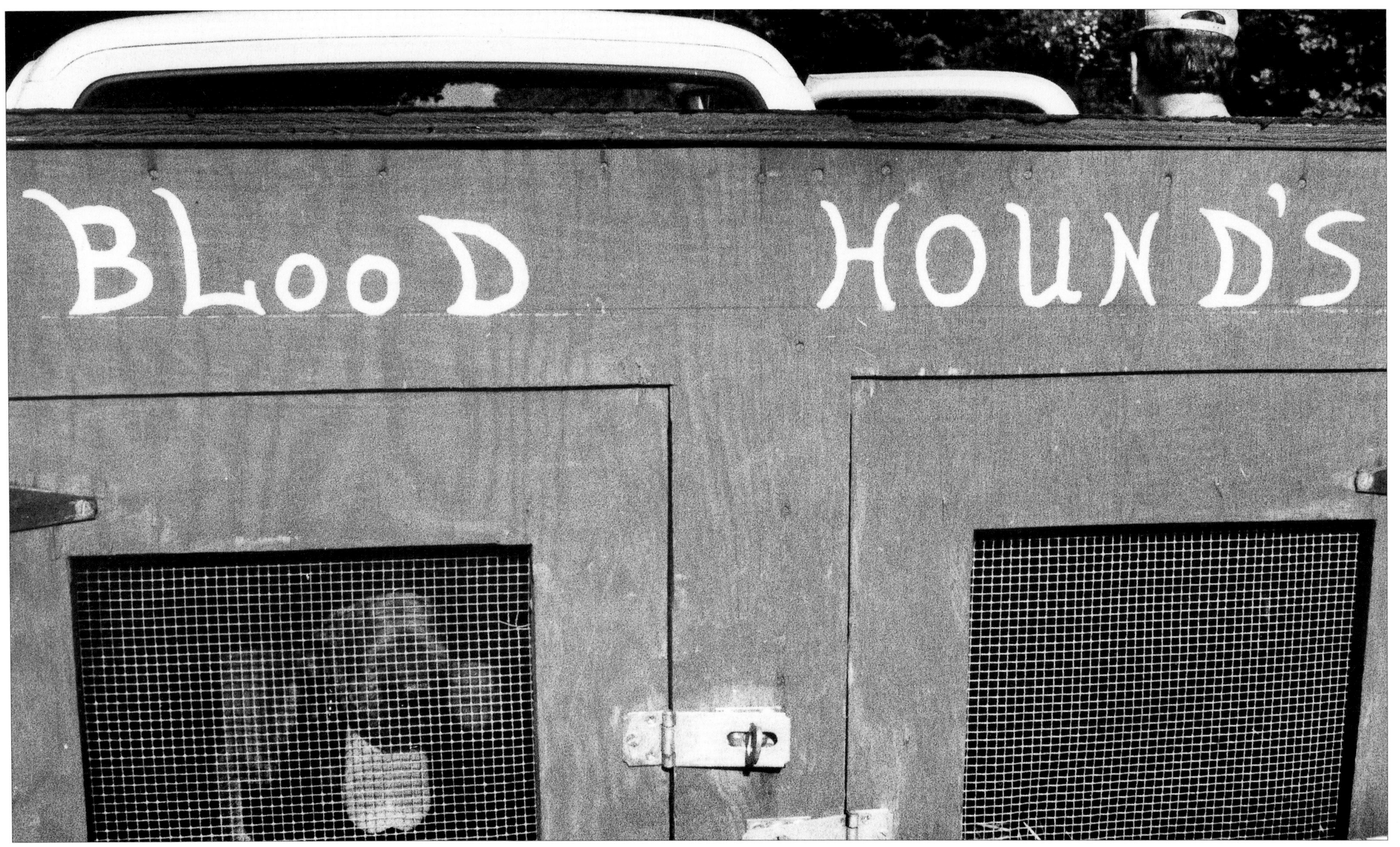

Above: In 1977, when James Earl Ray escaped from Brushy Mountain prison in Tennessee, locals quickly brought out bloodhounds to hunt for the escapee. In the olden days, whenever a prisoner escaped, a siren rang and women would start leafing through the Sears Roebuck catalogue, eager to figure out how to spend the prize money for a successful capture.

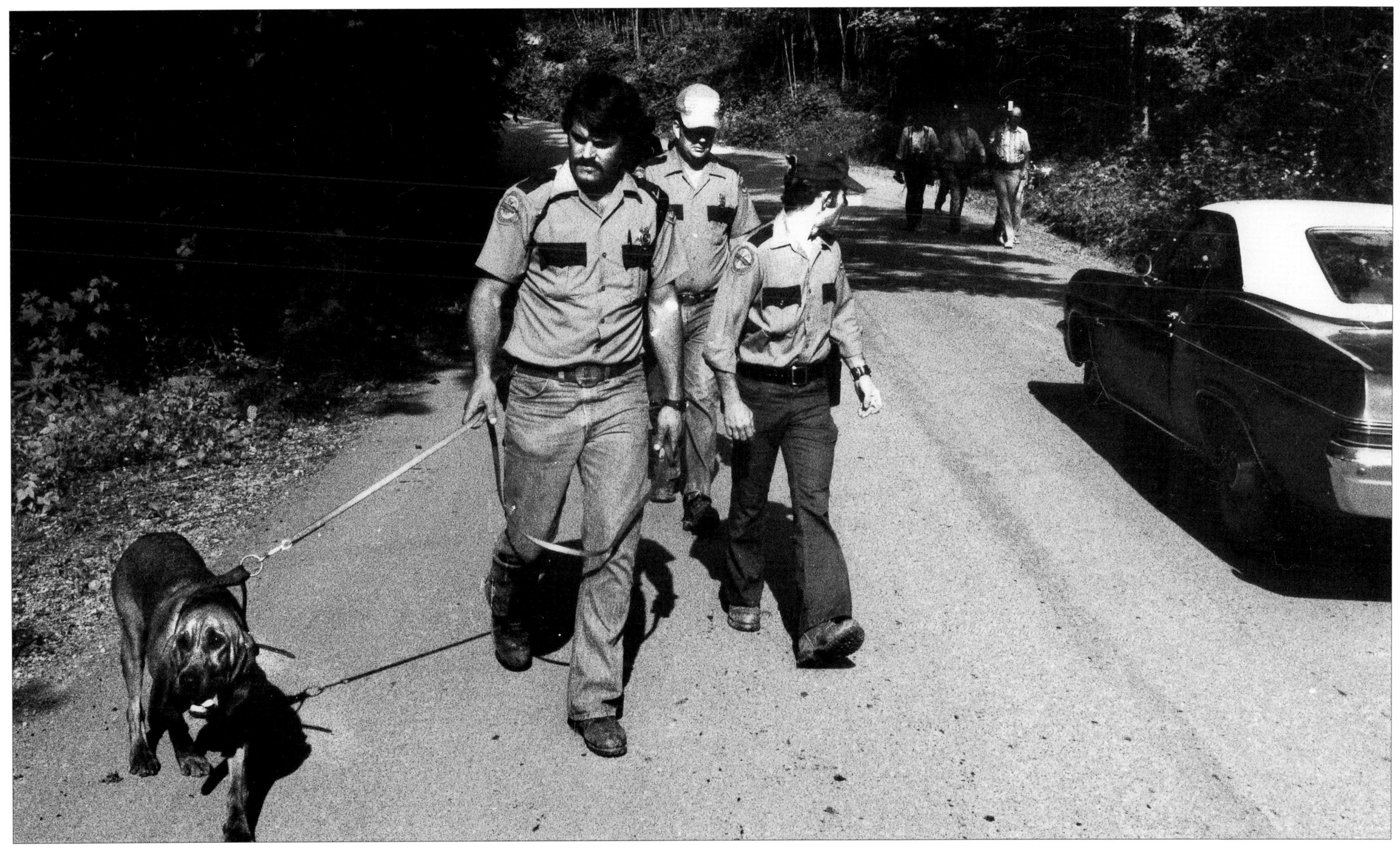

Above: Working hounds – may they be bloodhounds, hunting dogs or fox hounds –
are a pleasure to observe. Intent on their job and totally professional, these bloodhounds
chased James Earl Ray, who killed Martin Luther King, Jr..

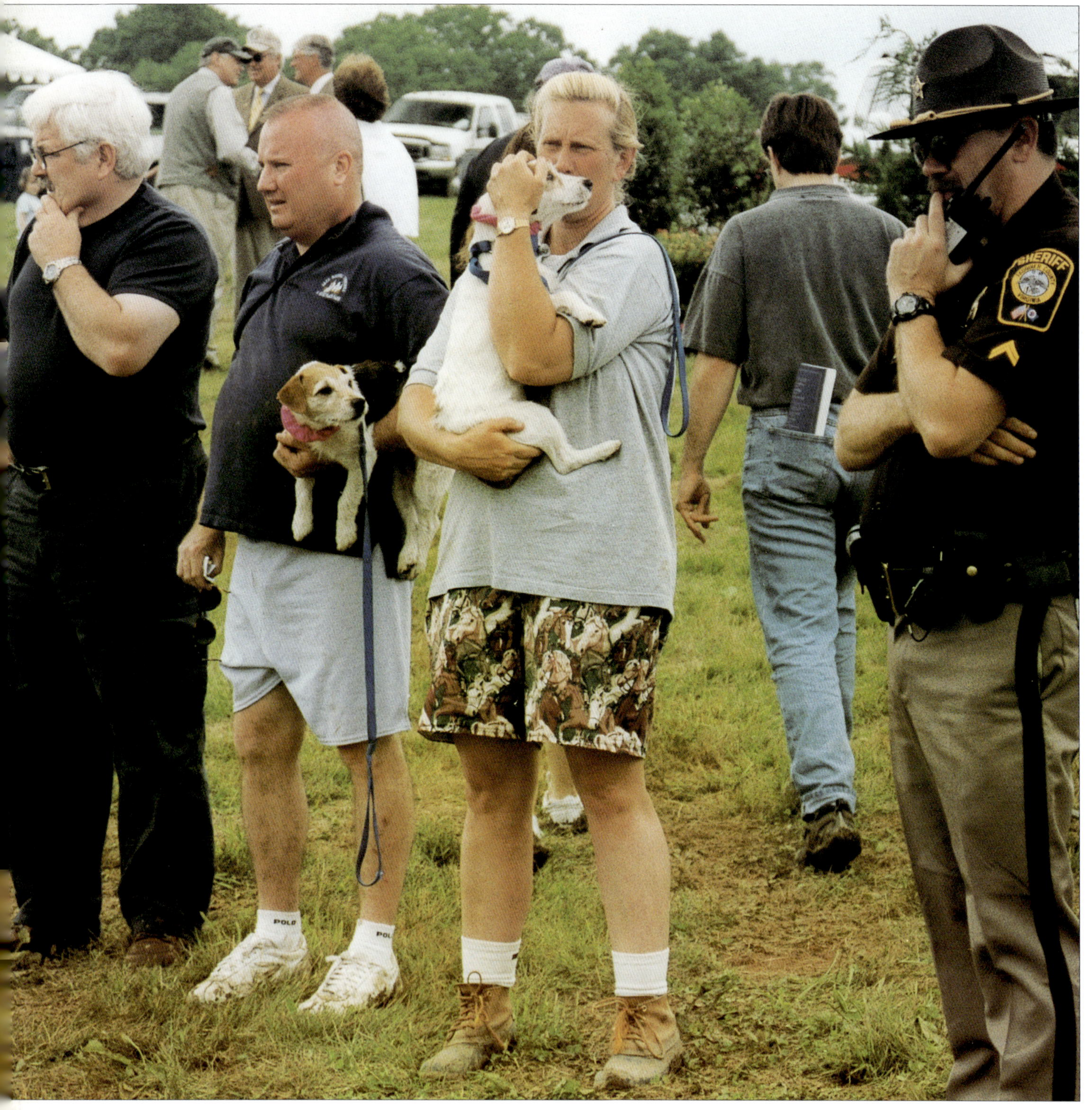

Left & Opposite:
Jack Russell Terriers are waiting to compete in a run during the Upperville Horse Show in Upperville, Virginia. They are feisty little assassins, trained to follow a fox into underground tunnels and flush out the fox so the hunt can continue. Hard to imagine that these nasty little creatures became a favorite pet – courtesy of a TV show – in big cities. Jack Russells typically get tucked into the jacket of one hunter known as the terrier man. Children may delight in them, but their aggressive spirit is hard to hide.

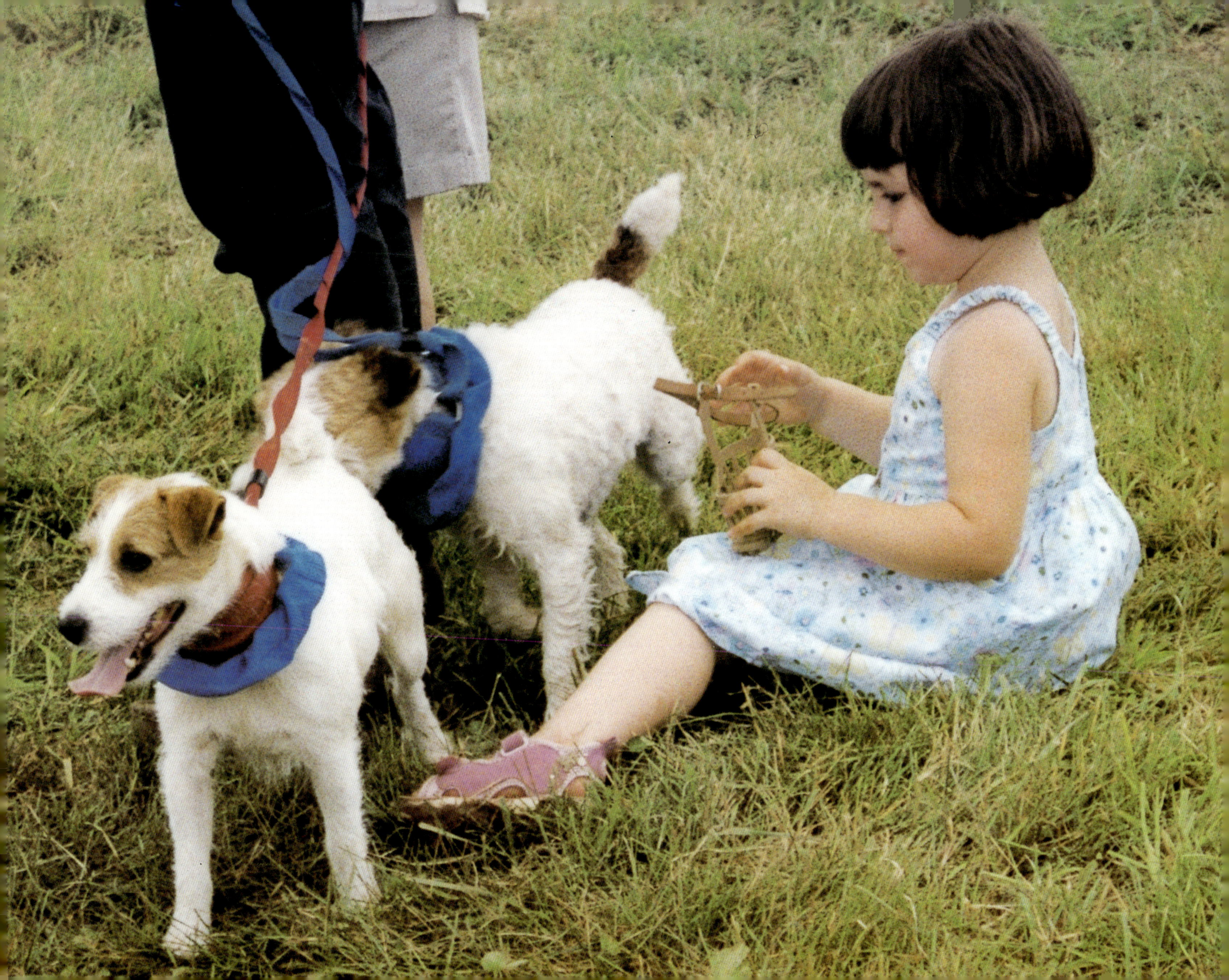

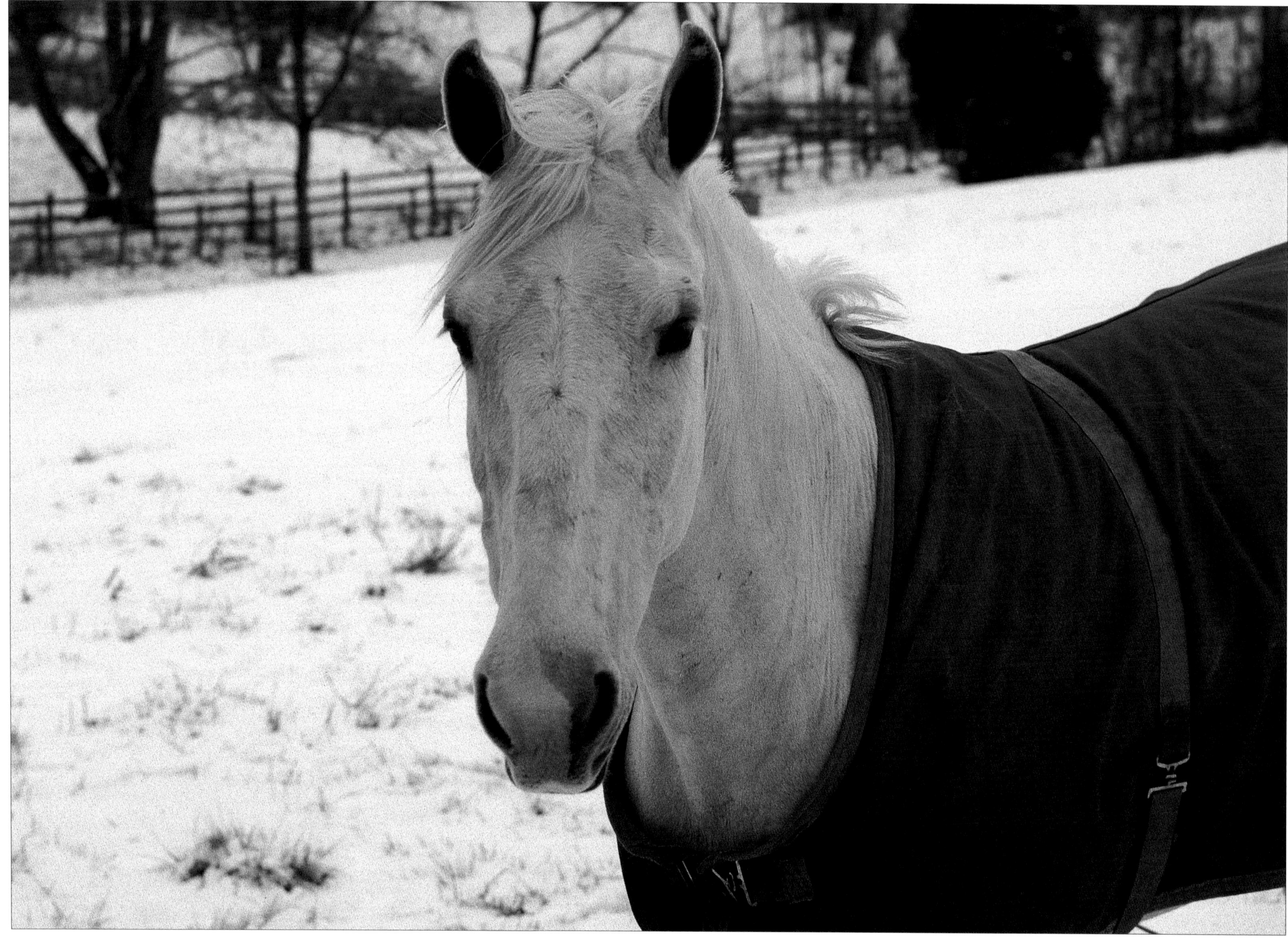

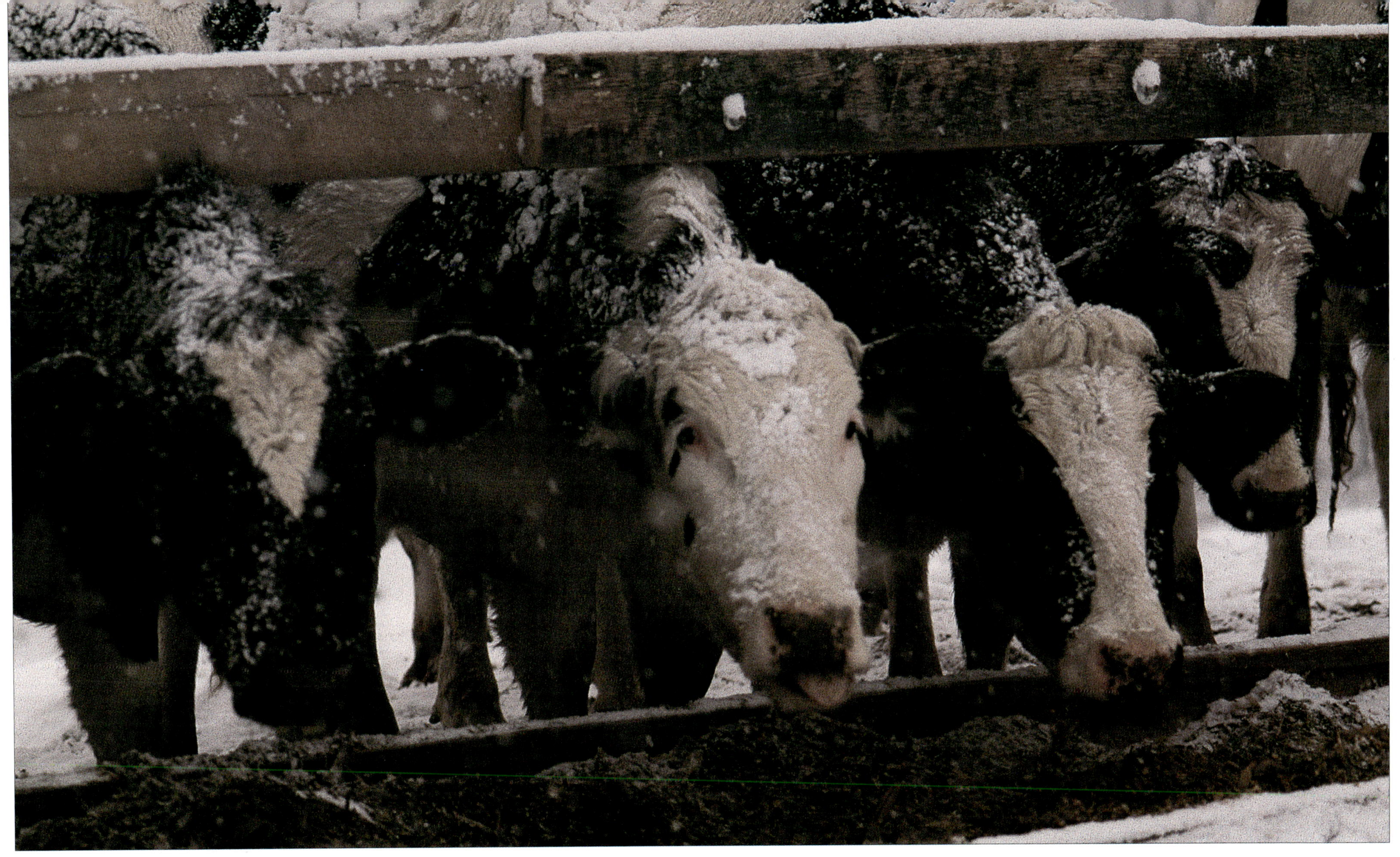

Above & Opposite: Animals in the winter are animals at rest. The work is done and all they are expected to do is eat the bounty of summer, feed corn and hay stacked in barns. Opposite, Madam Desiree casts a weary eye, concerned that her winter sojourn may be interrupted by work. And for the Holsteins above, the single biggest concern is the plentiful deer that share their feed troughs in the cold winters of America's northeast.

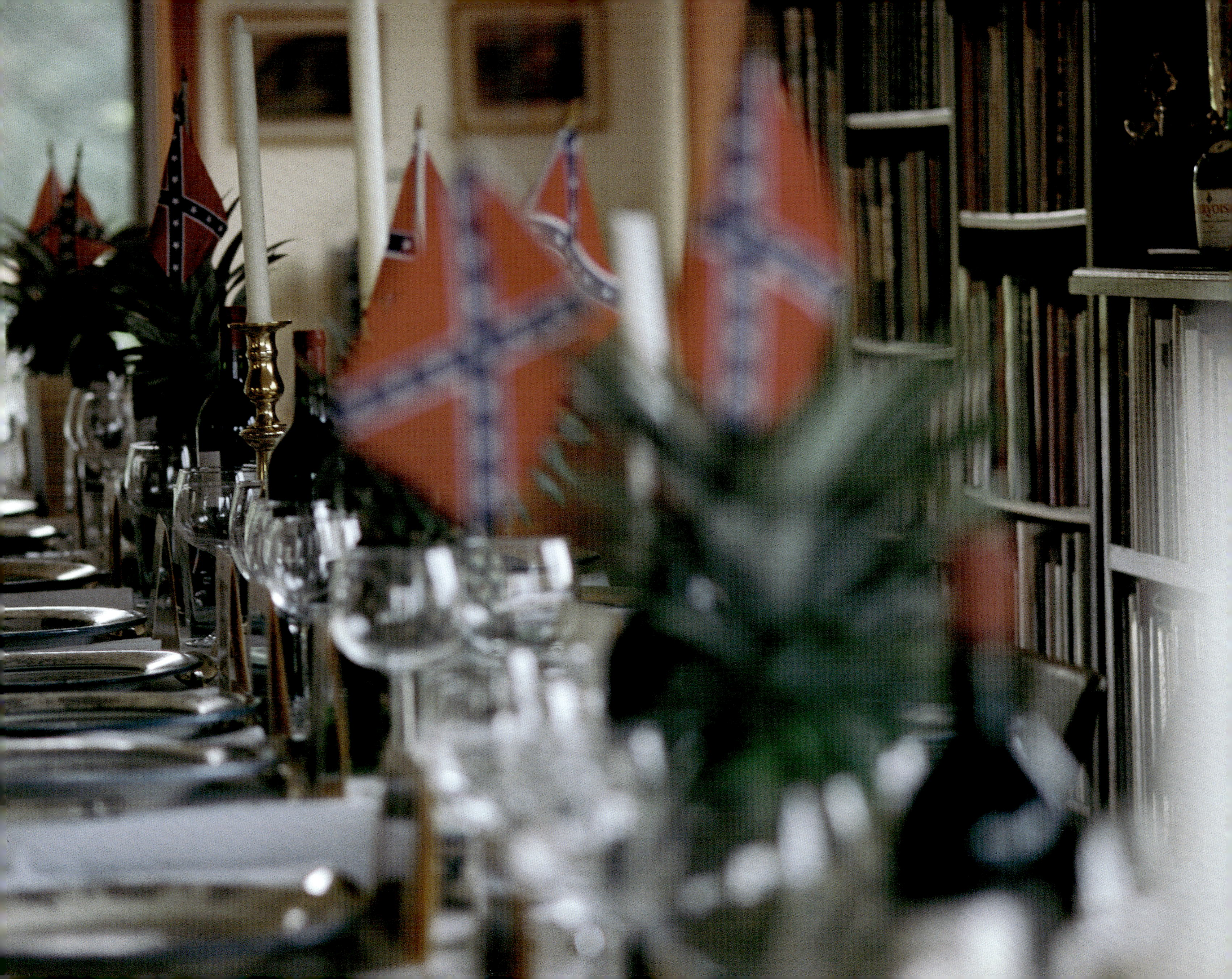

TRANQUILITY

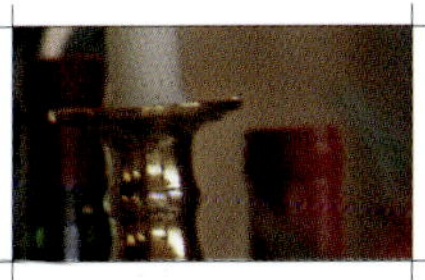

AMERICA MAY APPEAR TO BE CONSTANTLY CHANGING, IN PERPETUAL MOTION, BUT THERE ARE EXQUISITELY QUIET MOMENTS.

Opposite: Quiet celebration at simple yet elegant tables brings neighbors and friends together to remember the very old South and celebrate the future. America has the uncanny ability to take the best from a variety of cultures, cast away the rest and create something uniquely its own.

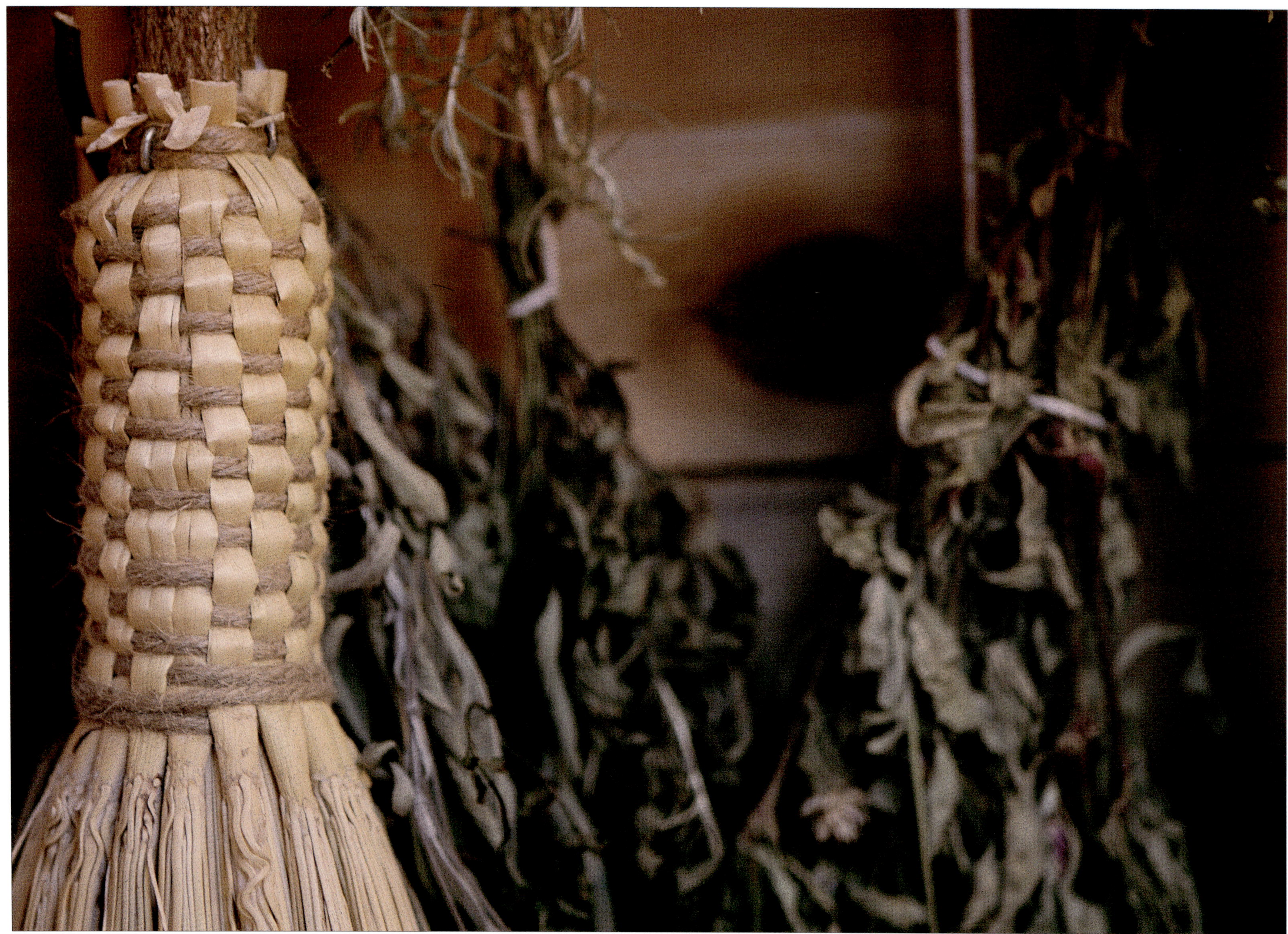

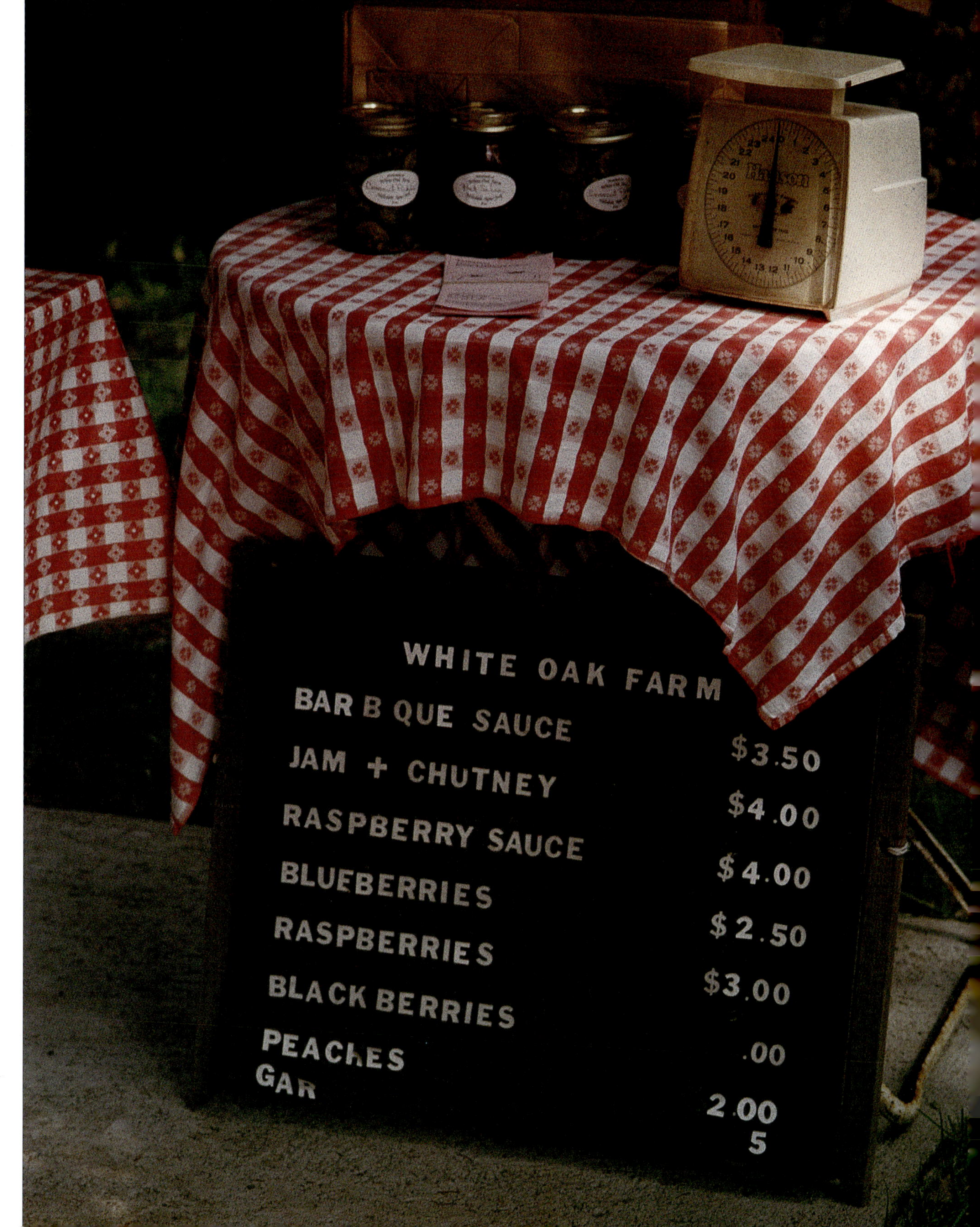

Opposite & Right: Herbs picked at their peak and carefully dried will infuse a pork roast with flavor and a sweet aroma. Produce stands with local fruits, vegetables and farm products are common throughout the United States. Many operate on the honor system, with customers dropping payment for the goods into a can or box. As William Shakespeare wrote: "Thy honesty and love doth mince this matter." Where else on earth could people run businesses based totally on trust?

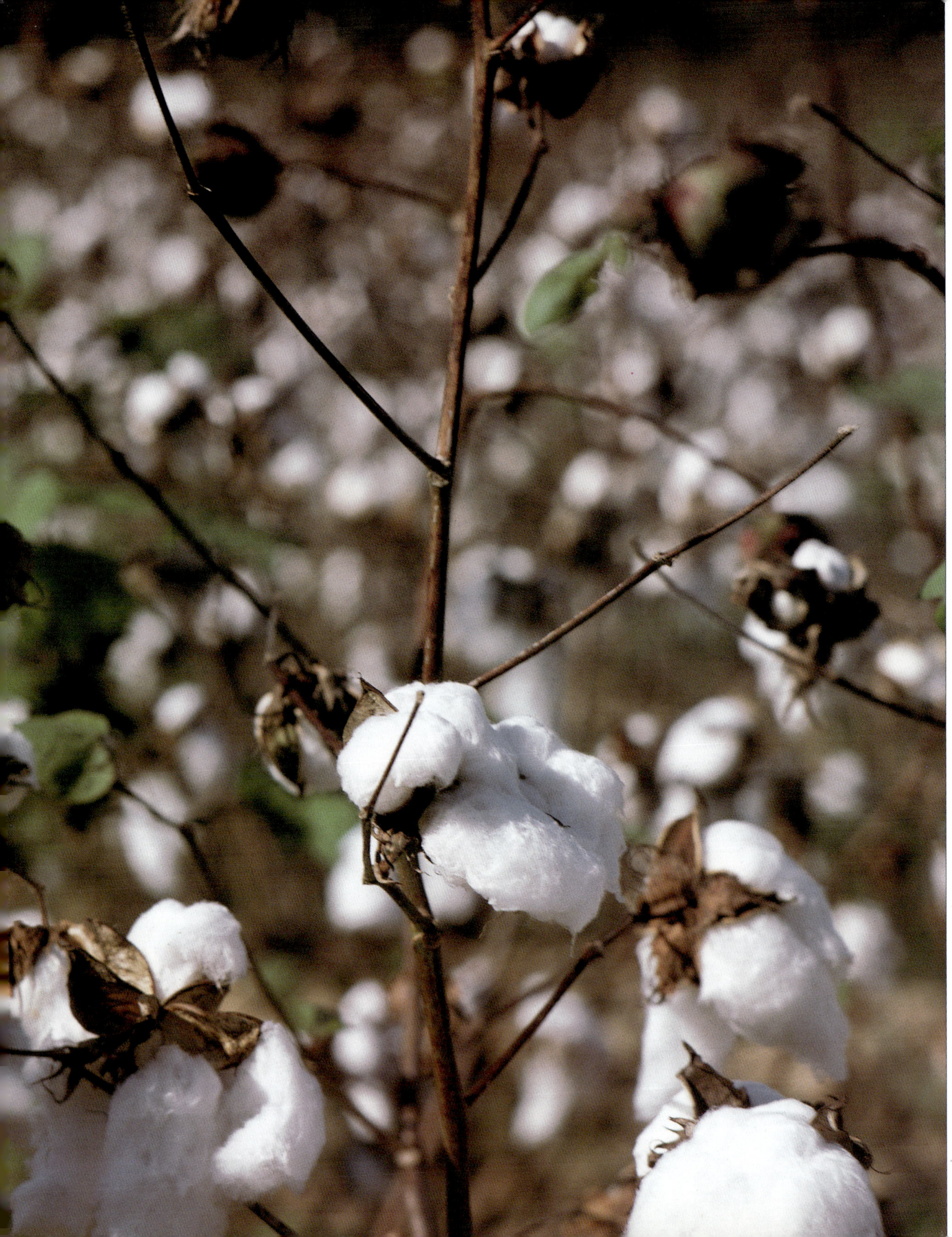

Left: "King Cotton" brought both misery and prosperity. It supported a cruel slave trade and created riches all over the Deep South. This cotton field in northern Mississippi stands in memory of both the bad and the good.

Opposite: America's industrial revolution helped improve the productivity of each acre of farmland. By the 20th century America could not only feed itself, but also export foodstuffs worldwide. The 1980s and 1990s saw corporate farming drive down food prices and undercut family-run operations. Thousands of families who had worked the land for generations lost their homes and their occupations to big business.

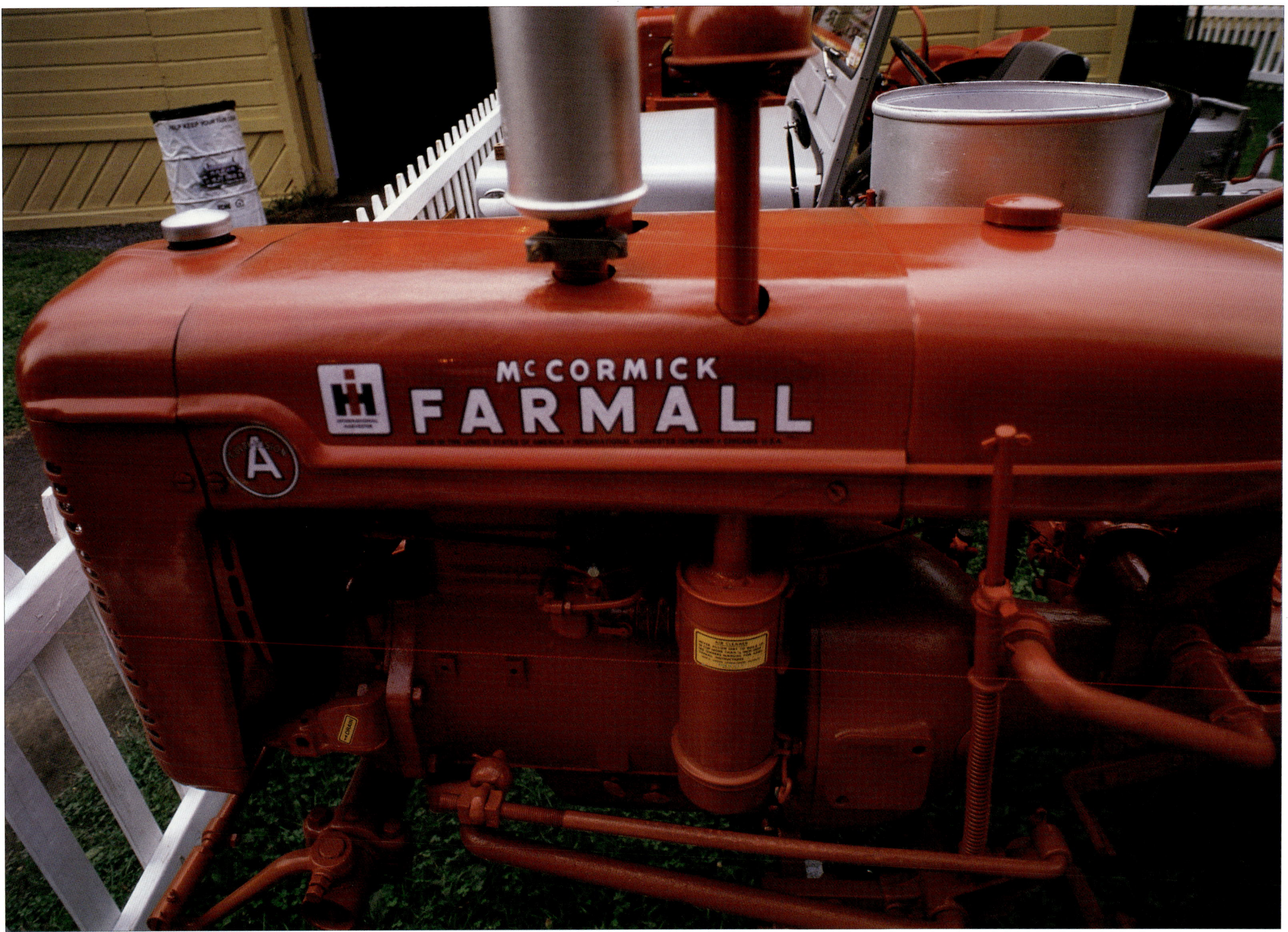

McCORMICK
FARMALL
A

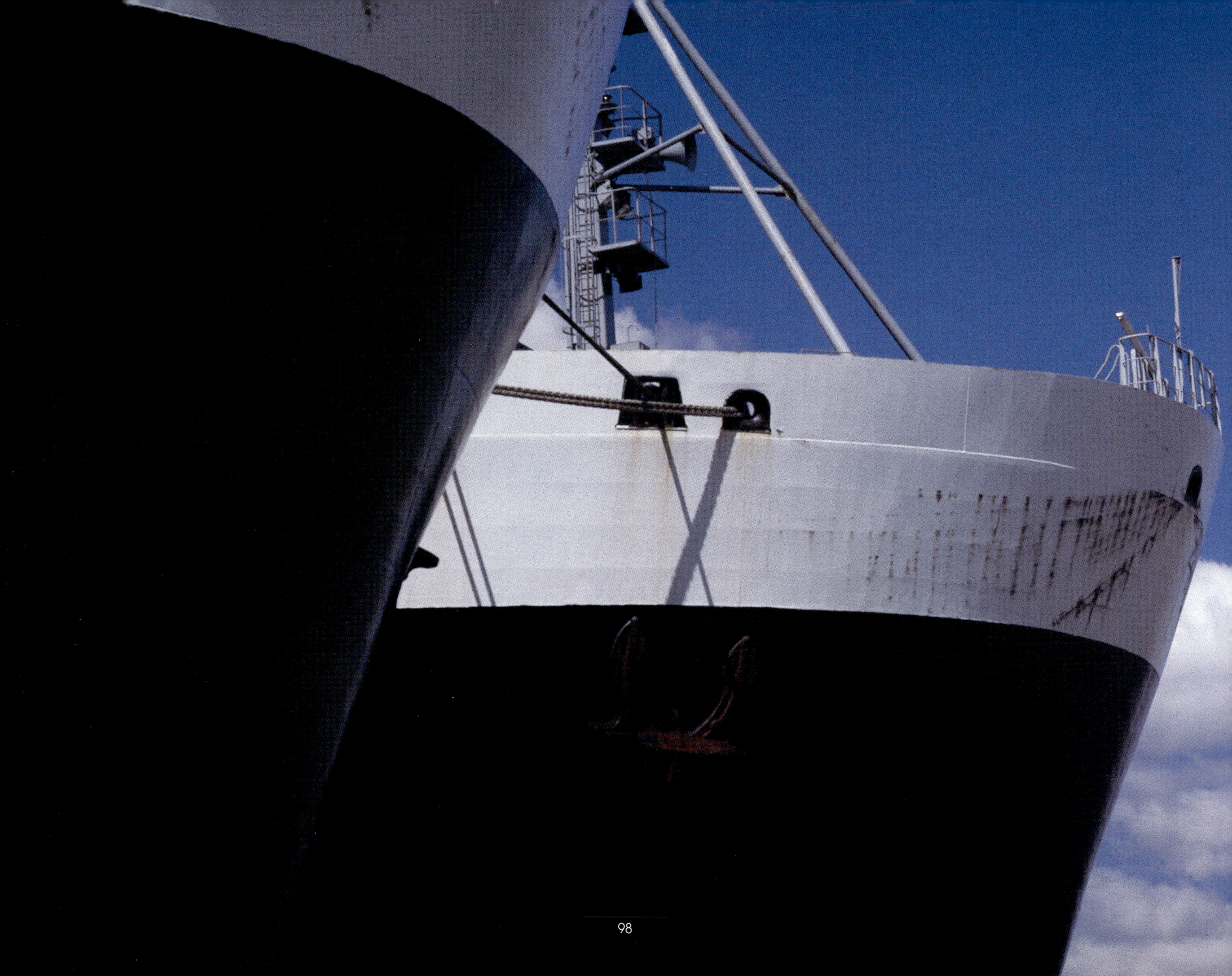

Opposite: Old ships are so very sad – like warriors out to pasture. These ships, now scrapped, were floating schools. The term "learning the ropes" originated at sea where each young man on board ship had to learn the importance and workings of hundreds of ropes so he could help in any location during an emergency.

Right: A knot is like a mystery and yet a promise. To this day Boy Scouts and Girl Scouts learn knot tying for use in camping, climbing and water sports, and Navy Midshipmen learn how to tie over 200 types of knots.

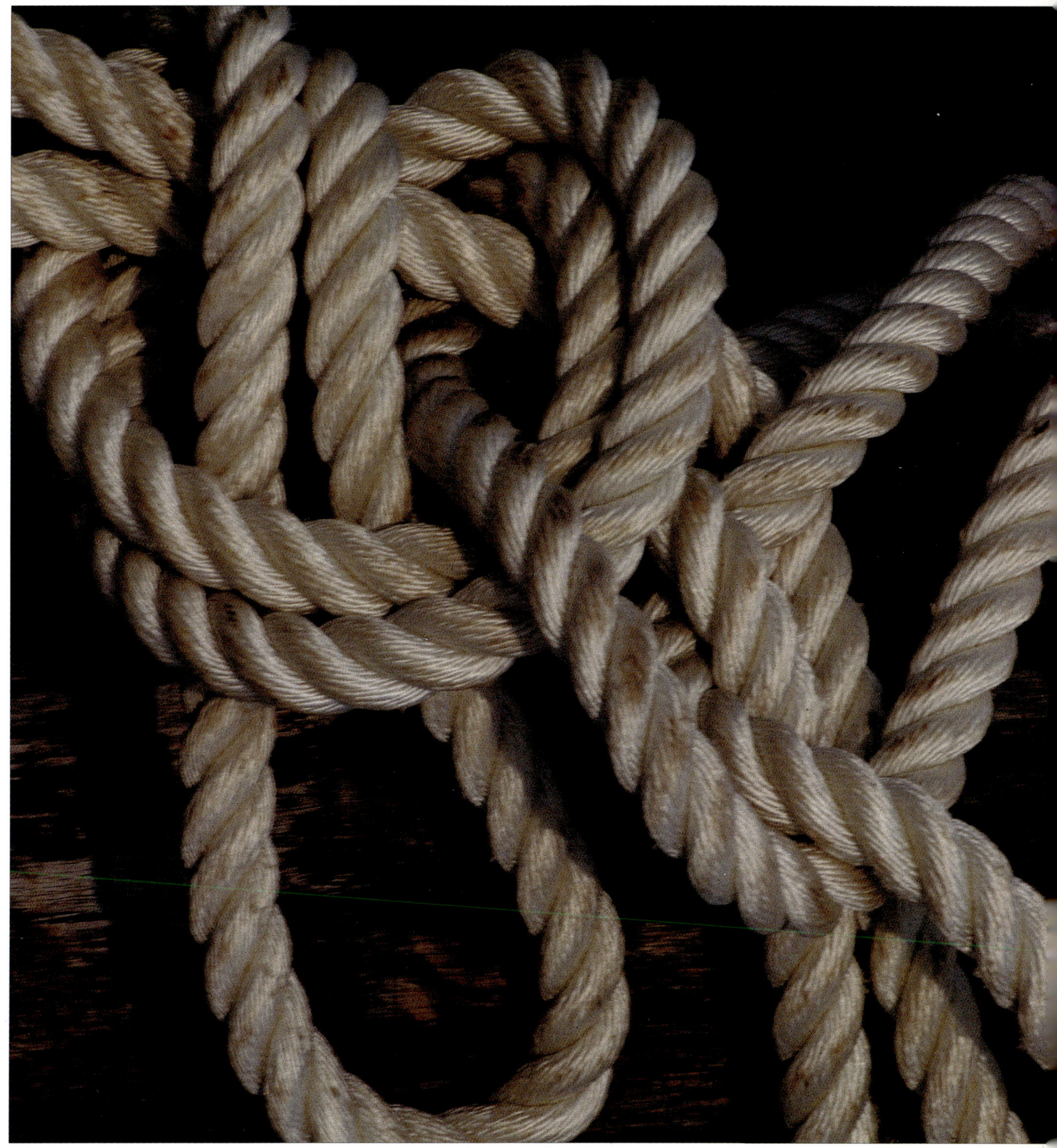

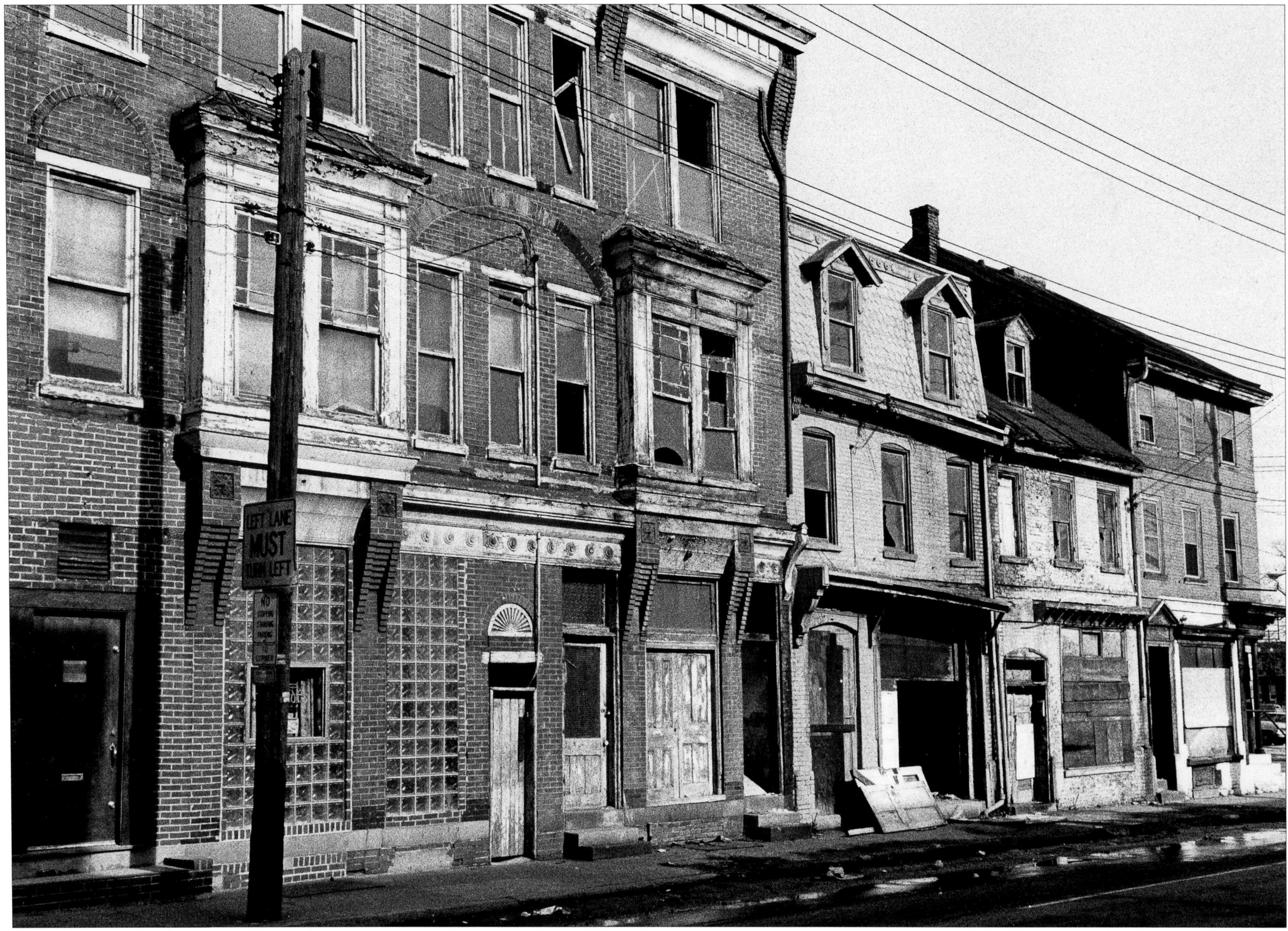
LEFT LANE
MUST
TURN LEFT

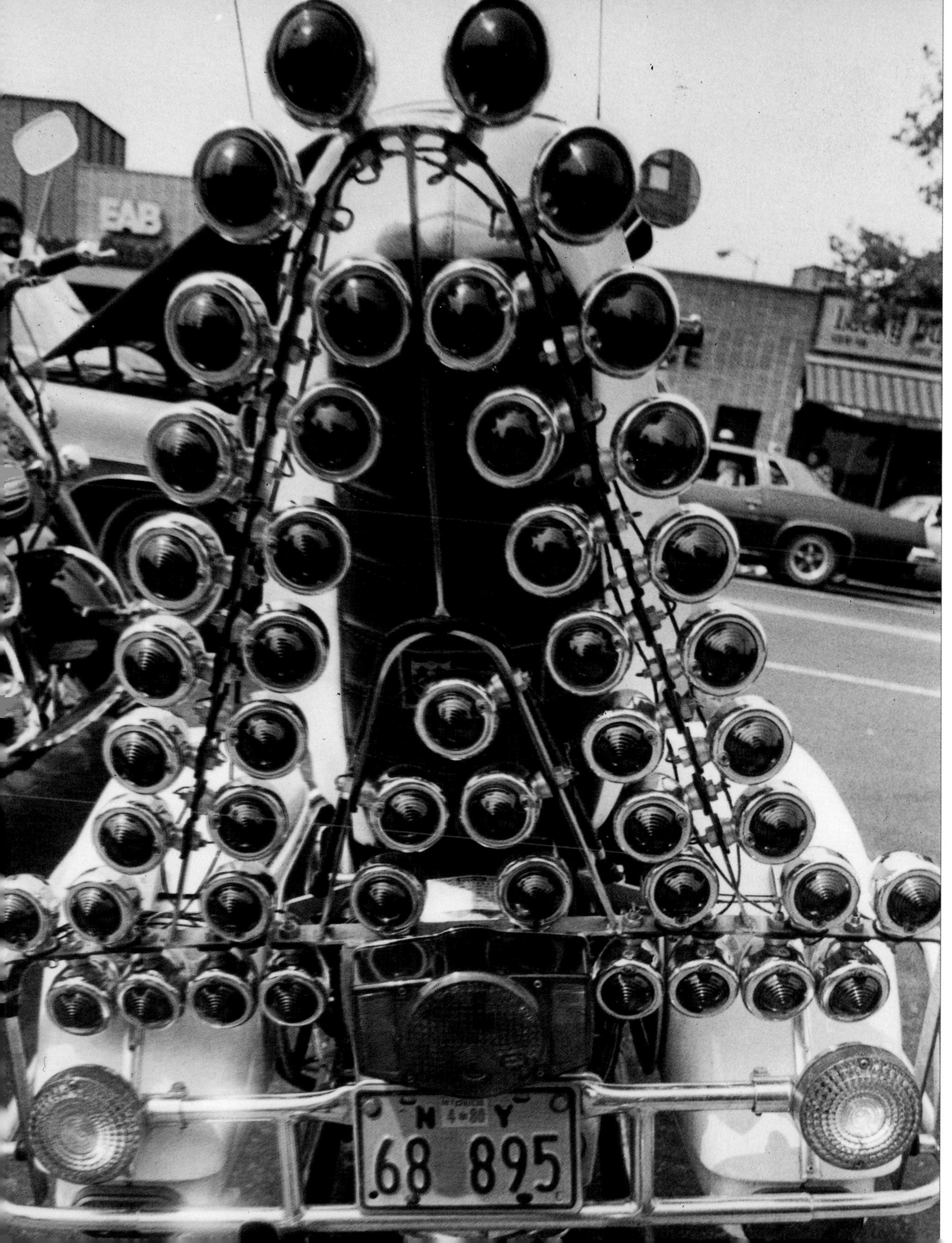

Opposite: Urban decline haunted American cities for decades. Fine houses – such as these in Harlem, New York – fell apart. Organizations like Habitat for Humanity and volunteers as prestigious as President Jimmy Carter have helped to rebuild urban America. Gentrification of formerly rundown neighborhoods has resulted in fine housing, restoring the old for a new generation.

Left: How dramatic do you want to get? America embraces splendor and gore, which explains the attraction and revulsion of the strip in Las Vegas and the Atlantic City boardwalk. Some individuals love excess and drama such as this motorcyclist who adorned his hog with more lamps than one can reasonably count.

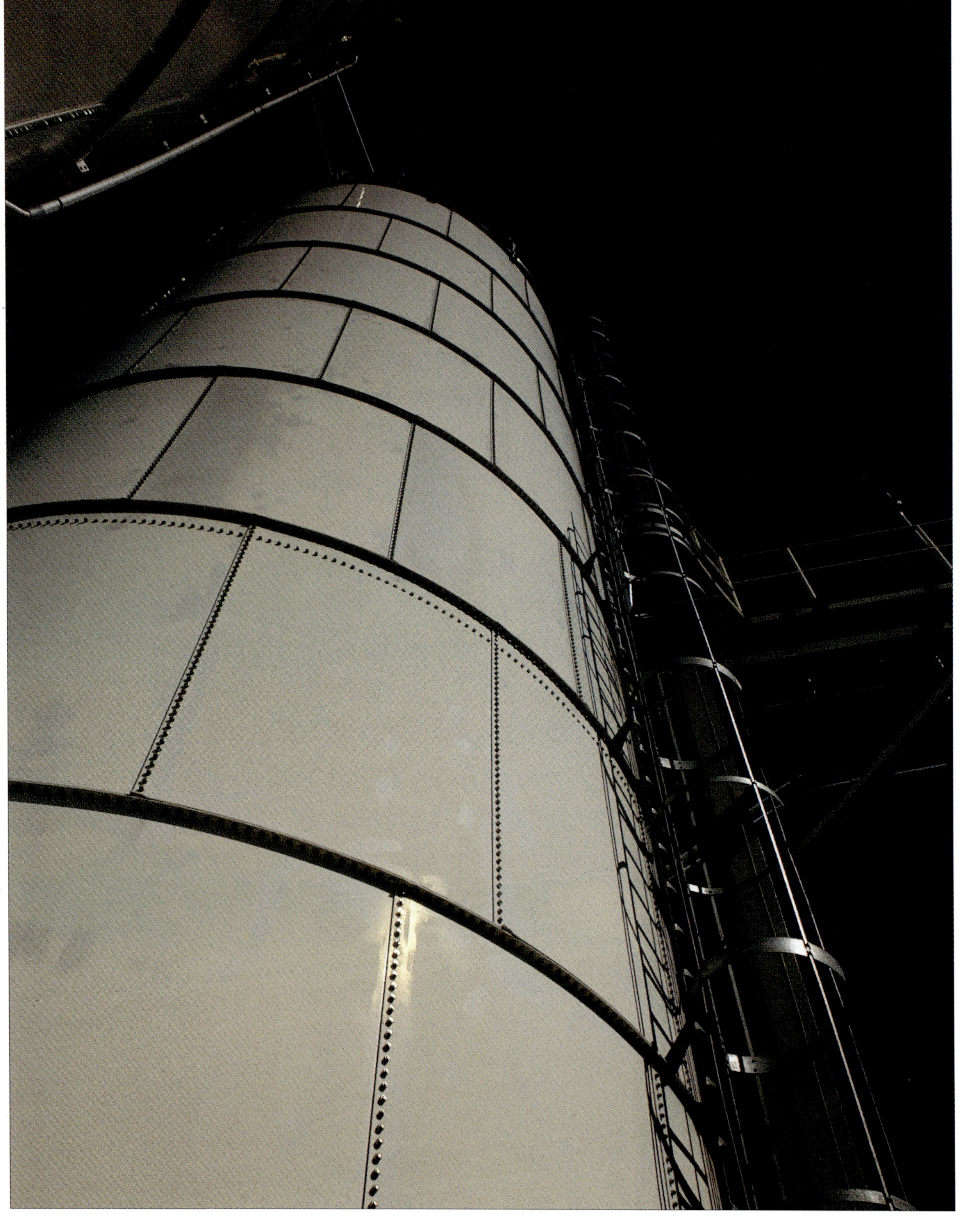

Left: Storage silos for corn and grain dominate the entirely flat lands in the Midwest, the great bread basket of the republic. This silo was photographed in Nebraska.

Opposite: Pine trees provide a memory of autumn and the promise of spring all winter long.

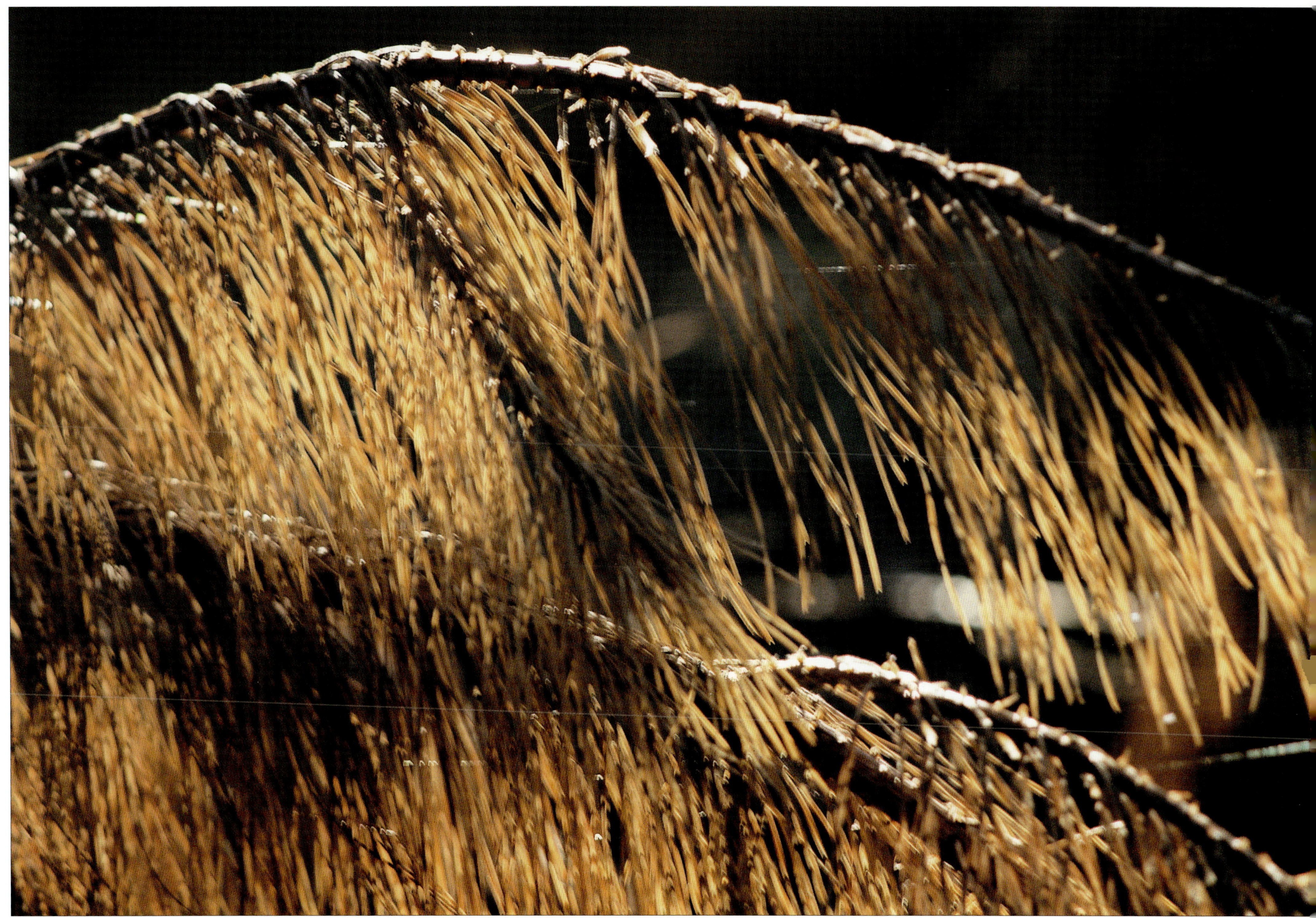

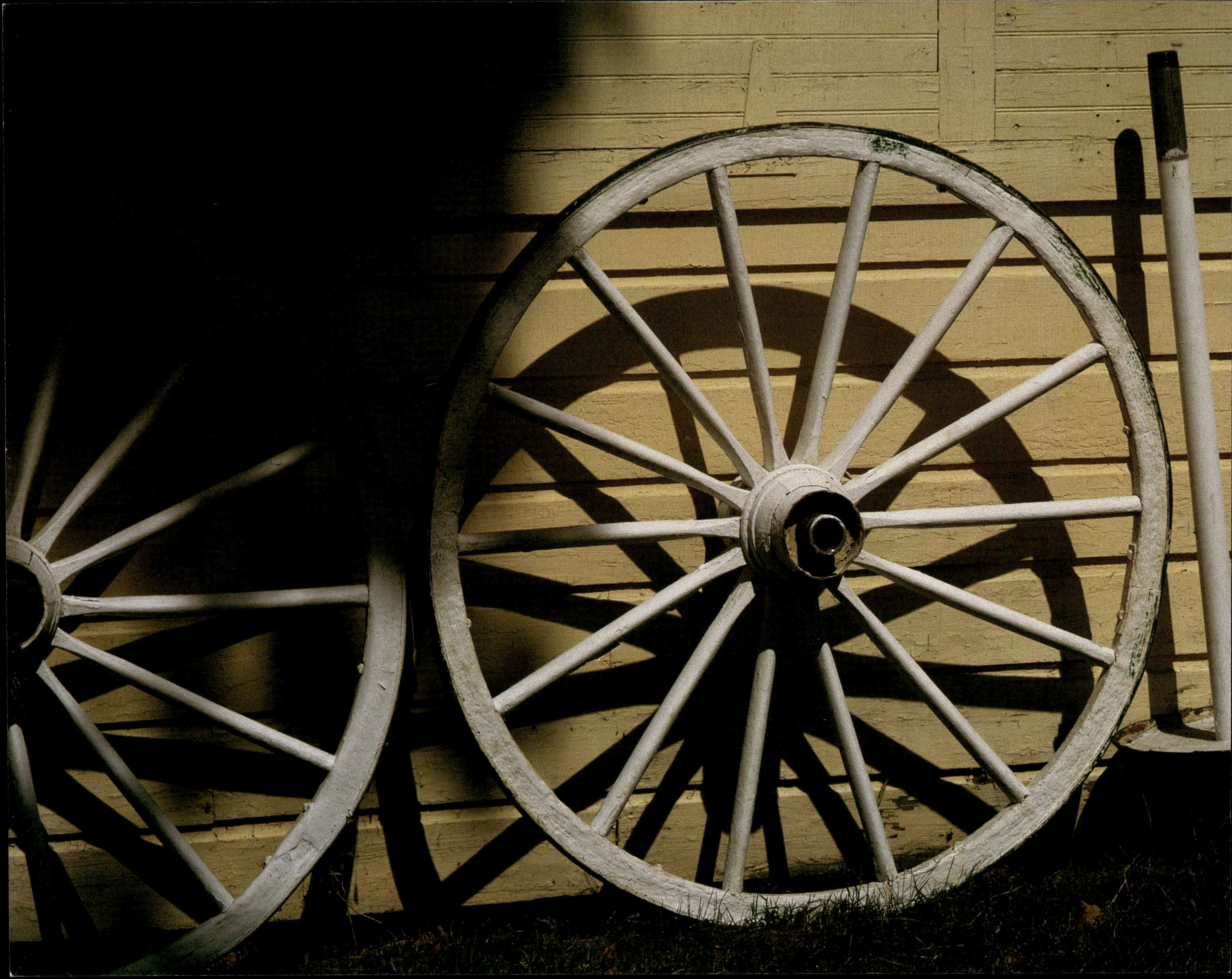

Opposite: Old wagon wheels remind the casual observer of the covered wagons that carried settlers across the Great Plains into the unconquered West. Wheelwrights combine functionality with artistry.

Right: "You should go to a pear tree for pears, not to an elm," wrote Livy around A.D. 17 in one of his maxims. He and others would always praise the greatness of the perfectly ripe pear.

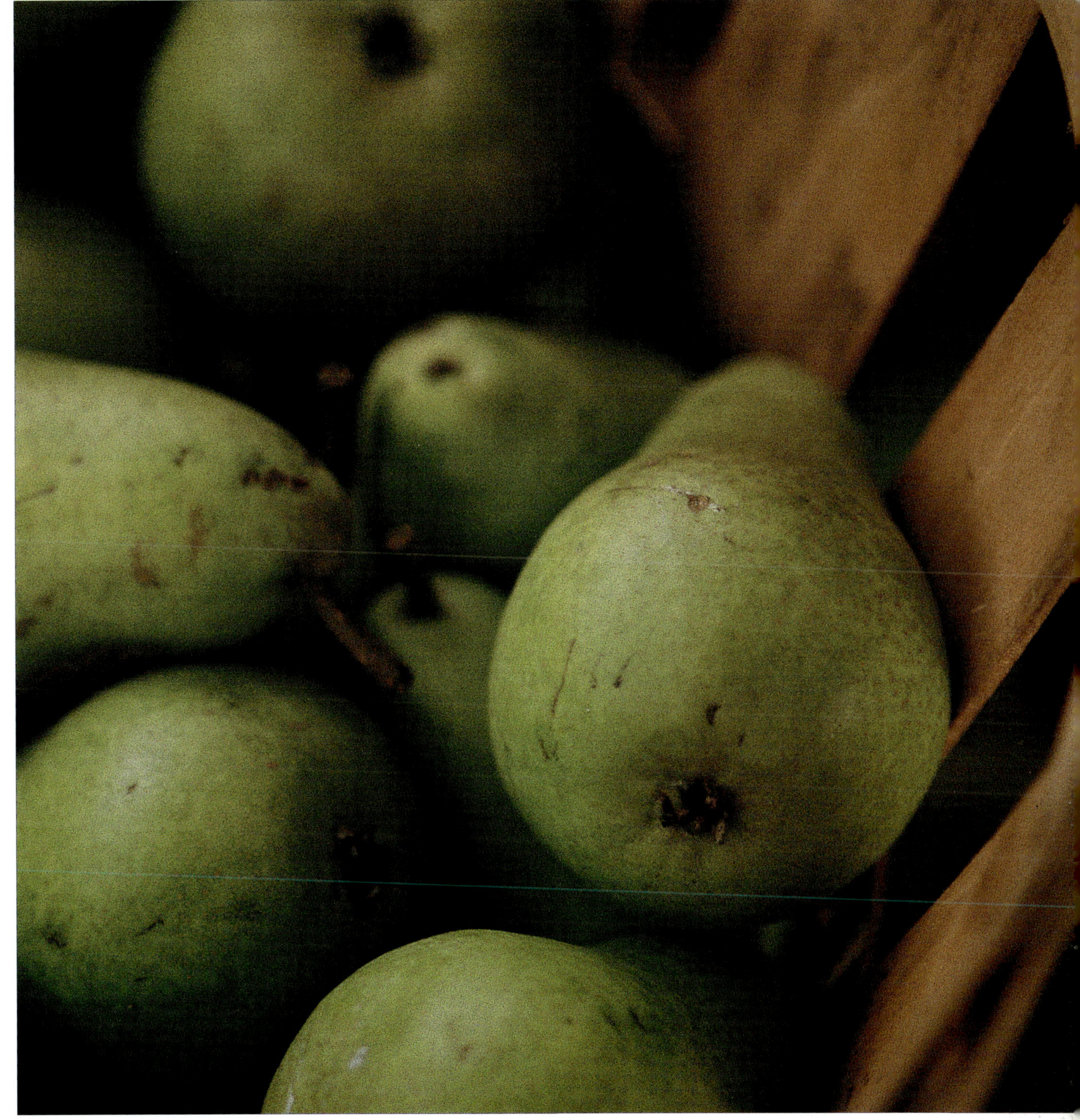

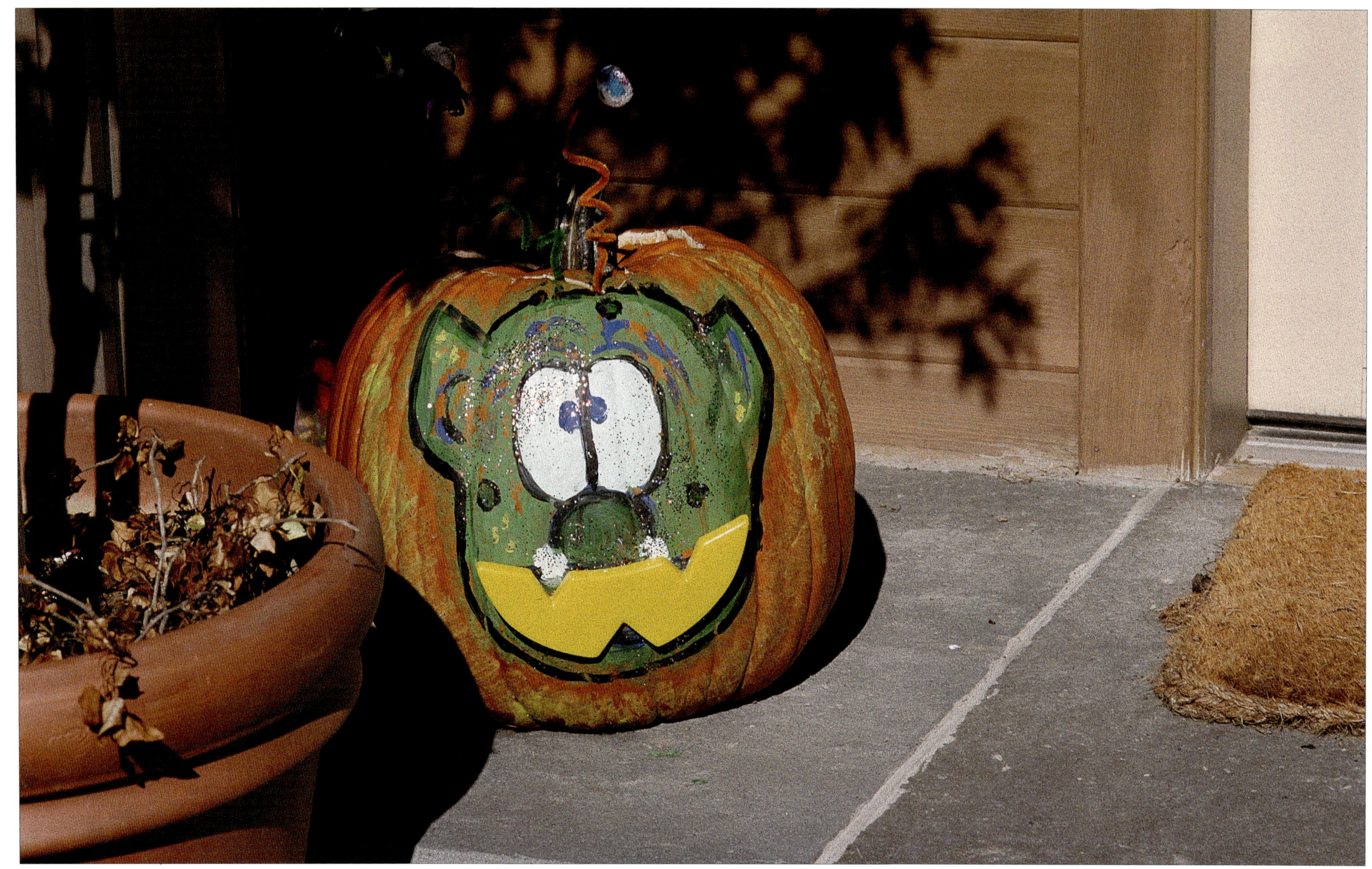

Above: American children celebrate Halloween with painted pumpkins, costumes and trick-or-treating. The last blast of fall colors ends at roughly the same time. Could the dreariness of winter be the work of ghosts and goblins?

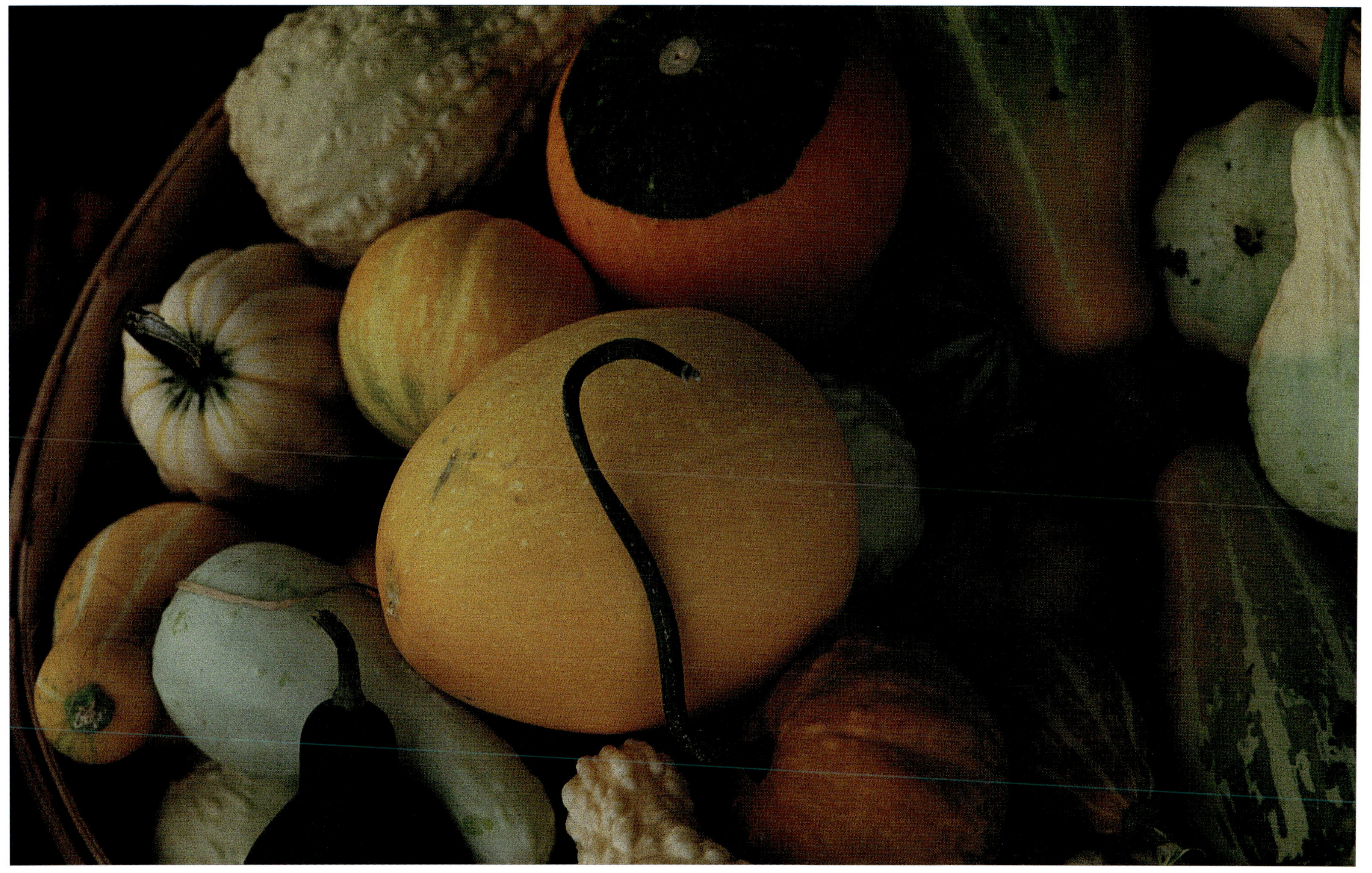

Above: The different varieties of squashes are a symbol of the bounty of nature and of the many plants this new continent gave to the world. Early American settlers depended upon vegetables such as squashes and gourds as both food and tools.

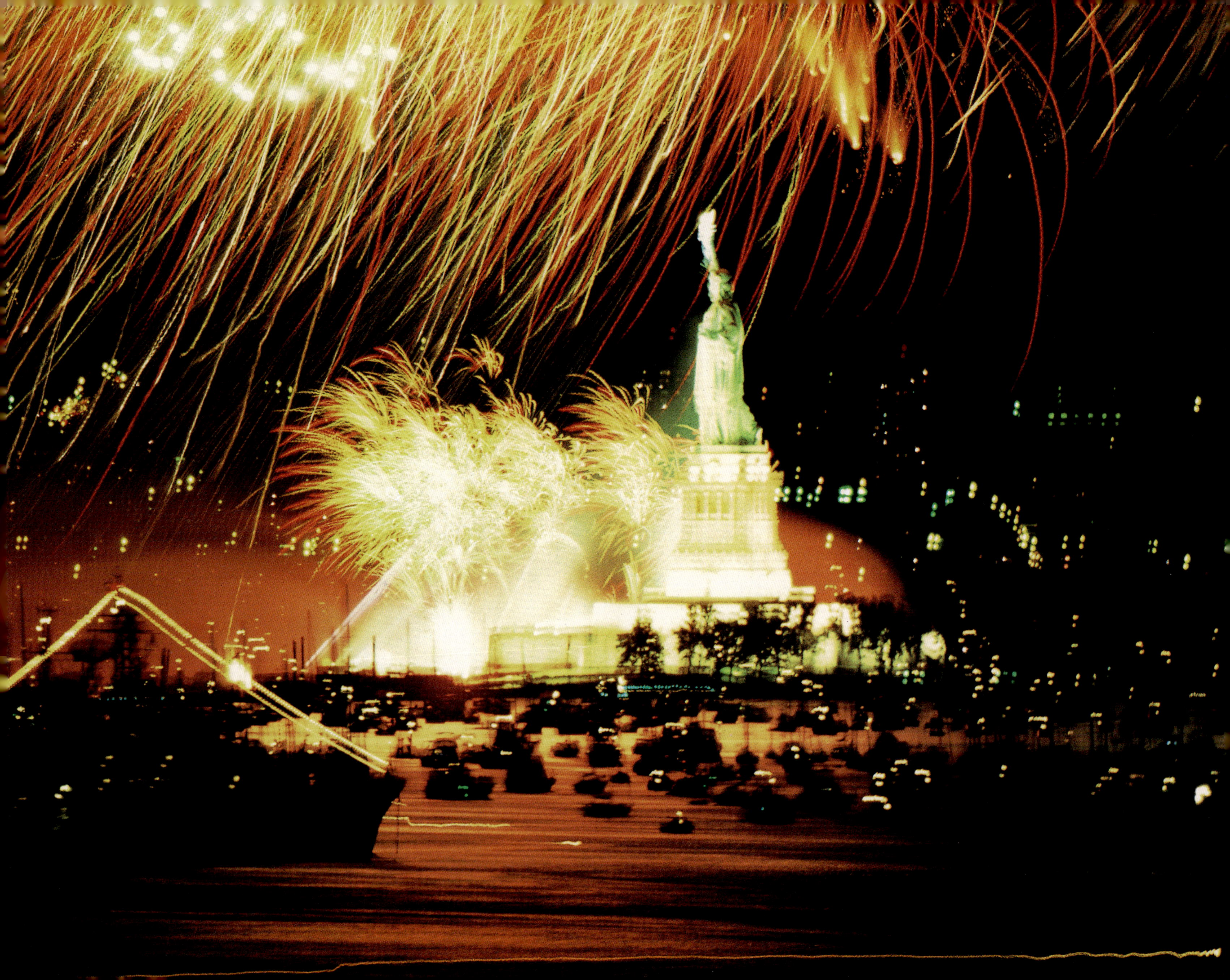

FREEDOM

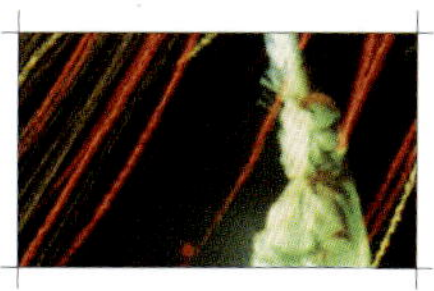

"IT IS FITTING, THEN, THAT THIS PROCESSION SHOULD TAKE PLACE IN HONOR OF LADY LIBERTY AND, AS THE WIND SWELLS THE SAILS, SO TOO MAY OUR HEARTS SWELL WITH PRIDE WITH ALL THAT LIBERTY'S SONS AND DAUGHTERS HAVE ACCOMPLISHED IN THIS, THE LAND OF THE FREE."

— PRESIDENT RONALD REAGAN, JULY 4, 1986

Opposite: Fireworks celebrating the nation's birthday and the renovated Statue of Liberty in New York Harbor on July 4, 1986.

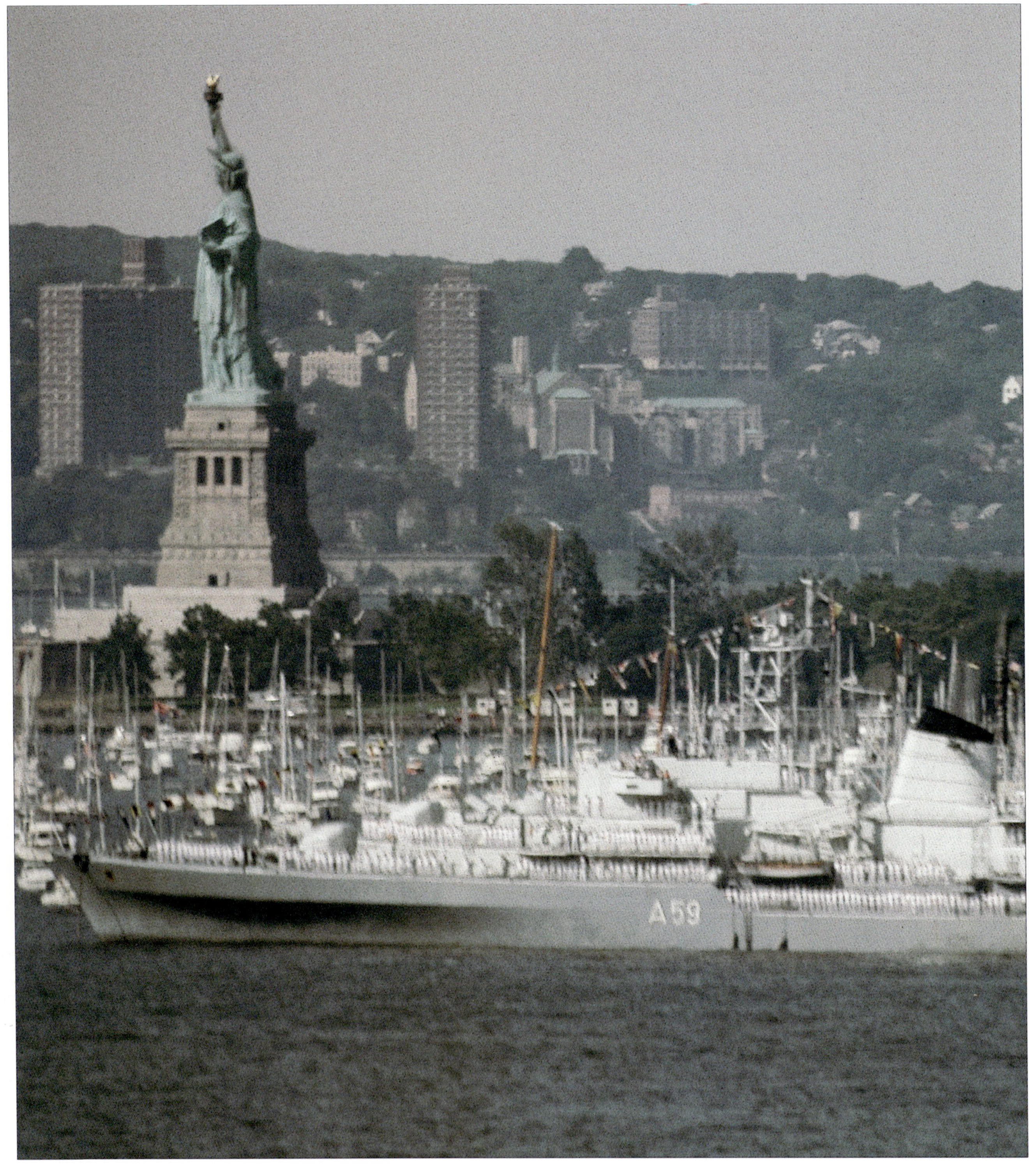

Left & Opposite: Ships from all over the world assembled in New York to honor the Statue of Liberty on July 4, 1986. The statue was rein-augurated after extensive repairs. Opposite, the majestic USS *Iowa* passes in procession. "Perhaps, indeed, these vessels embody our conception of liberty itself—to have before one no impediments, only open spaces to chart one's own course, to take the adventure of life as it comes, to be as free as the wind, as free as the tall ships themselves," said President Reagan.

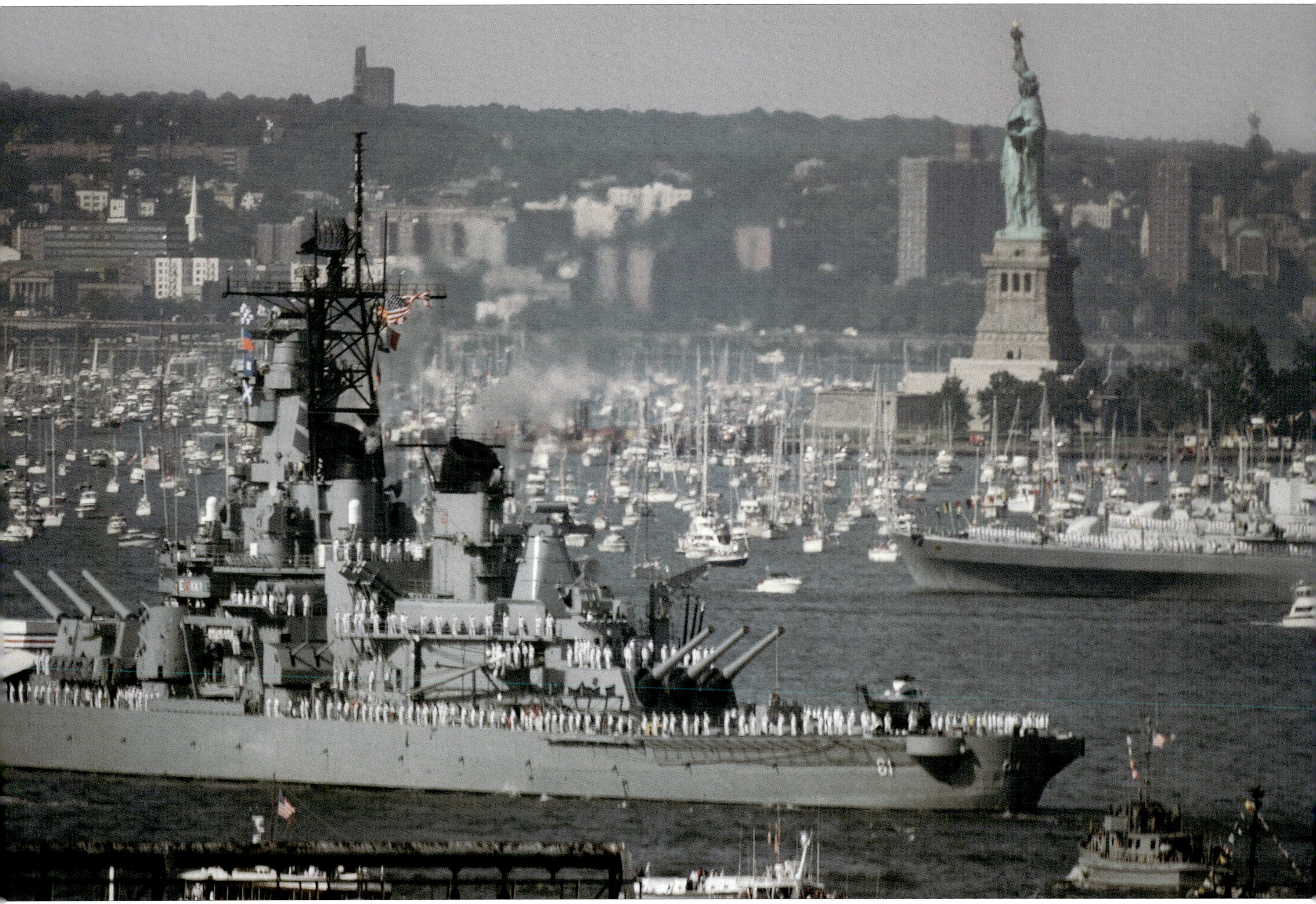

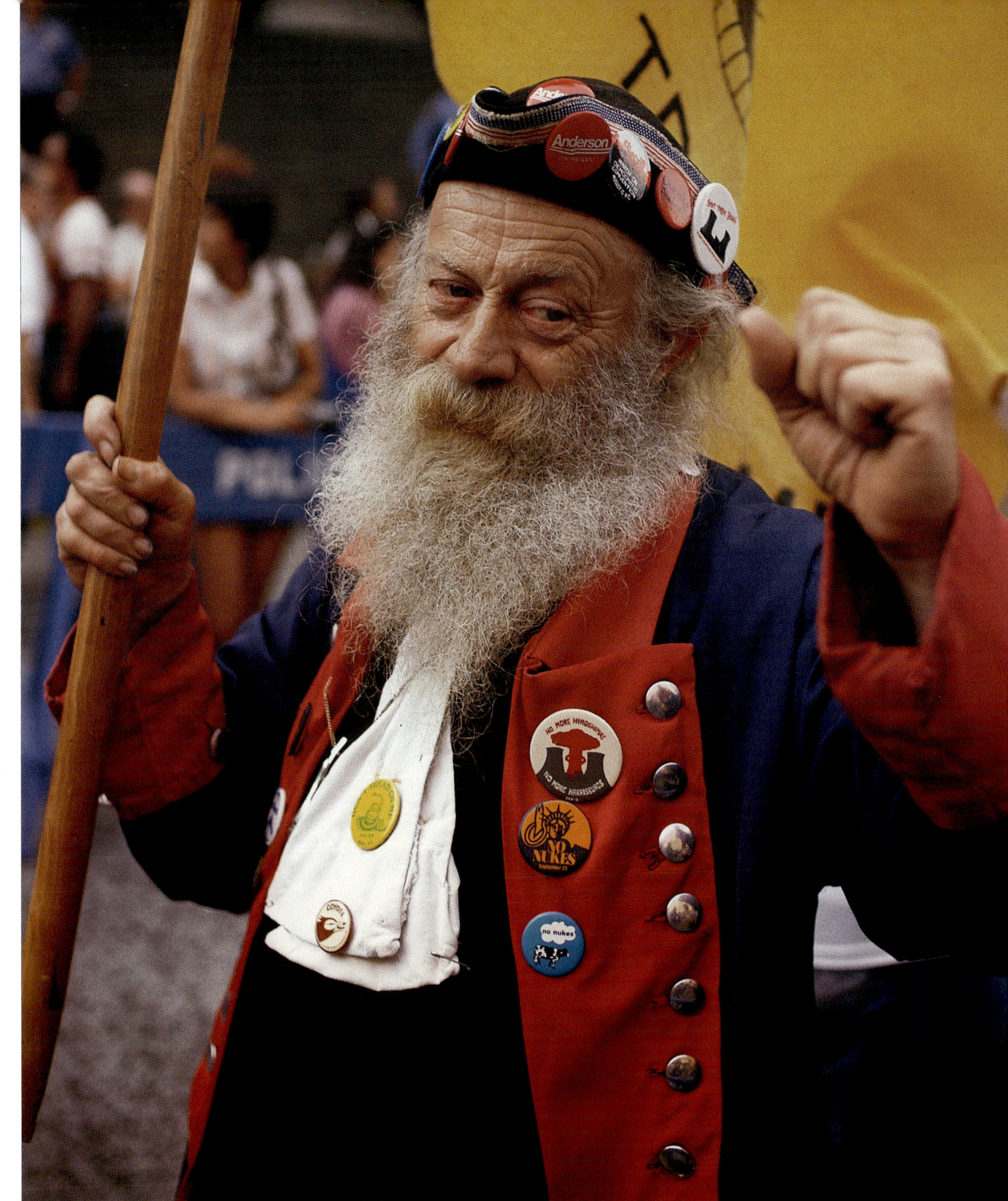

Right & Opposite: How shall we define the American spirit? We are full of cheer and full of joy. We take pride in our differences and our traditions. We do not shrink from duty, and we embrace humanity. Photographed in New York City (right) and Los Angeles (opposite).

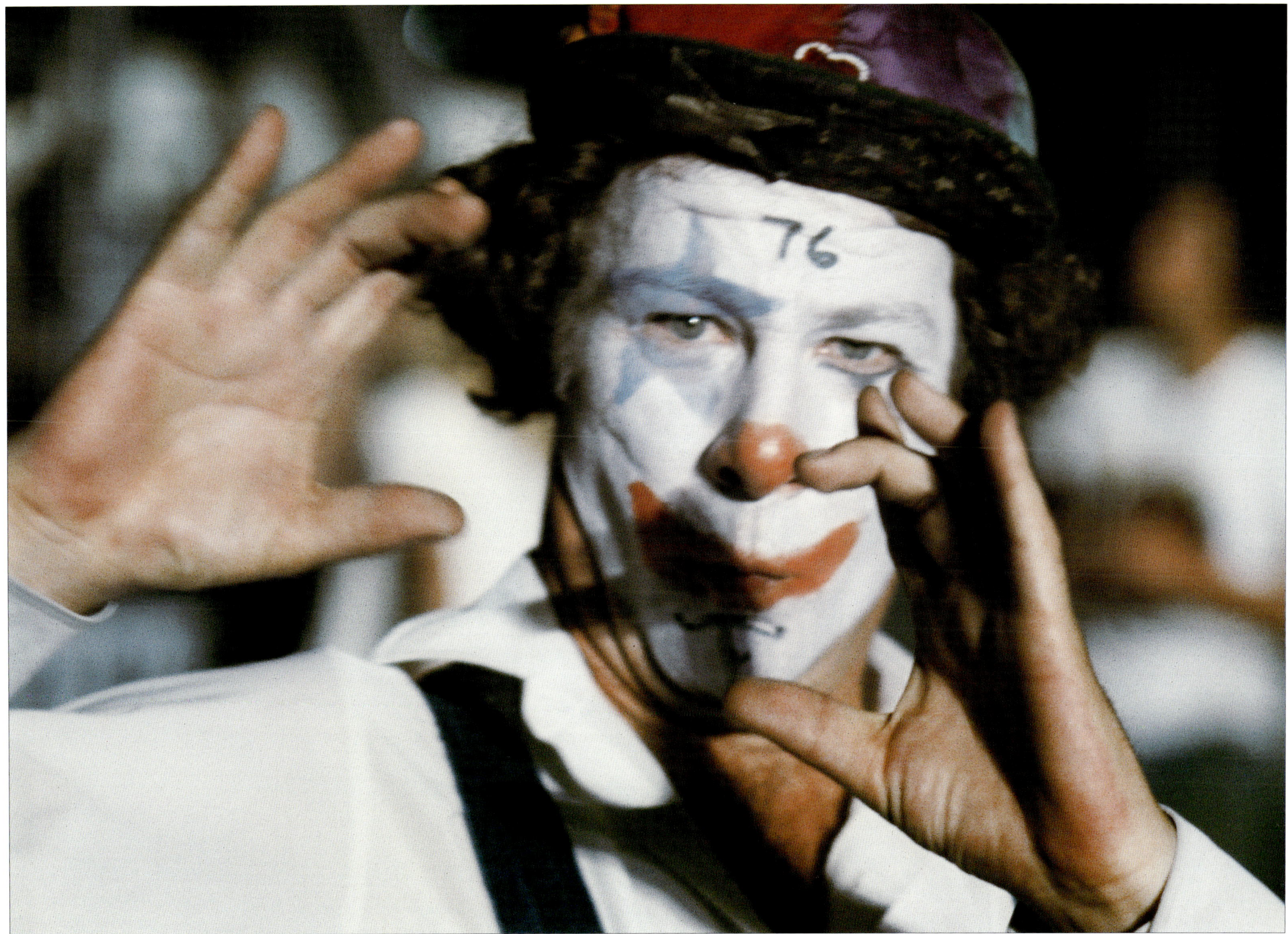

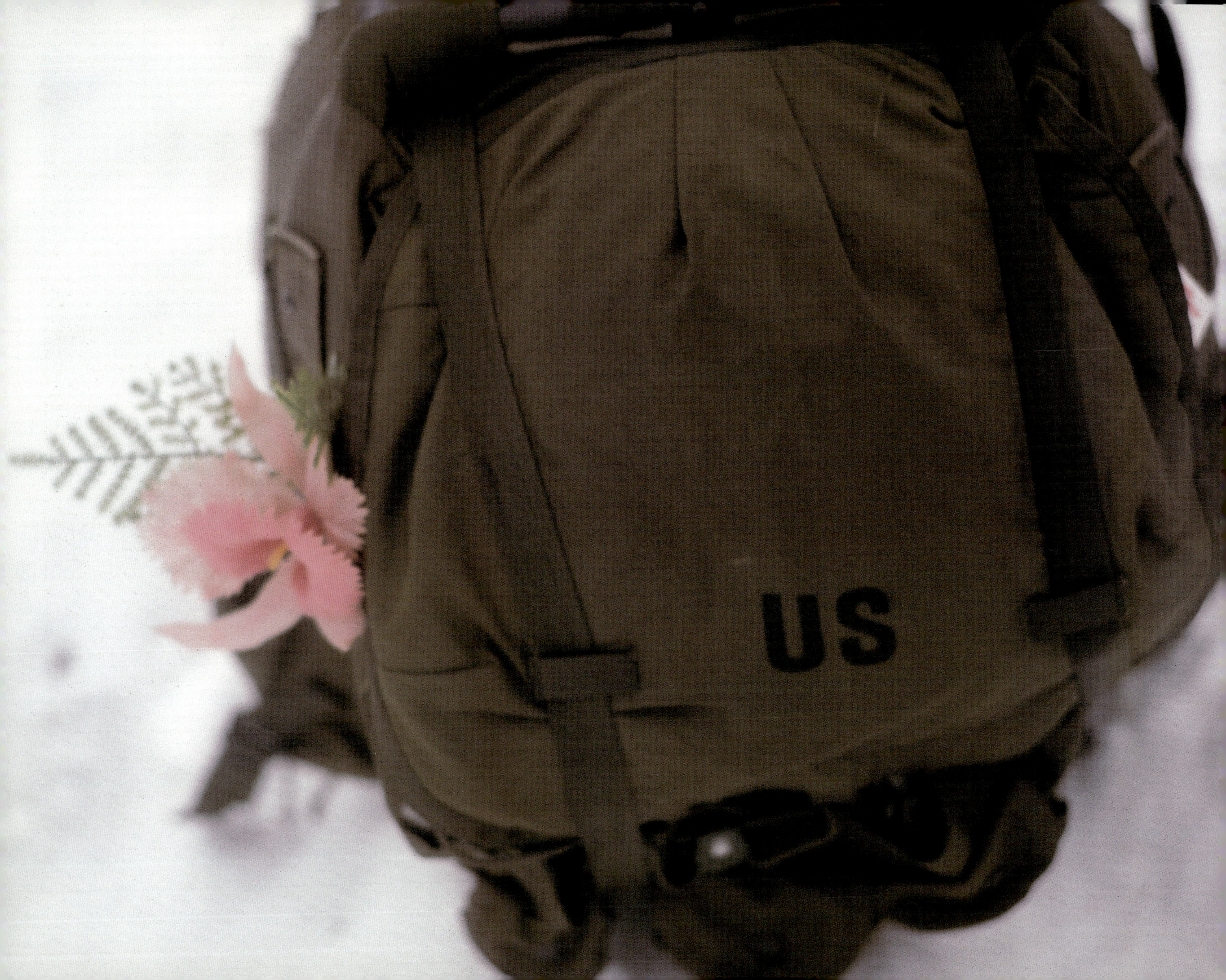
US

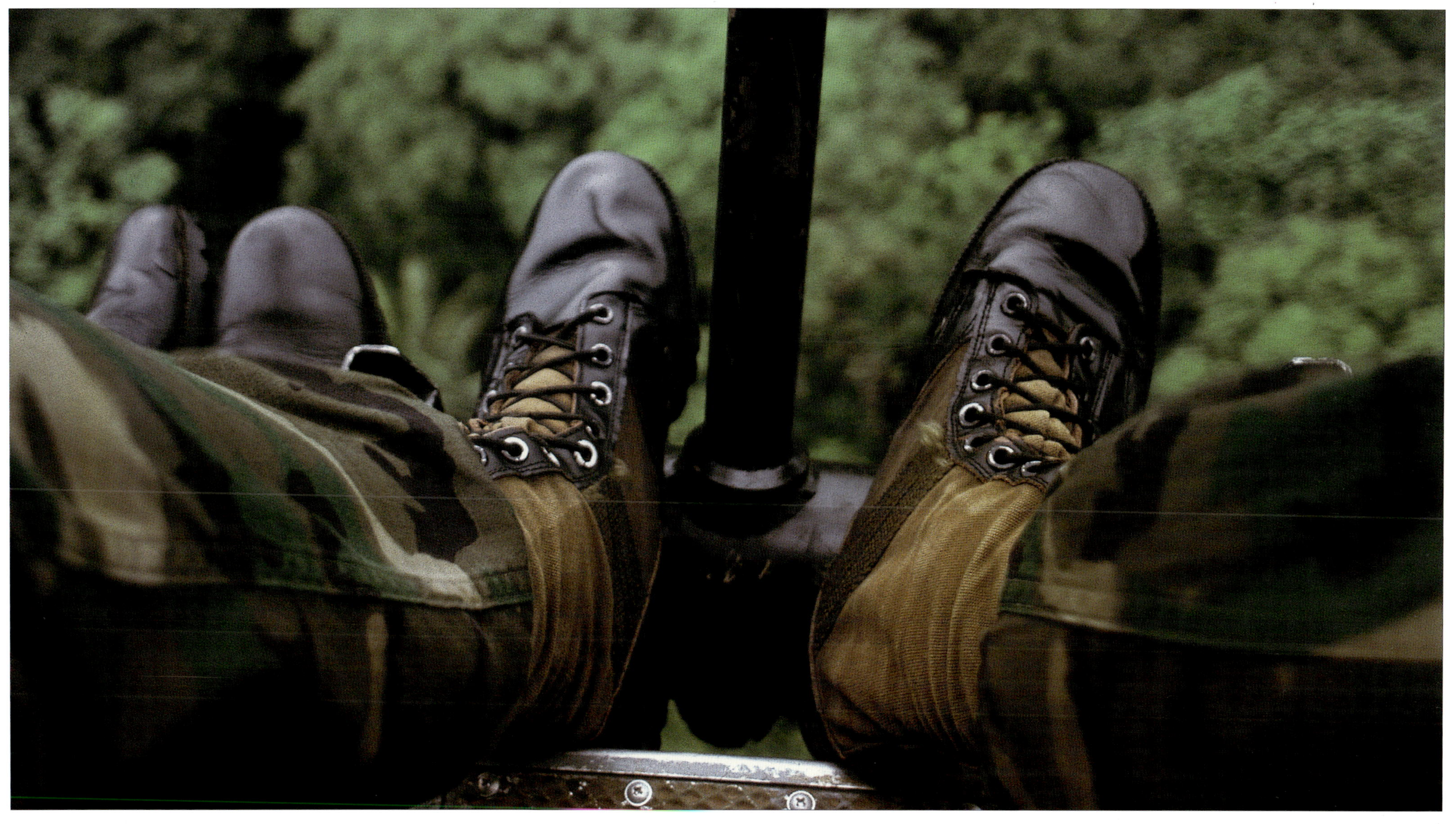

Opposite & Above: So how does one have fun in misery? Take an ugly, cheap plastic flower and decorate an overly heavy pack you drag about during winter warfare operations in Northern Norway with the United States Marines. Or sit in a helicopter, dangle your legs over the lush Panamanian jungle and admire your perfectly shined boots. The polish job took close to 45 minutes and you know full well that as soon as you land these jungle boots will be covered in mud. Does it make sense? No, but creating your own fun is part of American ingenuity.

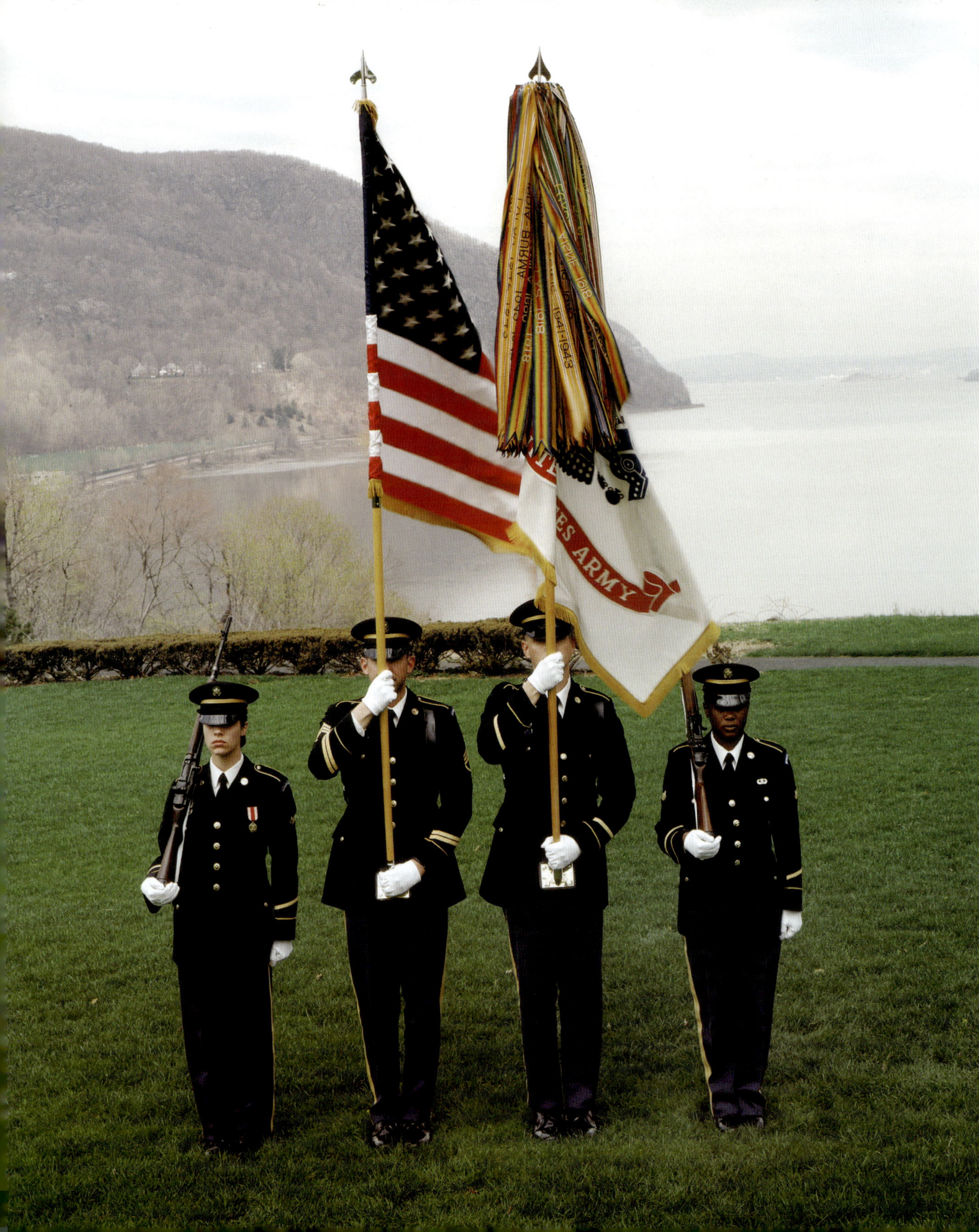

Left: The military police unit of the United States Military Academy at West Point stands with pride. In back of them you see the Hudson River – and that is the origin of West Point. A sharp turn in that river provided an opportunity for colonial patriots to block a feared attack from the British ships. A heavy chain was stretched across the Hudson, from the "West Point," a lonely rock, across to Constitution Island.

Opposite: Honor, Duty, Country – the motto of the military academy is inscribed on this grave for West Point graduate and first American astronaut to walk in space, Edward H. White II.

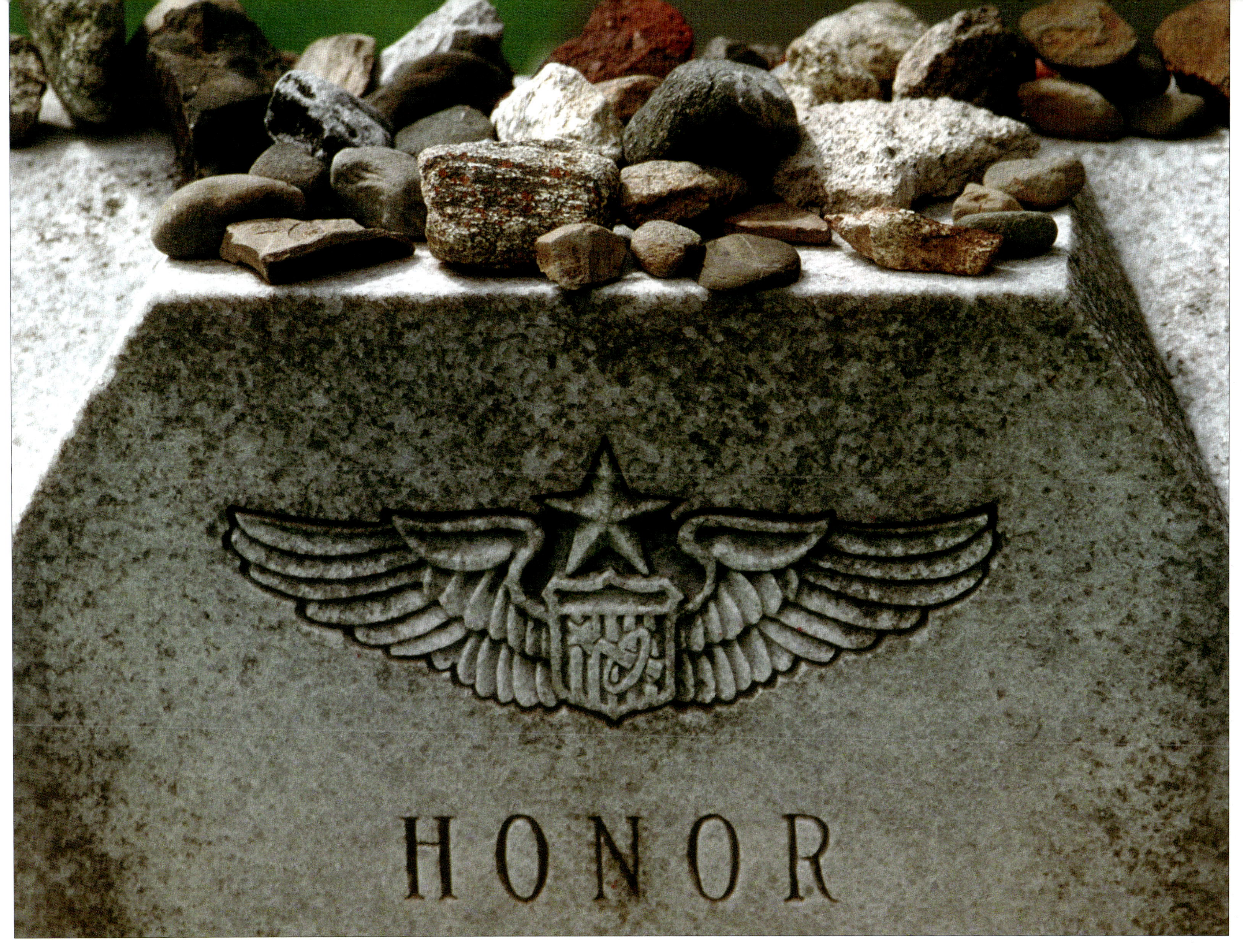

HONOR

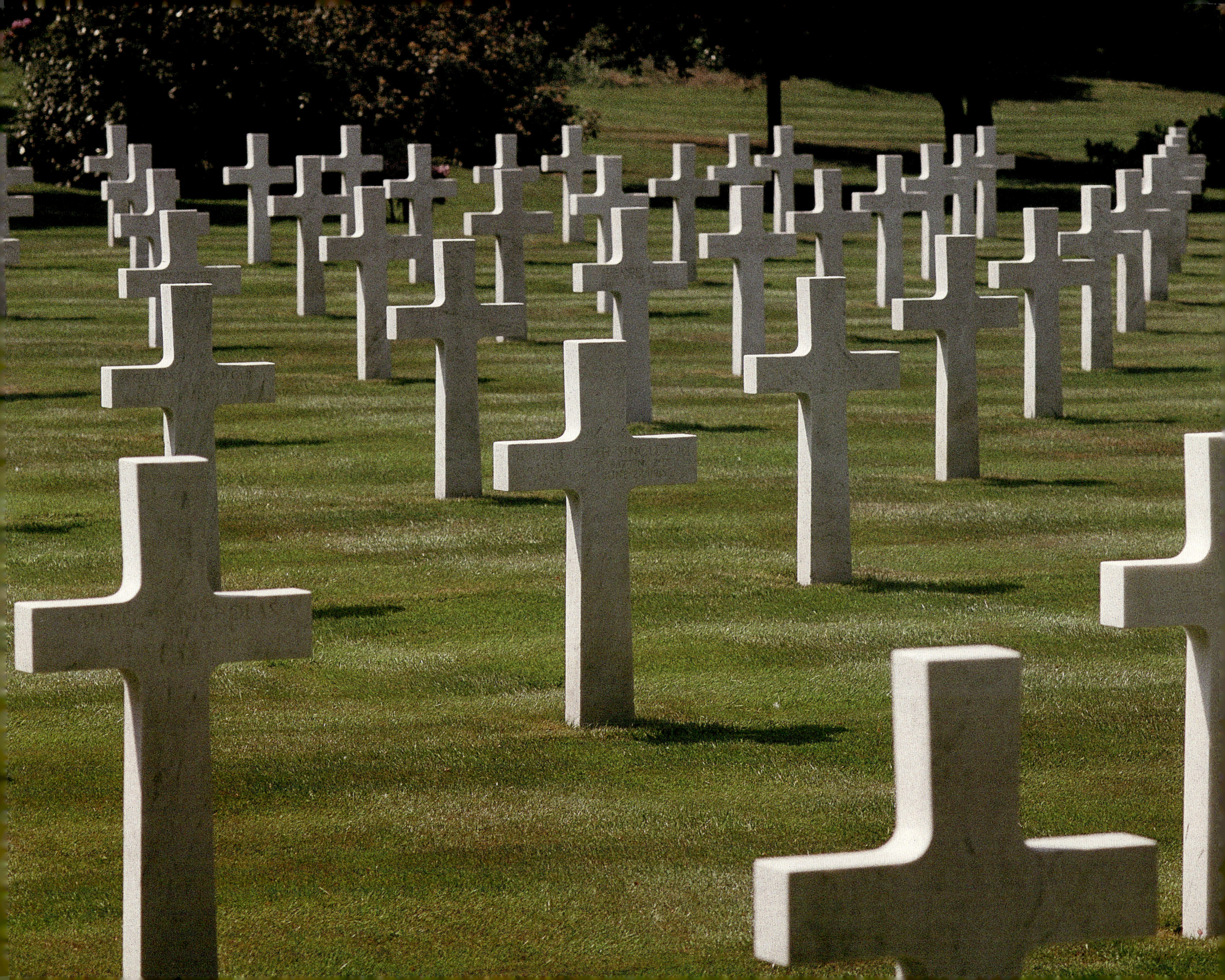

Opposite & Right: In July 1918, and on the front with Austria, Italian soldier and poet Giuseppe Ungaretti wrote this poem:

Soldati	Soldiers
Si sta come	They are like
d'autunno	in the Fall
sugli alberi	on the trees
le foglie.	The leaves

These images are from the cemetery of the World War One Battle at Belleau Wood in the Champagne Region of France. It is here that two regiments of Marines fought a pitched battle against elite Prussian and Bavarian units. The woods were secured in late July, at the cost of over 2,000 Marine souls. This battle, which "saved Paris" in the words of French Prime Minister Clemenceau, stopped the final advance of Germany's troops. France, it appears, has forgotten the American sacrifices of the First and Second World Wars.

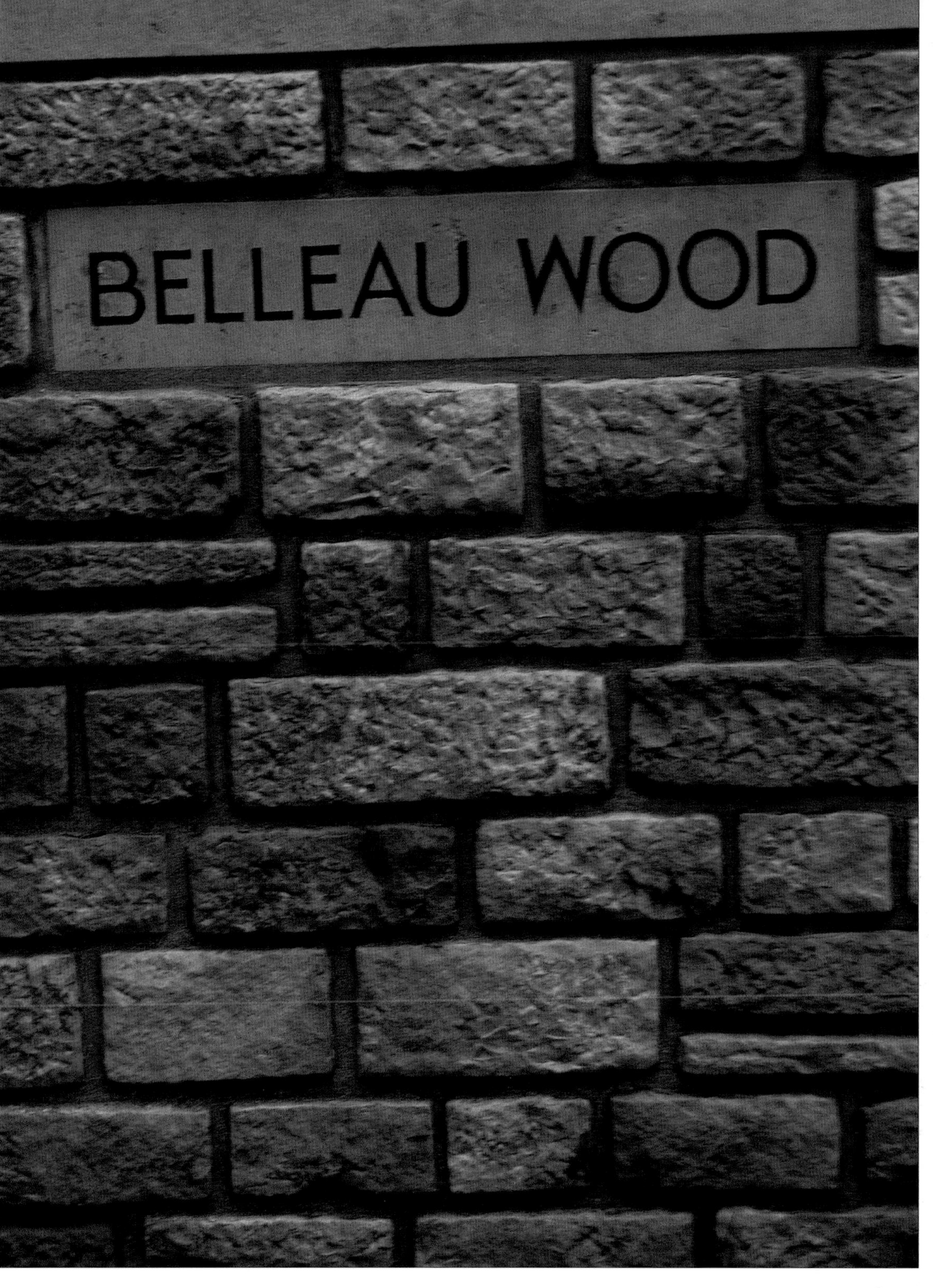

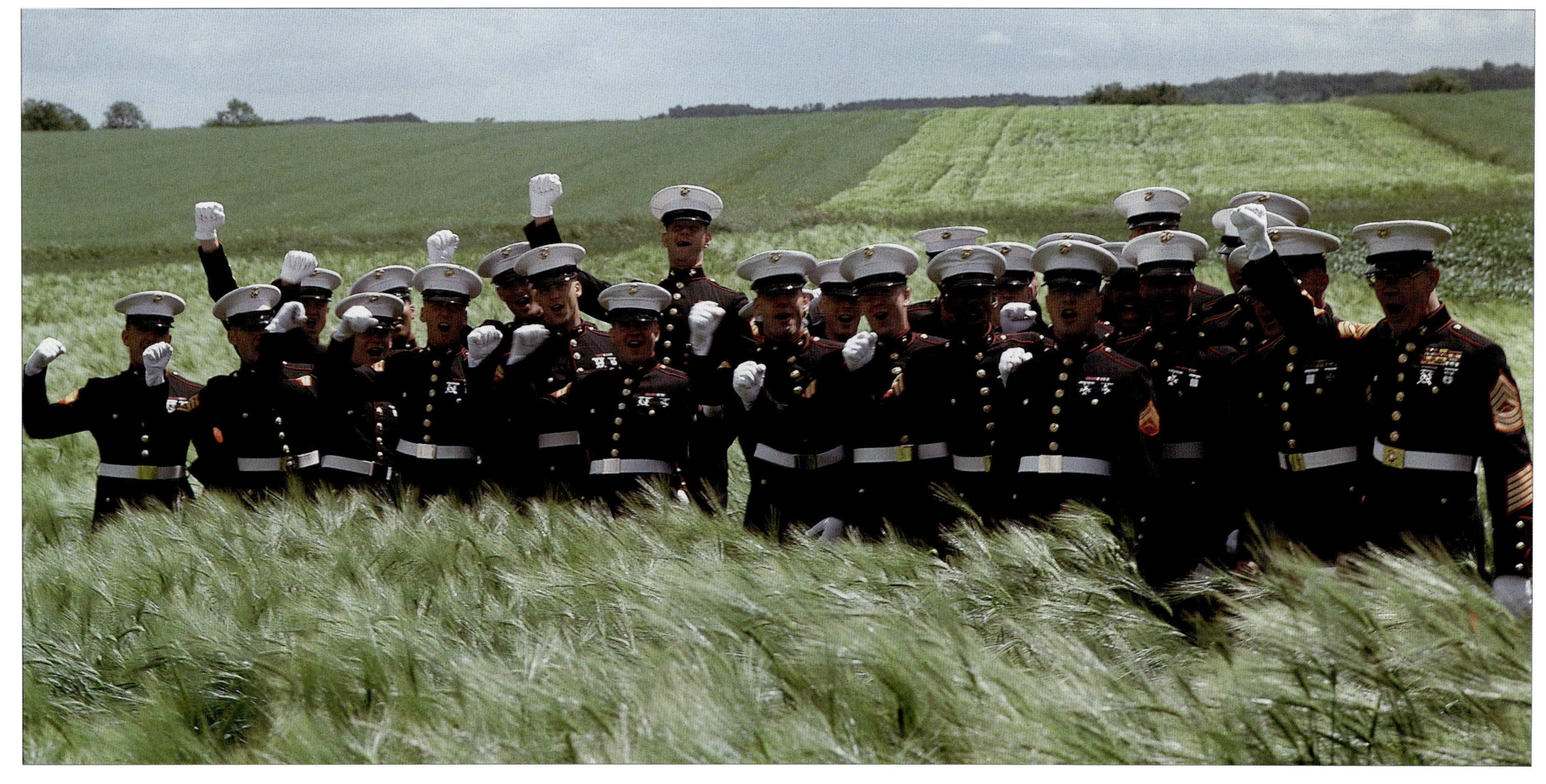

Above: Marines from the U.S. Embassy in Paris, France, cheer their forefathers
who fought across this wheat field on June 6, 1918, against massed machine gunfire
from German troops defending Belleau Wood.

Opposite: Tradition, history and never letting your Corps down are lessons instilled into every Marine.
Here the commanding general of the Recruit Depot at Parris Island, South Carolina, addresses
young recruits on the importance of leadership, sacrifice and tradition. All of them, the general
and his Marines, had gone on a long run on a humid South Carolina morning.

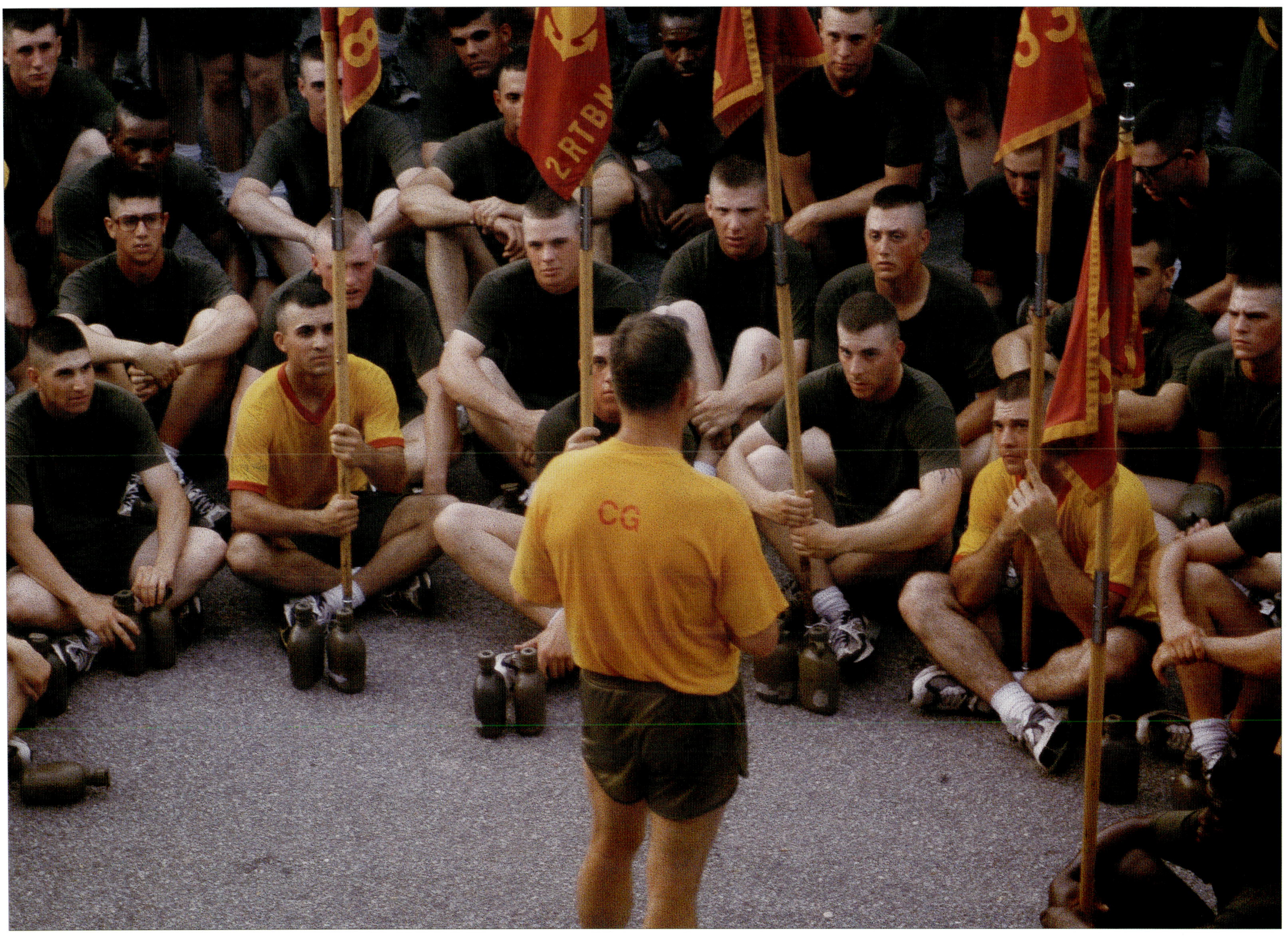

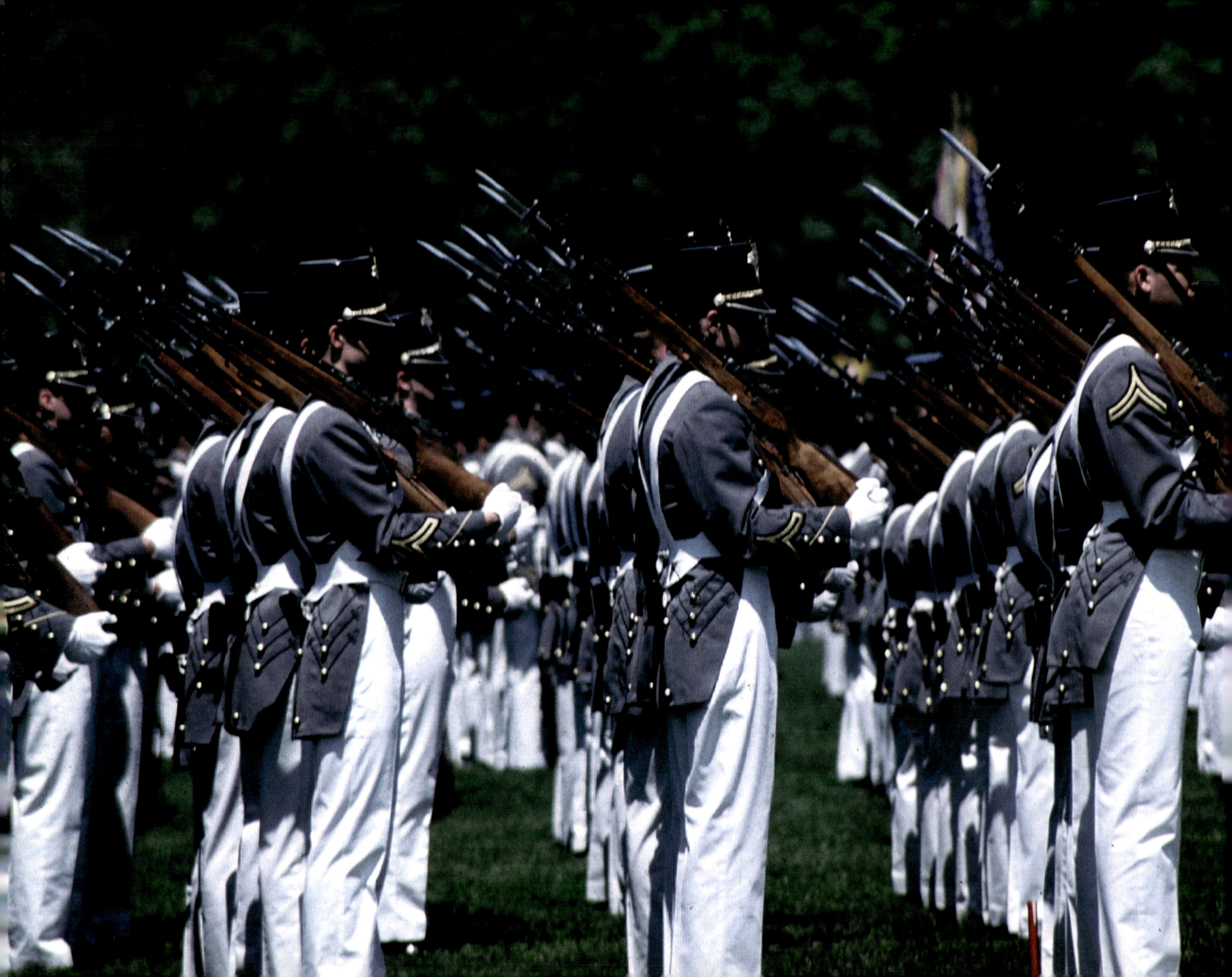

Opposite & Right: It is a tradition as old as this nation: to parade in honor of America and to fly the star spangled banner. Opposite, cadets stand in a silent salute to our nation's colors on The Plain of West Point. The large flag (right) flutters above the roof tops of Greenwich Village, New York.

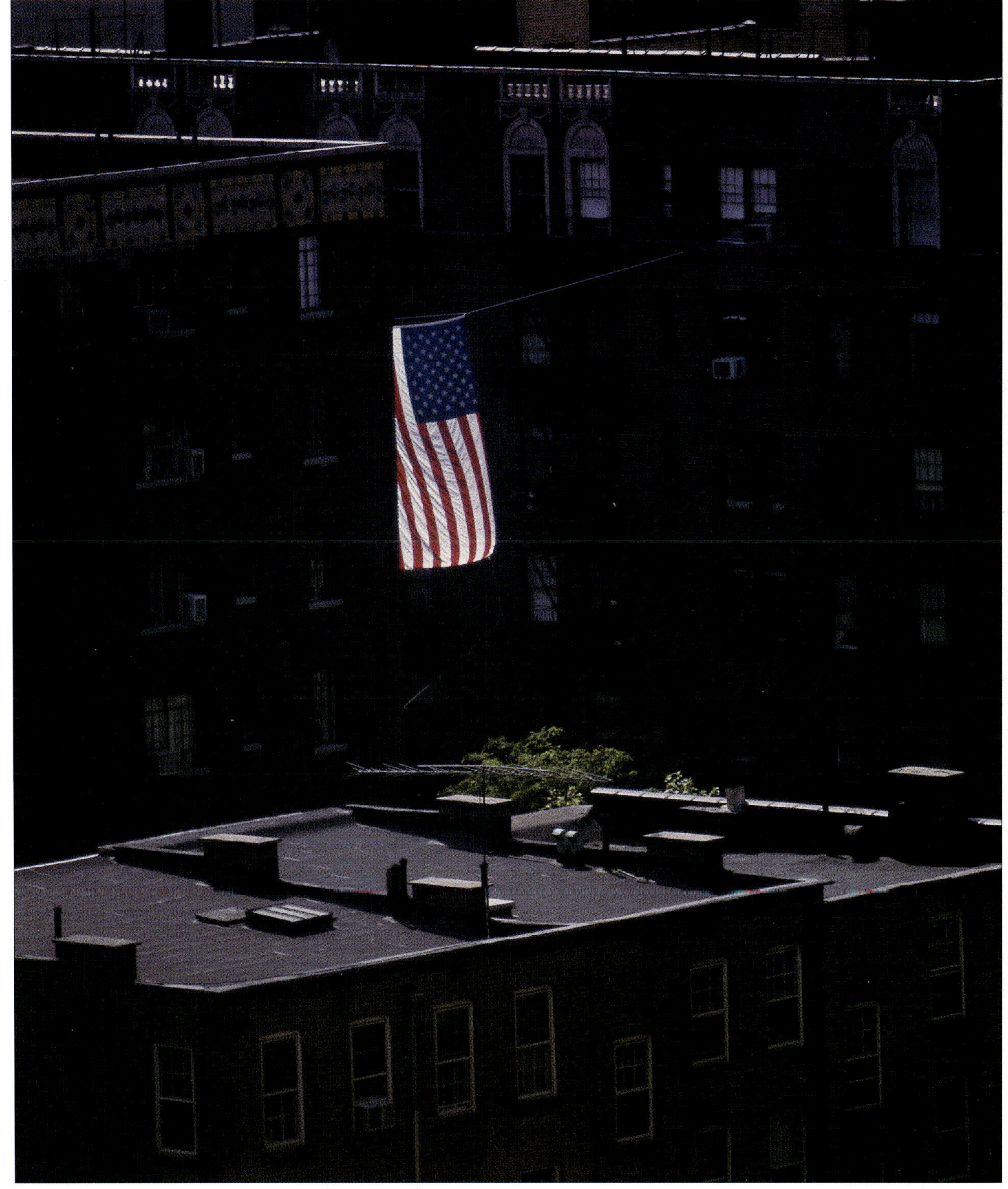